FROM SLAVERY
TO UNCERTAIN
FREEDOM

Black Community Studies

WILLARD B. GATEWOOD
General Editor

OTHER TITLES IN THIS SERIES

Ambiguous Lives
Free Women of Color in Rural Georgia, 1789–1879

The Other Brahmins
Boston's Black Upper Class, 1750–1950

Black Charlestonians
A Social History, 1822–1885

Black Savannah, 1788–1864

FROM SLAVERY TO UNCERTAIN FREEDOM

THE FREEDMEN'S BUREAU IN ARKANSAS, 1865–1869

RANDY FINLEY

The University of Arkansas Press
Fayetteville   1996

00   99   98   97   96   5   4   3   2

Designed by Liz Lester

♾ The paper used in this publication meets the minimum requirements of the American National Standard for Permanence of Paper for Printed Library Materials Z39.48-1984.

Library of Congress Cataloging-in-Publication Data

Finley, Randy, 1954–
        From slavery to uncertain freedom: the Freedmen's Bureau in Arkansas, 1865–1869 / Randy Finley.
            p.   cm.
        Includes bibliographical references and index.
        ISBN 1-55728-423-7 (cloth : alk. paper)
        1. Freedmen—Arkansas. 2. Reconstruction—Arkansas. 3. United States. Bureau of Refugees, Freedmen, and Abandoned Lands. 4. Arkansas—History. I. Title.
        F411.F445   1996   96–761
        976.7—dc20   CIP

For my mom and dad

ACKNOWLEDGMENTS

Most of all in this book, I wanted to forego economic reductionism and focus on the people of Arkansas, particularly the freedpersons, during Reconstruction. At times I think I made them live again, but at other times I failed, abysmally, to touch them.

Many thanks are in order. Willard Gatewood supervised my dissertation and read with great care innumerable drafts of this manuscript. I am among scores of students at the University of Arkansas who cannot imagine what their life would be like if Professor Gatewood had not returned to the history seminar room after a sojourn as chancellor. He is a superb scholar and a good friend.

Nancy Bercaw, Pete Daniel, Gretchen Munson, Hartwell Quinn, Daniel Sutherland, and Jeannie Whayne also read various drafts of the manuscript and offered critical insights. Karen Johnson of the University of Arkansas Press edited the manuscript judiciously and improved it with her considerable talents. None are responsible for my errors, but all are thanked for their perceptive comments and encouragement.

Generous aid for this research was afforded by Mary Hudgins research grants, by a University of Arkansas Medical Sciences History of Medicine research grant, and by a Smithsonian Institution Pre-Doctoral Fellowship. Research, writing, and fellowship at the Smithsonian were stimulated at the National Museum of American History by Pete Daniel, who deserves much praise, especially for his establishment of the Tuesday evening seminars at the Irish Times. He, too, is a genuine scholar and friend.

Thanks to editor Jeannie Whayne for permission to publish revisions of chapter five which previously appeared in the *Arkansas Historical Quarterly.*

Colleagues and students at Ashdown, Arkansas, High School, the University of Arkansas, and DeKalb College have constantly asked me challenging questions and sustained my love for history. They have often endured my thickheadedness and deserve much thanks. Special thanks goes to Hartwell Quinn, my mentor at DeKalb College, who made my transition to college teaching successful.

I wish history professor Bill Snodgrass, English teacher Barbara Minnick, and my two grandfathers were still here to read this. They would grin. I wish to thank my parents, Joe and Sue Finley, Mamaw Finley and Mamaw Sutton, and my sister, Debbie, who have contributed great joy to my life. My debt to them all is immense. And I owe even more to my nephews, Josh and Casey, who remind me every ten weeks at break that a meaningful life has to include baseball games where right field is a cornfield at my Pap Finley's farm. Thanks.

CONTENTS

TABLES AND MAPS

PREFACE

Black and white Arkansans struggled to discover the meanings of freedom in the aftermath of the Civil War. Freedpersons tested their freedom in many ways—by assuming new names, searching for lost family members, moving to new residences, working to provide for their families, learning to read and write, forming and attending their own churches, creating their own histories and myths, struggling to obtain land, and establishing different nuances in race, gender, and class. Under slavery, such decisions ran the risk of being overturned by the master if discovered. The multiple revolutions spawned by the Civil War included a demand by freedpersons that choices previously camouflaged be revealed. Freedpersons forged a new place for themselves in Southern society in war's wake. The struggles on diverse fronts to create that place was a central theme of Reconstruction.

New choices abounded for whites as well as blacks. Planters searched for ways to renew the plantation system while maintaining their political, economic, and social hegemony. New forms of paternalism and control of freedmen and yeomen whites were fashioned. White subsistence farmers also wondered where they fit into the postbellum world. White men and women questioned antebellum notions of gender after the Civil War had thrust women into spheres previously ordained "manly." Whites of all classes warily eyed freedpersons who now often disdained the role of "Uncle" and "Mammy." Whites were as unsure as blacks as to who precisely exercised power in this strange, new, postbellum world.

In revolutionary times such as the Civil War, choices proliferate. Freedpersons faced staggering numbers of personal and group decisions. Under slavery, blacks lived where masters decided they needed them most. Freedom offered blacks the chance to move to urban areas, to remain in a rural environment but move to a different farm, to journey to areas with richer economic opportunities, or to stay put. Under slavery, paternalism and its myths forged slave mentality. Freedom ensured freedpersons that they could create new heroic myths which celebrated their endurance under slavery and extolled their new empowerment and freedom. Masters had dominated much of a slave's conceptions of the future. Freedom meant that freedpersons controlled their own future, at least to some extent, and could envision a time when they would control far more of their own destiny than ever before.

Freedpersons also made critical choices about family relationships. Although a black family structure definitely existed under slavery, it often had to be disguised from planters. Freedom meant that African Americans could now openly and confidently develop lasting relationships which could not be destroyed by masters. Freedpersons developed new roles of motherhood and fatherhood and demanded that they be respected. Blacks nourished new bonds between parents and children. The Civil War revolutionized the black family by bringing previously hidden relationships and deep affections out into the open.

Blacks existentially determined for themselves what they thought it meant to be a man or a woman. Under slavery, masters and the dominant white culture defined and mythologized black sexuality. Freedpersons faced choices about how to openly respond to the dominant culture's stereotypes, fears, and anxieties while battling their own insecurities. New understandings of self-worth or self-loathing emerged with the choices they made.

Race confronted Arkansas's newly freed. A color code had existed during slavery which signaled superiority or inferiority. White revealed superior; black indicated inferior. But the Civil War demolished such simplistic demarcations. Both whites and blacks now wrestled with the new realities which seemed to demand a literalist interpretation of the

Declaration of Independence—that all men were created equal. Freedpersons engineered new understandings of their race and of their humanity.

African Americans created new communities to reenforce their new identities after emancipation. In the antebellum days, whenever two or three slaves gathered together, this disturbed their masters. Freedom allowed freedpersons to join churches, political clubs, and fraternal organizations. With such group empowerment, blacks thwarted their former masters' desires to keep them isolated and powerless. When some whites responded to black assertiveness with the formation of the Ku Klux Klan, many Arkansas blacks countered and formed all-black paramilitary organizations to protect themselves. Freedpersons created new communities which nourished and defended their newly gained freedom.

Blacks recognized the need for schools. Under slavery, masters considered books as dangerous as guns. With freedom, blacks, too, realized that books would be as beneficial as guns in the struggles to preserve their freedom. Freedpersons not only decided to have schools but donated generously from their limited economic resources to bring school buildings for blacks to Arkansas.

Freedpersons became responsible for the health of each other. In the antebellum South, a sick slave meant lower profits to a master. Planters responded by feeding slaves adequately, by improving sanitation in the slave quarters, and by summoning a doctor when necessary. After emancipation, planters grew far less concerned about black health. Freedpersons assumed much of the responsibility of caring for the sick and destitute.

Underlying all of these choices about residency, family structure, sexuality, race, associations, education, and health care was the struggle for economic survival. A starving man or woman loses interest in clubs to join, books to read, or responsibilities to others. Poverty often constricts choices and narrows freedom. If planters regained control of the Arkansas economy, then freedpersons would find their freedom diminished. Blacks struggled to see that this did not happen. They moved, demanded landownership, and diligently chopped and picked their own cotton to guarantee the economic underpinnings of their freedom.

But freedom, the fundamental of much popular culture during the Civil War, is an extraordinarily complex psychological reality. If Southern whites historically gained an understanding of their own freedom by contrasting it to enslaved, "inferior" blacks, how would emancipation alter their perceptions of freedom and of themselves? Would poor whites recognize their own forms of past enslavement in a world where blacks now struggled to be free? Would new psychological struggles be added to their daily existence? Would black freedom entail revenge against whites who had denied their freedom for over two centuries? Or would the past have to be forgotten or defanged—and can those forced to become historically amnesiac ever be truly free?

Freedpersons did not struggle alone as they sought to maintain and extend their new freedom. The Freedmen's Bureau, a federal government enterprise monitoring the South from 1865 to 1870, tried to ensure blacks a modicum of freedom. The mere presence of such a federal agency effectively checked much white animosity against blacks. What if there had been no Freedmen's Bureau in the South after the Civil War? It is easy to imagine that planters would have reenslaved blacks and denied them economic freedom, opportunities, the hope for change, or new work roles; that black churches would have been controlled, as in antebellum days, by white planters; that schools for blacks would have remained chimerical; that black families would not have been protected; that black men would neither have registered nor voted; that without the bureau, thousands of additional freedpersons would have died due to lack of medical care, clothing, or food. In such a confrontational context, the achievements made by freedpersons, often with the aid of the Freedmen's Bureau, are remarkable.

This study attempts to analyze Reconstruction from a bottom-rail perspective. It deals with the structure and influence of the Freedmen's Bureau, the federal agency designed to ease the transition of black Arkansans from slavery to freedom, but it does not purport to be another institutional study of the bureau at the state level. This work also attempts to avoid the rendering of judgments from a late twentieth-century perspective. Rather, the intention is to explore the ways in which Arkansans—black and white, men and women, rich and poor—refashioned themselves and their world in the years immediately following the Civil War when the Freedmen's Bureau operated in

Arkansas. The assumption is that the essential story of Reconstruction is not so much about abstractions as it is about *people* in the process of coming to terms with the revolutionary implications of emancipation. Which people were to gain power? Who would really become free? The major theme of life after the Civil War comprises the struggle for economic, political, and social power and the search for freedom.

To refer to the accomplishments and failures of the Freedmen's Bureau suggests that the agency was not powerful enough to have decisions made in Washington carried out uniformly in all areas of Arkansas. In reality, a flawless agency did not exist, at least not in Arkansas, where the assumptions, ambitions, fears, and prejudices of local bureau personnel largely determined the action or inaction of the bureau in crucial areas. To appreciate the meaning of Reconstruction in Arkansas, it is essential to understand the roles and interaction of three principal sets of participants in the drama as it unfolded in different locales: freedpersons both as individuals and groups; an assortment of whites of disparate backgrounds and classes; and the bureau officials in charge of particular districts or local offices. The interplay of these forces went far toward determining the realities of the world refashioned by Arkansans of both races in the wake of a war that did indeed leave "things tore up."

CHAPTER 1

PRELUDE TO FREEDOM, 1862–1865

Arkansas's 110,000 African Americans eagerly embraced freedom as Northern armies conquered Confederates in Arkansas between 1862 and 1865. No one knew what to expect as Yankees tramped southward. Blacks and whites pondered the perimeters of freedom. Confusion, ambiguity, and uncertainty reigned.

Freedom came to Arkansas slaves at different times and in different places. Blacks reacted to their emancipation uniquely. Ida Harper's mother "dropped her hoe and danced up to the town road and danced right up into old master's parlor." An all-night celebration followed. Laura Abramson's mother "bawled in the field, cried, laughed, hollered, and danced" when notified of emancipation. Charles Anderson of Helena thought "freedom was something mysterious. Colored folks didn't talk it. White folks didn't talk it." Irene Robertson also recalled the uncertainty but insisted, "We was glad to be set free. I did not know what it would be like. It was just like opening the door and lettin' the bird fly out. He might starve, or freeze, or be killed pretty soon but he just felt good because he was free." Patsy Moore of Madison captured the uncertainty best, noting:

> When freedom come, folks left home, out in the streets, crying, praying, singing, shouting, yelling, and knocking down everything. Some shot off big guns. Den come the calm. It was sad then. So many folks done dead, things tore up and

nowhere to go and nothing to eat, nothing to do. It got squally. Folks got sick, so hungry. Some folks starved nearly to death. Times got hard. We went to the washtub onliest way we could live.[1]

Over five thousand Arkansas freedmen joined the Union Army as it trekked across Arkansas from 1862 to 1865. General Lorenzo Thomas recruited Arkansas blacks in 1863 for the Army of the Mississippi. Used primarily as laborers and garrison guards on burial details, and in similar capacities, they found themselves in regions as far-flung as Vicksburg, Mississippi, Memphis, Tennessee, Brownsville, Texas, and Milliken's Bend, Louisiana. Although white soldiers frequently disdained their black comrades, African-American soldiers often won praise from their white officers. Captain James Talbot in Pine Bluff complimented Arkansas black troops who exceeded his highest expectations during their initial combat experience.[2]

Arkansas's black soldiers endured Confederate atrocities, as when Rebels massacred over eighty African-American soldiers at Poison Springs near Camden, Arkansas. John Edwards witnessed a similar event at Mark's Mill, in south central Arkansas between Camden and Monticello, in April 1864 and recalled that "the battlefield was sickening to behold. No orders, threats, or commands could restrain the men from vengeance on the negroes, and they were piled in great heaps about the wagons, in the tangled brushwood, and upon the muddy and trampled road." If black Arkansans wondered what these brutalities meant, they nonetheless continued to fight.[3]

Not only did freedmen enlist in the Union Army, but many blacks worked for white Northerners who began to lease abandoned plantations in 1862. By 1864 freedmen labored on over one hundred leased plantations. Most worked in large gangs under white lessees, but several blacks leased small tracts of land and labored by themselves. Other African-American men and women also joined contraband labor camps supervised by army personnel while the war continued. Colonel John Eaton, placed in charge of the Arkansas camps, detected "no plan in their exodus, no Moses to lead it. There were men, women, and children in every stage of disease or decrepitude, often nearly naked, with torn flesh by the terrible experience of their escape. Sometimes they were intelligent and eager to help themselves; often they were bewildered or stupid or possessed by the wildest notions of what liberty might mean." Labor not only provided revenue for freedmen but also inculcated discipline and a "proper" respect for the work ethic.[4]

Colonel Eaton divided "his" contraband into five categories. New arrivals to camps became stevedores, hospital attendants, officials' servants, and commissary and quartermaster employees. Town residents continued their services as bakers, hackmen, draymen, porters, carpenters, shoemakers, blacksmiths, tailors, seamstresses, nurses, laundresses, waiters, cooks, and teachers. Woodcutters stayed in the abundant Arkansas forests and supplied the army and contraband camps with much needed fuel. Eaton persuaded plantation laborers to remain in the fields. Blacks acquiesced with his orders and successfully farmed over one hundred plantations of more than fifty thousand acres during the war. The black work ethic impressed Eaton as he witnessed freedpersons who "returned to their work after being repeatedly driven away by guerrillas, and when no white dared to go in."[5]

Pay scales fluctuated as Treasury and War Department bureaucrats assessed "fair" wages. Pay began at $7 per month for able-bodied men and $5 per month for women, with half-pay for children. The Treasury Department recommended wage increases to $25 per month for men, but a compromise forced the wages back down to $10 for men, $7 for women, and $5 for children. Although fearing that these leases would prove to be facades for forced military services, many blacks signed up and accumulated unprecedented sums of money. Helena blacks, for example, earned over $40,000 in 1864.[6]

But not every black could contribute to the work force. Caring for the sick and supervising the sanitation of the contraband camps became a major concern for Eaton and the U.S. Army. Maria Mann, niece of American educator Horace Mann, discovered patients "eaten up with vermin" in Helena, and A. N. Harlan observed a White River camp where blacks' cabins consisted of "an incongruous assemblage of miserable huts no attempt haveing been made towards introducing any system whatever their floors are on or quite near the ground they have no windows and are lighted by holes in the roofs consequently in raining weather most of their scanty bedding is wet their floors are damp and no wonder that from this little community they have already furnished 116 subjects for the graveyard." In Pine Bluff, American

Missionary Association representative David Todd reported that "the mortality rate here in the Freedmen's Camp is astonishing" and recorded over one hundred deaths in May and June of 1864. George Palmer, an army officer at Little Rock, observed that the Little Rock camp was "really in fact nothing more nor less than one vast hospital, strictly speaking, it is a grave yard rather than the residence of human beings. There is scarcely one family in camp that can boast of all of its members being well."[7]

Freedpersons died most often from measles, mumps, whooping cough, pneumonia, and dysentery. Mortality statistics from the Little Rock Freedmen's Home Farm in June 1864 reveal the pandemics freedpersons faced (see Table 1.1).[8]

The army experimented with different measures to combat the sickness and death so pervasive during the war. Colonel Eaton levied taxes on healthy blacks to support visiting physicians sent to contraband camps. An officer in Fort Smith in western Arkansas detailed a surgeon to vaccinate soldiers and citizens and to inspect daily all camps, tents, and clothing for cleanliness. To deter epidemics, Little Rock provost marshall M. L. Andrews ordered the collection and removal of all garbage, the cleaning of privies, and an end to animals running at large. Lieutenant Henry Sweeny of Helena burned all dwellings contaminated with smallpox. Nearly all officers distributed rations and sur-

TABLE 1.1

**Little Rock Freedmen's Home Farm
June 1864**

Cause of death	Number dead
Diarrhea	119
Rubeola	112
Dysentery	32
Intermittent fever	15
Pertussis	14
Typhoid fever	2
Cholera	1

plus bedding and clothing to blacks in an attempt to alleviate suffering and prevent disease and death.[9]

Northern humanitarian and religious agencies joined the army in trying to stymie skyrocketing mortality. Quakers, the American Missionary Association (AMA), and the Western Sanitary Commission sent medical supplies and food to counter the poverty and sickness faced by Arkansas blacks. Northern humanitarian subscriptions funded artisans, carpenters, farmers, preachers, teachers, and adventurers for Arkansas in an effort to improve the quality of life for Arkansas freedmen.[10]

Of these Northern sojourners, teachers made the most lasting contributions to Arkansas blacks. Toiling in a state where the legislature had never adequately funded public education for either whites or blacks, teachers such as E. A. Young of Little Rock noted that blacks seemed "very proud to have an opportunity to educate their children 'like white folks.'" Over seventeen hundred blacks attended schools in Little Rock, Pine Bluff, De Valls Bluff, and Helena in May 1865, revealing the commitment of blacks to education. Pine Bluff and Little Rock blacks contributed over seven hundred dollars in May 1865 to AMA educational enterprises in Arkansas. But many white Arkansans resented these intrusions and feared that educated blacks might become more powerful than they. A Camden teacher and missionary sensed no sympathy whatever among whites for this educational mission.[11]

Northern teachers and black students faced problems other than whites' disapproval in establishing schools in Arkansas. Since schoolhouses did not exist, teachers often appropriated abandoned white churches for new black schools. Little Rock teacher and pastor Hugh Brady lamented that many of his students learned "to write very fast but we have no desks yet except a few small tables." Northern teachers, unacclimated to the South, often became ill, making it impossible for them to continue classes. The army added to teachers' burdens by conscripting older black students for foraging details which disrupted classes and the students' progress.[12]

In 1863 and 1864 the eventual fate of the South's four million slaves enmeshed with marches to the sea, confrontations over habeas corpus, deaths, wranglings with England and France, struggles concerning presidential and congressional sovereignty, the transcontinental railroad, the

Homestead Act, and a thousand other perplexities. In such an environment Senator Charles Sumner of Massachusetts held clearly in focus the problems and hopes of freed black men and women. Sumner converted to abolitionism in the 1840s and throughout the Civil War kept the plight of Southern blacks before Congress and the nation. "It is well known," he warned the Senate, "that among the former slavemasters there are many who continue to count upon appropriating the labor of their slaves, if not under the name of slavery, at least under some other system by which the freedmen shall be effectually bound to serve. There must be no slavery under another *alias.*" Sumner searched for a bridge, "a way from slavery to freedom."[13]

To prevent the reenslavement of freedpersons, Sumner persuaded Secretary of War Edwin Stanton to appoint a three-member panel, known as the American Freedmen's Inquiry Commission, to tour the South to investigate the plight of the freedmen. Dr. Samuel G. Howe, Robert Dale Owen, and Colonel James McKaye, who made up the commission, brought their Boston Brahmin world view southward. Howe revealed the committee's philosophy by endorsing the idea of "sinking the differences of race." "It is only in this way," he insisted, "that we can leave free an unobstructed course to that natural law by which the weaker and poorer race is to be absorbed by the stronger and better one to the improvement of humanity, and to the glory of God." The committee in May 1864 recommended the establishment of a Freedmen's Bureau "not because these people are negroes, only because they are men who have been, for generations, despoiled of their rights." Although the committee feared "that there is as much danger in doing too much as in doing too little," they still believed a Freedmen's Bureau would offer blacks "a fair chance."[14]

Radical Republicans began immediately the congressional fight to enact the committee's proposals. Congressman Thomas D. Eliot of Massachusetts, a leading proponent, warned his colleagues that "the shackles have been loosened from the slave, but the conquering armies would leave the defeated free to weld them on again with bolts that could not be stricken off." Senator Charles Sumner joined Eliot in support of the bureau and argued that "the service required is too vast and complex for unorganized individuals. It must proceed from the national government. The national Government must interfere in this case precisely as in building the Pacific railroad."[15]

Opponents challenged the committee's proposals and lambasted the Freedmen's Bureau. Some members of Congress, such as Senator William Richardson of Illinois, believed that the bureau's goal of equality would prove impossible to achieve. "God has made the negro inferior," he proclaimed, "and such laws cannot make him equal." Others castigated "the evils of race-mixing." Congressman Samuel Cox of Ohio asserted that "no government farming system, no charitable black scheme, can wash out the color of the negro, change his inferior nature, or save him from his inevitable fate." Several congressmen feared the bureau would become too expensive to operate or too powerful—"swallowing up people and states." Other opponents of the legislation, though friends of the freedmen, worried that the bureau would emerge as but another master—dictating where and how to work and live.[16]

Congressmen debated for nearly twelve months over which cabinet department would control the Freedmen's Bureau and finally chose the War Department in March 1865. The bill enacted by Congress established a "Bureau of Refugees, Freedmen, and Abandoned Lands," to continue for one year after the war's end, and provided for a commissioner salaried at three thousand dollars annually. Areas of concern for the bureau included issuance of provisions, clothing, and fuel for refugees and freedmen, the maintenance of order, and abandoned land rental to freedmen and refugees. As historian Richard Bensel notes, the law expanded central government authority "in areas previously exclusively controlled by the individual states." Still, legislation enacted by Congress was one thing; realizing the goals of the legislation in Osceola or Jacksonport, Camden or other places in Arkansas was quite another.[17]

Secretary of War Edwin Stanton chose Oliver Otis Howard to head the Freedmen's Bureau. Born in 1830 in Leeds, Maine, and educated at Bowdoin College and at West Point, Howard displayed a self-righteousness and religiosity that alienated him from many classmates and fellow officers but made him a natural choice to lead the Freedmen's Bureau. Leading troops at Chancellorsville, Antietam, Fredericksburg, Gettysburg, Chattanooga, and in the March to the Sea, Howard impressed superiors. Such leadership, coupled with his moralism and humanitarianism, clearly recommended Howard for the position. The man who had solved tactical dilemmas at Chancellorsville and

Gettysburg was now called upon to solve, with equal efficiency, the problems of the freedmen. The military's penchant for moral dichotomies and for eschewing ambiguity and uncertainty comforted Howard, steadying him with confidence. He viewed the Civil War as "an awfully calamitous breaking up of a thoroughly organized society; dark desolation lay in its wake." Freedmen "had drifted into nooks and corners like debris into sloughs and eddies," Howard asserted, and his duty— and destiny—was to move freedmen toward their rightful freedom. William T. Sherman warned Howard, "It is not in your power to fulfill $^{1}/_{10}$ part of the expectations of those who formed the Bureau"; but Howard believed otherwise and dedicated himself to this crusade of bringing real freedom to blacks. What remained to be seen was whether Howard's or Sherman's vision for a postbellum world was realized.[18]

As long as the Civil War continued, the army and the federal government could not make treatment of freedpersons the top priority. But with the war's end in April 1865, the powers in Washington, D.C., turned their attention from blockades and military maneuvers to deciding what to do for freedpersons in the South, including Arkansas's 110,000. For Arkansas blacks, their treatment in the army, in the persistent plantation economy where many still chopped cotton and hoed corn, and in schools and hospitals which continued paternalism and neglect provided ample evidence that emancipation was not freedom. And there were thousands of freshly dug graves for acquaintances and relatives. They wondered if a new dawn would likely appear, if Lincoln's "new birth of freedom" would have any reality for them. In April 1865 Arkansas blacks and whites pondered what life would be like now that the war and slavery had ended. Congressmen and the new president, Andrew Johnson, also puzzled over what the future would bring. The military campaigns of the Civil War were over as of April 1865, but the struggle for freedom had just begun.

## CHAPTER 2

BUREAU BEGINNINGS AND IDEOLOGICAL UNDERPINNINGS

As head of the Freedmen's Bureau, Oliver Otis Howard confronted enormous obstacles and opportunities as he began to find personnel to organize the bureau in Dixie. Howard chose three subordinates between 1865 and 1869 to lead the Freedmen's Bureau in Arkansas: Brigadier General John W. Sprague, Brevet Major General E. O. C. Ord, and Brevet Major General Charles H. Smith. Officers in the occupied South needed tact, calm, patience, and discretion, not necessarily the abilities needed in the recent war. In restructuring the army in 1866 and 1867, the War Department slashed the number of officers to 1,530. Sprague, Ord, and Smith competed for promotion or at least to maintain a position in the army. Such rivalry stimulated some officers to be innovative in dealing with the freedmen in order to impress their superiors. In others who clung to the status quo, it caused timidity. General Sprague faced the unique difficulty of creating the bureau in Arkansas. Howard wanted Major Henry Hitchcock, a subordinate of General William T. Sherman, nominated as leader of the Freedmen's Bureau in Arkansas and Missouri, but when Secretary of War Edwin Stanton actively lobbied for Sprague, Howard eventually acquiesced. Howard noted that Sprague was "distinguished in the Army of the Tennessee for decided ability as a general, and meritorious conduct which he showed at all times, and for his dignity and carriage and thought"—a good bureaucrat's way of staying in favor with superiors.[1]

Born April 4, 1817, in White Creek, Washington County, New

York, Sprague attended the Rensselaer Polytechnic Institute and demonstrated Yankee ingenuity and practicality by successfully building one small business after another in the antebellum years. He joined the Seventh Ohio Volunteers in 1861 and rose from colonel to brevet major general during the fighting. After his Freedmen's Bureau tenure from June 1865 through October 1866, he managed the western division of the Northern Pacific Railroad and was influential in establishing the city of Takoma, Washington. Sprague demonstrated the Victorian era's devotion to moneymaking as a means to create one's personal identity and worth. Revealingly, he envisioned the state of Washington and western railroads, rather than his post in Arkansas, as a venue for economic success. He administered the bureau for the critical first sixteen months, but did he, even then, hear train whistles and clinking gold?[2]

Edward Otho Cresap Ord, unlike Sprague, committed his life to the military, serving in the army from 1835 to 1880. Born in Cumberland, Maryland, on October 19, 1818, Ord followed in his father's footsteps with military training, graduating from West Point in 1839. He served most notably at Harper's Ferry, Virginia, in 1858 during John Brown's failed rebellion. Severely wounded at Hatchie, Mississippi, and injured again at Fort Harrison, Virginia, in 1862, Ord served in Kentucky, Tennessee, Louisiana, and West Virginia in the last two years of the war. After his stint as the Freedmen's Bureau head, which lasted for but six months in 1866 and 1867, he commanded troops in Texas and on the Great Plains until his forced retirement in 1880 (a retirement opposed by the International Great Northern Railroad Company, indicating that Ord had won the favor of big business in the Indian Wars). Ord contracted yellow fever in Havana in 1883, died, and was interred at Arlington National Cemetery.[3]

Charles Henry Smith became captain of the First Maine Regiment in 1861 and fought at Second Bull Run, Antietam, Fredericksburg, and Gettysburg. He received the Congressional Medal of Honor after receiving three wounds at the Battle of St. Mary's Church in June 1864. He volunteered to head the Twenty-eighth U.S. Colored Infantry, indicating that he saw the war as something other than just a conflict to save the Union. He served, after his twenty-six month tour in Arkansas from March 1867 to May 1869, in Michigan, the Dakotas,

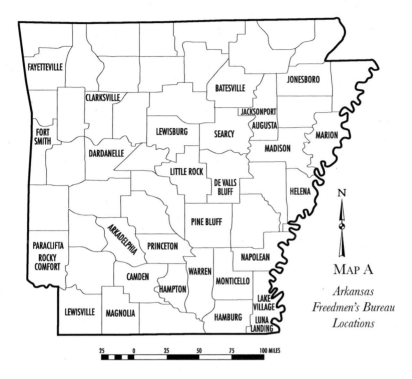

MAP A

Arkansas Freedmen's Bureau Locations

Texas, and New York City until his retirement in 1891. He died in 1902 and was, like General Ord, buried at Arlington National Cemetery.[4]

Local agents, far more than the state's bureau head, forged the fate of the Freedmen's Bureau and of freedpersons in Arkansas. Orders could be transmitted from Washington, D.C., to St. Louis or Little Rock with some clarity, but getting those orders to De Valls Bluff, Paraclifta, or Augusta posed a major dilemma for the Freedmen's Bureau in its effort to reconstruct Arkansas. Seventy-nine men, thirty-six civilians and forty-three army officers, headed the local bureaus from July 1865 until December 1868. Excluding Little Rock and Pulaski County in the state's center, the northeastern quadrant of Arkansas contained thirteen agencies, the southeastern and southwestern quadrants housed nine agencies each, and the northwestern quadrant, home of fewer freedmen, maintained only five agencies (see Map A). Agents remained at their post an average of nine and one-half months, their tenure varying from as little as one month to as long as thirty-four months (see Table 2.1).[5]

TABLE 2.1

Bureau Agent's Tenure: Local Agency Vacancies, 1865–1868

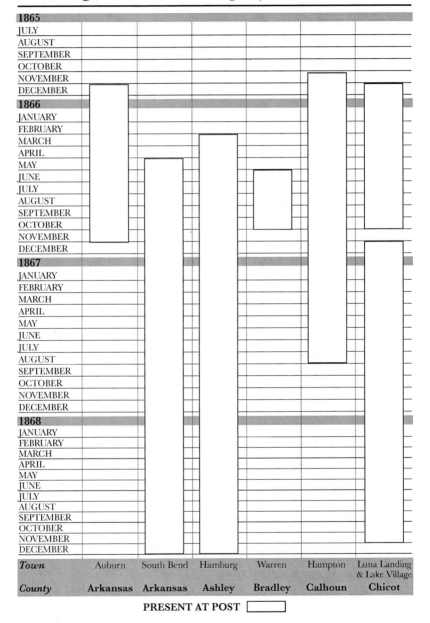

PRESENT AT POST [   ]

TABLE 2.1 *continued*

Bureau Agent's Tenure: Local Agency Vacancies, 1865–1868

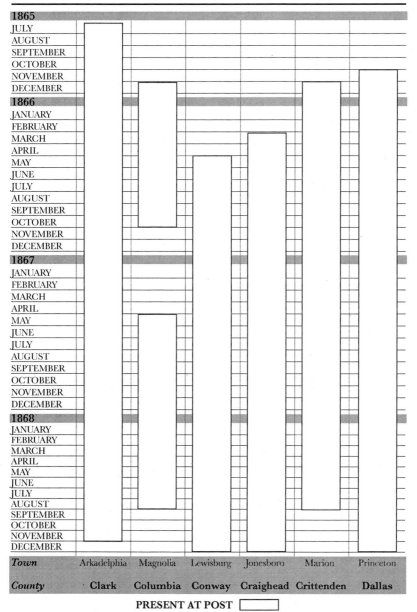

	Arkadelphia	Magnolia	Lewisburg	Jonesboro	Marion	Princeton
Town						
County	Clark	Columbia	Conway	Craighead	Crittenden	Dallas

PRESENT AT POST

TABLE 2.1 *continued*

Bureau Agent's Tenure: Local Agency Vacancies, 1865–1868

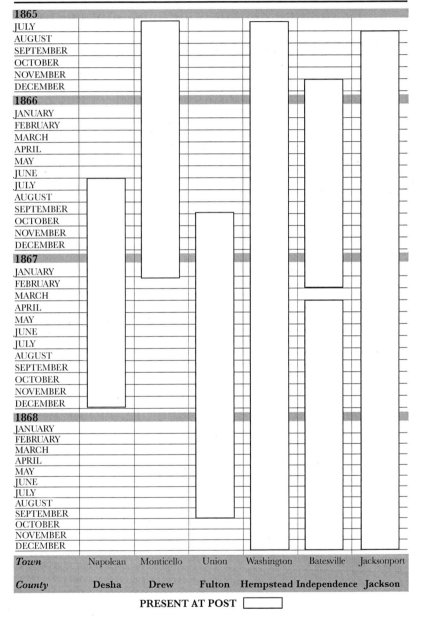

	Napolean	Monticello	Union	Washington	Batesville	Jacksonport
Town						
County	Desha	Drew	Fulton	Hempstead	Independence	Jackson

PRESENT AT POST ☐

TABLE 2.1 *continued*

Bureau Agent's Tenure: Local Agency Vacancies, 1865–1868

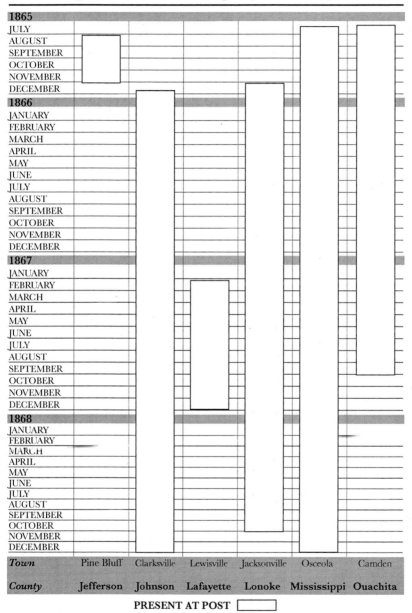

PRESENT AT POST [ ]

TABLE 2.1 *continued*

Bureau Agent's Tenure: Local Agency Vacancies, 1865–1868

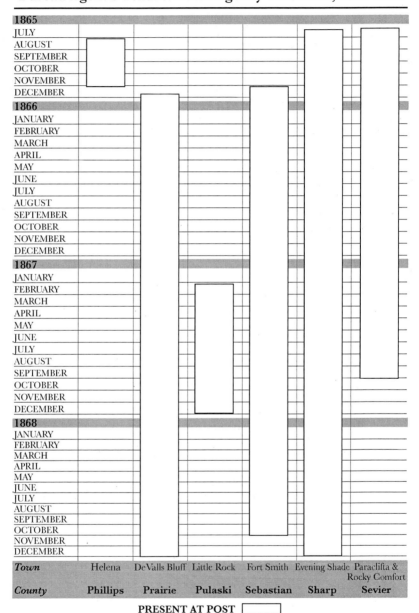

	Helena	DeValls Bluff	Little Rock	Fort Smith	Evening Shade	Paraclifta & Rocky Comfort
Town						
County	Phillips	Prairie	Pulaski	Sebastian	Sharp	Sevier

PRESENT AT POST ▭

TABLE 2.1 *continued*

Bureau Agent's Tenure: Local Agency Vacancies, 1865–1868

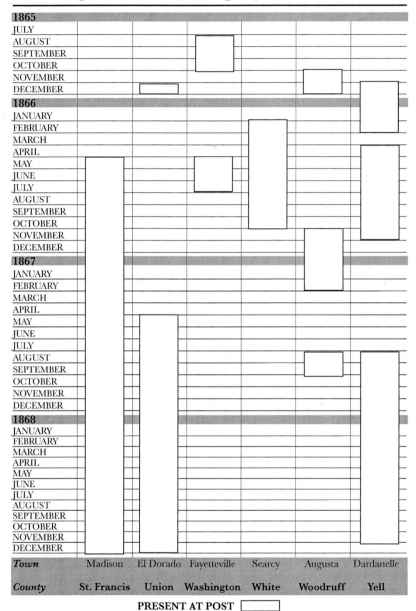

	Madison	El Dorado	Fayetteville	Searcy	Augusta	Dardanelle
Town	Madison	El Dorado	Fayetteville	Searcy	Augusta	Dardanelle
County	St. Francis	Union	Washington	White	Woodruff	Yell

PRESENT AT POST

Fierce intra-army competition raged for Freedmen's Bureau assignments. Within six months of Appomattox, the army dwindled from one million Union soldiers to two hundred thousand, declining to twenty-five thousand within ten years of the war's end. Since far fewer officers were needed, a variety of contacts and ploys were used to gain appointment. Thomas Hendricks recommended Edward T. Wallace because he was "the son of Governor Wallace of Tennessee and in politics, strictly conservative." Fort Smith merchant William Walker championed Fred Thibaut since he was "*nearly* related to the most distinguished officers in the Prussian and Austrian armies." Mrs. Frank Gross urged General Grant to appoint her husband since "my father and your father are friends." For others, such as Francis Springer, a Lutheran minister, patronage ties proved far less nebulous. "I personally know Mr. Springer to be an excellent man, and if he can be appointed consistently, I shall be glad," penned Abraham Lincoln, Springer's Springfield acquaintance. Springer received appointment to Fort Smith in October 1865.[6]

Henry Sweeney, Helena agent, epitomized the successes and failures a bureau agent faced. Born in Dublin, Ireland, in 1833, Sweeney trained as a druggist and migrated in 1864 to New York City where he enlisted in the army. Serving as a hospital steward in the West in the years before Fort Sumter fell, he worked his way from lieutenant to captain of U.S. Colored Troops during the Civil War. Placed in charge of the Freedmen's Bureau in Helena, this bureau agent favorably impressed blacks and whites with his behavior and demeanor. In 1866, however, planters accused him of accepting bribes from freedmen. Black elites responded and orchestrated a mass meeting in his behalf which persuaded officials of his innocence. Not above backstabbing a rival, Sweeney reported to his superior that another agent had been seen "in the streets of Memphis in a state of intoxication." When he left Helena in 1867, the local newspaper eulogized him and claimed, "It would be difficult, we think, to find an officer whose duties have been so delicate, and often so complicated, as those appertaining to the office of the Superintendent of the Freedmen's Bureau, that has pursued a course as singularly faultless or devoid of criticism. We cherish him with feelings of respect and admiration." Whether one held in such high esteem by the town's white elite adequately protected the rights of freedmen highlights the problems bureau agents faced, but

Sweeney garnered praise from both blacks and whites, an extraordinary accomplishment in such troubled times.[7]

Sebastian Geisreiter, an officer and agent in Pine Bluff, became one of the leading citizens and entrepreneurs of Jefferson County after his tenure in the Freedmen's Bureau. Born in Bavaria, Germany, in May 1840, Geisreiter moved with his parents to New York City in May 1854. Working there as a salesman and bookkeeper until 1857, he then joined those heading west in search of fortune as the United States experienced one of its cyclical economic depressions. Finding neither gold nor silver, he joined the Second Minnesota Cavalry during the Civil War and fought Indians on the Great Plains. At war's end, he received orders sending him to Arkansas where he served as a bureau agent until 1868. Having offended few in Jefferson County as a bureau official, he began selling insurance and accumulating the wealth he had unsuccessfully sought in the West. Marrying into a prominent Pine Bluff family in 1877, Geisreiter used the Freedmen's Bureau as a stepping-stone, a way to make contacts in southern Arkansas.[8]

Only biographical shards of other Freedmen's Bureau agents remain. Civilian agents included antebellum physicians, lawyers, merchants, farmers, tailors, bootmakers, and, inexplicably, an overseer. But regardless of their former occupations, their ideologies and philosophical world view critically shaped postwar Arkansas.[9]

Agents' philosophies molded policies and procedures in the local bureau offices. The two lodestars of Southern history—race and class—confronted agents with Gordian knots to unravel. Agents displayed, as did most of the population, a keen awareness of color. Officials inscribed in marriage records the color of the bride and groom and of their parents. Typically, one agent noted:

> I have this day united in matrimony Henry B. Smith of County D—— and Mamala Johnston of Pine Bluff Arkansas age of man twenty-one years color Brown and of his father Brown and of his mother Yellow age of woman twenty years color Yellow and of her father Yellow and of her mother Yellow.

Entries grew more precise, with terms such as "black, white, mulatto, quadroon, octoroon, ¾ black, and mixed" frequenting agents' records.[10]

Many agents believed color signaled inferiority. Bureau head

General Sprague equated African Americans to Native Americans and insisted that the flaws of blacks, like those of Indians, would make it easy to transform freedmen into "a class of drunkards." Sprague despaired to the point of writing a Chicago philanthropist that the freedmen's behavior "will almost force the conclusion upon any one that it were better to let them perish from the earth." Lieutenant William Tisdale, stationed in Little Rock, lamented that blacks were both "shiftless and lazy." Pine Bluff agent Sebastian Geisreiter concluded after a few months in the field that "there is always room for apology on behalf of the negroes, but the patience of the agent is at times sorely tried." Captain Edward T. Wallace grew exasperated at a black who, when told to leave his office, responded to Wallace, "Shit. A nigger is as good as any damned son of a bitch." "No sooner was the remark made," Wallace noted, "than I thrashed him soundly." If any African American dared challenge agents' notions of a hierarchy of black inferiority and white superiority, they were likely to feel the sting of whips or verbal abuse—just as under slavery.[11]

Views of blacks prompted some agents to attempt to continue the practice whereby a white man presumed a right to sexual intercourse with black women whenever he desired. Agent Thomas Hunnicutt in Lake Village forced freedwomen to engage in sexual activities in his office when they visited him on official business. One woman, Catherine Hanna, refused his advances by insisting "she didn't do that." Hunnicutt responded to her rejection by noting that "he treated white women so." Although Hunnicutt continued to pressure Hanna and swore that she was not "the first damn yellow woman he ever screwed," Hanna still resisted. A. A. Wright of Lewisville coerced black and white women and admitted having been with an army private and that "he had played on his banjo then, and would do so again." Albert Coats repeatedly engaged "in improper conduct with nearly every colored girl" he met. An eyewitness found Coats leaving his room "wearing only a shirt and drawers" and accompanied by a black woman. "I found my bed badly tumbled and many of the slats had fallen on to the floor," the witness alleged. Many agents consciously and openly expressed their contempt for Arkansas blacks, revealing a racism that permeated much of American life.[12]

Agents also manifested paternalism toward freedpersons, another more subtle form of racism. Bureau officials often perceived themselves as surrogate planters, white patriarchs taking care of infantile Sambos. E. G. Barker, Marion agent, confessed to a Northern friend that the "colored people having been suddenly changed from slaves to that of citizens of the U.S. are but *children* in their new position, and easily led astray." General Sprague cautioned local agents not to control freedpersons too much. He insisted they "should remember that they are in no sense the *master* or *overseer* of the Freed people. All are *free*. No rules or regulations can be made for the government and control of freedmen that do not legally apply also to whites." Repeatedly, agents' assumptions about black infantilism and subservience clearly hampered freedpersons in their attempts to clarify freedom for themselves. It is here that agents exerted their greatest influence at the local level.[13]

Bureau officials accepted nineteenth-century notions of hierarchies and recognized that Southern planters still controlled much of local life, even if their power rested only on memories of antebellum days. Agents and planters eyed each other warily, each trying to outmaneuver the other. Planters often co-opted agents and thereby controlled the bureau. Nathan Cole in Lewisville believed the bureau would succeed because "the better class of planters are disposed to aid in the work." Sebastian Geisreiter, a Pine Bluff agent who eventually became a "leading white citizen" of Jefferson County, enjoyed the "very cordial manner" in which local planters received him. Arkadelphia agent A. E. Habricht, stationed in Arkansas for twenty-seven months (perhaps because he understood the correct approach to take with Southern planters), inquired if a planter had "any charges to proffer against *your* freedmen."[14]

While some agents became the puppets of planters, others zealously loathed the old ruling class. The Chicot County agent conceived a list of the planters with his evaluation of each. He judged W. H. Anderson of Fawnwood Plantation as "a bad man and requires watching" and perceived J. McClemm of Dressim Plantation as "a whiskey drinking loafer who has not sufficient education to keep his own accounts properly. Down on the government and Nigger generally and on the bureau particularly." Curtis Garrett and Robert Clay "required strict watching," Clay because he failed to pay laborers properly and Garrett because he longed to whip freedmen as before. Lewis Cooper seemed "honest, hardworking" but loved Argyle bitters too much.[15]

The agents' conceptions of class structure also included a "better sort" of African Americans. George Benson of Chicot County requested a teacher for Lake Village after the county's "influential colored men" favored one. General Ord ordered the Ashley County agent "to notify the intelligent freedmen" of the arrival of a company of black soldiers. When General Sprague received complaints about Helena's agent, he interrogated "the most intelligent freedmen there" and dismissed the charge.[16]

This attachment to hierarchy that pervaded agents' mentalities is revealed not only in their recognition of white and black elites, but is also evidenced in their disdain for lower-class whites. Frank Gross of Little Rock worried that "only from that portion which have no interests at all—*the canaille of the community*—need any demonstration against the rights of colored people be feared." Sebastian Geisreiter compared lower class whites to vermin and noted that "a lower class of irresponsible white men of whom many *infest* the country" hindered labor at Fountain Hill. John Walker condemned "the worthless white vagabonds" that littered the Arkansas countryside. Such bureau condescension and loathing toward many Southern whites only exacerbated an already strained situation.[17]

Agents maintained and encouraged such hierarchies as reflections of their belief that God ruled the universe justly, that one indeed reaped what one sowed. Planters and the black elite possessed skills, talents, and morals which rewarded them with success, while poor whites had been created in God's image but had all but lost the divine stamp.

Racism, paternalism, and commitment to hierarchies combined to produce the agents' desires to foster a work ethic. Bureau chief O. O. Howard strongly encouraged state and local agents to preach the gospel of work. He repeatedly promised freedmen "nothing but their freedom, and freedom means work." "The Negro should understand," he insisted, "that he is really free, but on no account, if able to work, should he harbor the thought that the Government will support him in idleness."[18]

Local agents joined in the chorus which extolled work. Crittenden County agent E. G. Barker exhorted planters, "We must try to teach the colored folk that it is by the sweat of the brow that man eats bread." Hempstead County superintendent E. W. Gantt reminded blacks that "the Good Book tells us that we must 'earn our bread by the sweat of the brow.' If there were any other I would tell you."[19]

Self-reliance also dominated agents' philosophies. Bureau officials repeatedly reminded freedpersons that they had to protect their own freedom. General Sprague advised General Howard at the bureau's genesis in Arkansas, "I think it better that Freedmen should whenever practicable furnish their own clothes and if possible his board, also, thus acting for himself even in these things he will be taught to think."[20]

Agents' philosophies reflected dominant Northern ideologies which sustained racism, paternalism, "natural" hierarchies, a work ethic, and self-help sentiments. Dispensing such philosophies, the Freedmen's Bureau often became, for Arkansas blacks, the Freedmen's burden, adding to the challenges faced by freedmen. At other times, blacks accepted and embraced these sentiments as what they wanted for themselves. Still others undoubtedly accepted the agents' ideas unthinkingly and gladly. Most blacks, however, did not totally embrace the dogmas of their bureau benefactors. They created their own ideologies which co-opted or countered agents' assumptions and which critically determined their own futures.

Blacks developed their own ideological emphasis as a response to the opportunities offered at emancipation for the creation of new identities and self-concepts. Although former slaves plunged eagerly into the heady experience of a new beginning, a new birth of freedom, they obviously possessed no tabula rasa. Slavery had seared their consciousnesses. Former slaves readily recalled children's wails, the awful rips of whip on human flesh, and the hollow feeling in the stomach while longing for a recently sold spouse. Slave tales filled the crisp night air of many Arkansas evenings. Anna Huggins of Little Rock heard "lots of things about slavery" from her grandmother. What did Annie Hill of Nashville think and feel as she listened to her mother recall slavery? "The Leslie man brought her to Arkansas. When she was eleven," reported Hill of her grandmother's story. "That is what she always told us kids. She was eleven years old when they sold her. Just like selling mules." "I know too much of slavery to be a Democrat," Lewisburg freedman Sam Houston swore. Former slaves rejoiced at their emancipation but dared not forget what they had endured.[21]

While ever cultivating a remembrance of things past, freedpersons often chose to move from their old homes to distance themselves from painful memories and to prove themselves free. To a large degree, *where* a black or white lived determined the quality of their existence. More than just demographic concepts, white-black density and rural-urban demarcations not only determined the location of a Freedmen's Bureau office, but also whether a freedperson felt safe or isolated, and whether lucrative work opportunities or poverty prevailed. James Gill of Marvell recalled that most blacks left the plantation "like when you leave de let get open where is a big litter of shotes and dey just hit de road and commenced to ramble." Liddie Aiken of Wheatley remembered blacks scattered "for two years to get work and something to eat." Hammett Dale of Brasfield registered "droves [of] darkies just rovin' around."[22]

Freedpersons felt safer in areas of high black density and also appreciated the richness and diversity of larger communities. Blacks wanted to be with other blacks. J. L. Thorp, Camden bureau agent, complained that many freedmen seemed "infatuated with town life" where ten to twenty people rented and lived in a single unit to escape plantation life. The *Weekly Arkansas Gazette* lamented, "Freedmen throughout the state are hanging around the town and villages. Our city is unusually crowded with the poor devils."[23]

Regardless of whites' consternation at swelling black populations, freedmen continued to choose to empower themselves by living in areas of heavily populated African-American enclaves. Arkansas blacks made up over 25 percent of the population of southern and southeastern quadrants of the state (see Map B). For example, the black population of Pulaski County increased by 290 percent from 1860 to 1870 as the urban capital, Little Rock, drew farm blacks to its new opportunities and promised riches. The racial composition of the largest Arkansas communities was recorded in 1870 (see Table 2.2). Blacks and whites in towns such as Little Rock or Helena experienced different sensibilities about time, space, power, and class than did their counterparts in Council (population 312) or Dudley Lake (population 292).[24]

New self-concepts hinged on an emphasis of communities. Freedpersons developed and nourished group-reliance philosophies while they established new ties with new neighbors. John Goodrum of Des Arc believed blacks turned to each other at emancipation since freedmen "got just turned out like you turn a hog out the pen and say go on I'm through with you." Pine Bluff blacks assured an American Missionary Association representative, "We can take care of ourselves. We are in the majority in the county. We don't want any Carpet Bagger

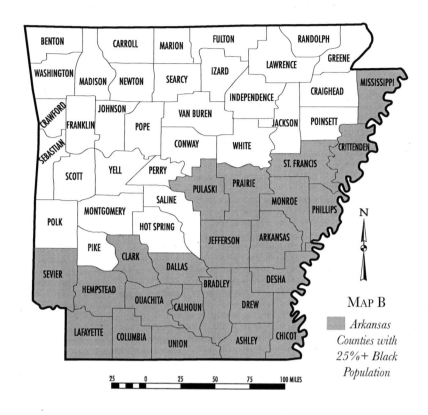

MAP B

Arkansas
Counties with
25%+ Black
Population

TABLE 2.2

Urban Racial Composition: 1870

City	# Whites	%	# Blacks	%	Total
Arkadelphia	680	72%	268	28%	948
Camden	998	62%	612	38%	1,610
Fort Smith	1,682	75%	536	25%	2,218
Helena	1,140	50.5%	1,109	49.5%	2,249
Little Rock	7,101	57%	5,274	43%	12,375
Pine Bluff	1,297	62%	800	38%	2,087
Van Buren	2,521	76%	768	34%	3,289

among us." Blacks carefully surveyed offers of help from whites and often decided to control their own destiny.[25]

The black family, nourished even in slavery under dire circumstances, became *the* treasure many blacks jealously guarded in the post-bellum world. It was *the* most important institution for sustaining the new personalities which emerged after emancipation. Caring for wife, husband, daughter, son, grandparents, uncles, aunts, and cousins loomed as far more significant for many African Americans than did accumulating greenbacks, bank credit, railroad stock, or capital. Freedpersons at emancipation began the diligent and heart-wrenching search for family renewals and publicly proclaimed just who composed their family. A Brinkley woman moved to Arkansas in hopes of finding her husband. Her child, Charlie Huff, recalled, "Ma heard somebody out here bought Pa. We kept inquiring till after she died." John Carroll notified Freedmen's Bureau personnel that "my wife and child are at Joshua Tatrus place in Union County Arkansas and I would like to have them with me here at Little Rock and should like to know by what route I can receive them they wish of course to be with me." Many freedpersons decided first and foremost to sustain and protect families so long disrupted by slavery.[26]

In order to protect their newly united families and to ensure freedom, blacks upheld their own work ethic. Many clearly recognized that the only way to guarantee freedom was to achieve economic self-subsistence. National African-American leaders such as Frederick Douglass exhorted freedmen that "if you would be prosperous, you must be industrious." Arkansas black elites joined Douglass and urged blacks to work so as to be able to provide for themselves. A black orator at a gathering of freedpersons on the Maxwell Plantation near Searcy insisted to his audience "that just because they were free, doves would not fly, roasted, into their mouths; that they must all work." An African Methodist Episcopal bishop, visiting Arkansas, urged freedmen to "work hard, save their money, and buy lands."[27]

If blacks agreed with whites about the importance of work, they did not, however, accept work rhythms dictated by whites. Freedom meant hoeing, fishing, and dancing when *they* wished. Freedmen's Bureau agent William Tisdale believed freedpersons often refused "to work merely for the sake of giving a more tangible form to the fact that they are free." William Stuart of Arkadelphia recognized that "the negro is full of the idea of controlling his own time and of being a planter." Complaints that freedpersons "will not work on Saturday, even when the crop needs getting in," filled both planter correspondence and Freedmen's Bureau reports. A Pine Bluff overseer on the Bayner Plantation recorded in his journal, "I have talked and talked it does no good about getting out of morning it does no good they say as soon as the weather clears that they will make it all up." Blacks often worked when and where they chose.[28]

Freedmen's Bureau agents often faced aggressive and assertive African Americans. Conflict between bureau agents and freedmen would have been inevitable even if they had been the only two groups in Arkansas. Blacks and bureau agents looked at the world and often defined freedom differently. But they, of course, could not write the rules for postbellum Arkansas alone. White Arkansans—poor, suddenly poor, wealthy, and suddenly wealthy—added their philosophies and agendas to the volatile situation.

Just as freedmen returned through memory to slavery, so too did planters and yeomen who had dreamed one day of becoming slave holders. John R. Montgomery of Washington, Arkansas, reported that many southwestern planters "had not yet realized the colored man was free." Bureau agent William Tisdale discovered similar conditions in the central portion of the state and observed that "slavery in its most servile form, is today as much in existence as it ever was in the days of King Jeff." The reactionary *Little Rock Daily Arkansas Gazette* editorialized, "We need the services of the freedmen; we can make them useful to us." Most planters dreamed of a return, in some form, to the days before 1860 when they and cotton were king.[29]

Many whites also could not yet forget their defeat in the hellacious Civil War. Thomas J. Reed, bureau agent in Lewisville, witnessed "a great deal of hostility on the part of the people from Ashley County to the government," with many returning Rebels still sporting their Confederate uniforms. Opponents of the Freedmen's Bureau serenaded agent Volney Voltaire Smith nightly with strains of "Southern Rights" and "Get Out of the Wilderness." Napoleon's J. C. Predmore testified that many people harbored "a bitter feeling against the bureau" which intensified because its officers were "northern men."[30]

The so-called "meddling" by the Freedmen's Bureau proved especially loathsome to the white elite. Planters openly boasted to Lafayette County agent V. V. Smith that "they can handle any damned nigger [bureau] agent that can be sent here." Marion County sheriff I. M. Stinnett informed Colonel C. H. Smith that "no negro agent shall visit Marion County without being mobbed." Arkadelphia whites referred to the bureau in the most scathing epithet Southerners used: "the nigger amongst us."[31]

Lower-class Southern whites at times accepted and at other moments rejected planters' efforts to resurrect antebellum philosophies. Crittenden County agent J. P. Walker feared that "the lowest order of whites some without a visible means of living who neglect no opportunity when it presents itself with safety to annoy and molest industrious Freedmen" influenced freedpersons toward lethargy and leisure. Poor whites could no longer ignore their black competitors, and they now often feared that industrious blacks would force them to abandon their lives of ease. Freedmen's Bureau head General E. O. C. Ord witnessed "many poor and laboring white men who feel themselves aggrieved and degraded at having to compete with negroes as tenants and laborers." Lower-class whites offered freedmen either an alternative to ponder, a competitor to face, or an enemy to conquer.[32]

If the Civil War erupted over cultural values, then the cessation of the fighting did not end the conflict. Humanitarians, Freedmen's Bureau agents, freedpersons, white planters, and poor whites all continued to assert their own ideologies and demand empowerment. The Freedmen's Bureau particularly faced gargantuan difficulties as it tried to implement its philosophies in Arkansas.

Each bureau agent upheld his own particular ideological perspective and never clearly grasped the goals of the bureau. V. V. Smith succinctly stated the problem: "Every agent that has had charge of the affairs of the bureau in this country has had different ideas as to the manner in which the duties on him should be discharged." Nathan Cole cursed "the poor records" he inherited from his predecessor which made his task doubly difficult since he could not be sure what had and had not been tried previously. Even the leaders of the bureau complained of inadequate local assessments. "I am yet without reports of any kind from Arkansas," groaned General Sprague in June 1865.

When reports finally arrived, Sprague found them "about as useful as the Greek alphabet in enabling me to get an idea of the progress of the work."[33]

Many agents suffered moral myopia and never captured a vision of what the bureau attempted or of the new worlds struggling to be born in Arkansas. E. G. Barker of Monticello in November 1865, only five months after Appomattox, informed his superiors in regard to a specific plantation classified as "abandoned" that "this plantation is not used by the Bureau *and will not be needed* next year." Such certainty that he would not need the land for freedmen reveals the deadening conservatism that hampered bureau activities.[34]

The bureau served as a steppingstone to other, more lucrative opportunities for some agents; for others it became a final post before retirement. White citizens of Paraclifta complained that agent H. W. Ballard made "his own interests the object of his stay." Thomas Hunnicutt collected "large sums of money as black-mail" from planters for whom he supplied black laborers. Agent Thomas Reed levied a two dollar tax on freedmen until reprimanded by bureau officials. John Thorpe of Camden assessed a marriage fee until he, too, received orders to cease. The Lafayette County register of "letters received" recorded page after page of translations of Spanish to English phrases, hinting that the agent dreamed of the day when he lived far, far away from Lafayette County. Other agents hoped to persevere until retirement. Some officers grew senile and did not readily adjust their world view to the new environment forged from war. Colonel Pinkeny Lugenbeel of Fort Smith seemed outdated to bureau superiors. They judged him "an old Army officer of the old school" who believed "if a man goes to the Episcopal Church and votes the democratic ticket he cannot materially err."[35]

Even if the local agent dedicated himself to honestly aiding freedmen, logistics thwarted his efforts. Limited numbers of men faced impossibly large areas to supervise. Lewis Carhart of Camden admitted there existed "sections where our troops have never been." Poor roads hampered bureau activities and forced General Ord to complain: "I might as well send snails to catch antelopes as send Infantry to arrest violators of laws in Arkansas." Flooding, a common occurrence along the Mississippi River, forced Isaac Adair of Chicot County to "go every place in a canoe." Agent H. C. DeWolf of South Bend ruined an artificial leg crossing a swollen stream in an attempt to check on freedmen in his area. Overcrowded and unfurnished offices also added to officials' burdens. Problems abounded as agents began their work in Arkansas in 1865.[36]

Ideologies clashed and difficulties soared as the Civil War ended in Arkansas. Planters, freedmen, freedwomen, Freedmen's Bureau agents, carpetbaggers, and poor whites each dreamed their separate dreams—haunted by the past and unsure of the future. Just who were freedmen in 1865? What did it mean to be a black man or woman in 1865? Freedpersons, bureau agents, planters, and white yeomen addressed the basic question of identity first. Blacks confronted not only their old masters' yearnings to reenslave them, but also wrestled with their self-images established under the paternalism and violence of slavery, self-images often reinforced by bureau agents. A basic dilemma—Who am I?—perplexed freedpersons in the days after Appomattox. The decisions reached in the period between 1865 and 1868 regarding identity would crucially shape African-American life for years to come.

CHAPTER 3

IDENTITIES AND THE FREEDMEN'S BUREAU, 1865–1868

Although most historians today deny that slavery inevitably produced pathological personalities, the "I" which metamorphosed under slavery was often limited in viable alternatives and therefore sometimes stunted. Eugene Genovese correctly insists that slaves asserted their humanity in a thousand ways—creating their own work rhythms, worshiping their own God, respecting their own family mores, subtly controlling overseers and masters, to name but a few. And Genovese's thesis has been richly corroborated by historians George Rawick, John Boles, Charles Joyner, John Blassingame, Lawrence Levine, Deborah White, and Elizabeth Fox-Genovese. But although slaves displayed far more resiliency and humanity than historians such as Ulrich B. Phillips indicated, the truth remains that no one would choose to be a slave. Slavery *did* hinder and cripple both black and white personalities. If this is denied, the hardships of emancipation—the successes and failures—dim, diluted by a Carlislean view of the "slave as superman." If, however, Reconstruction is viewed as a wrenching struggle by freedpersons to forge their own personalities, less fettered by masters, whips, and white expectations of innate inferiority, then the struggle takes on more realistic and heroic dimensions.[1]

Although African Americans most likely carried from Africa a question better phrased as Who are we?, their forced arrival in the Western hemisphere dictated their confrontation with the European variety of identity: Who am I? During slavery, the overwhelming domination of whites constrained slaves' answers to the questions. Their "I" was molded and shaped by their own choices to a degree and by their own skilled subterfuge, but it was also formed as much by decisions made by masters, their children, overseers, or Adam Smith's "Invisible Hand." Yet at emancipation, identities camouflaged under slavery could now be unmasked. Who am I? demanded new individual and communal answers. Freedom demanded renewed searching. Although influenced by African cultural linkages which predisposed African Americans toward certain answers, their recent history in the United States where both Northerners and Southerners treated them as unwanted stepchildren and their own physical and psychological limitations and potentials were also influential. In a real sense freedpersons guarded and created their new identities often by *their* choices. A major aspect of Reconstruction in Arkansas involved the ways in which the Freedmen's Bureau and Arkansas freedpersons struggled with African-American identity.

It is a daunting task to attempt to ponder the identities of others. Even though it is impossible to *know* the freedpersons or their former masters, the processes they used to reconstruct themselves may be glimpsed. There are further complications in a study of self: Were these new identities which freedpersons in 1865 and 1866 so openly displayed the same selves which had been camouflaged under slavery? Or were these new identities masks devised by blacks to test the boundaries of freedom? Or were they not masks at all, but rather the genuine African American, revealed at last? The study of identities is crucial in understanding Arkansas blacks and Reconstruction, but it is a very complex inquiry.

In reconstructing identities after the Civil War, freedpersons first selected their new names. Slavery ideology denied surnames to imply subhumanity. Sallie Crane recalled that under slavery "we hardly knowed our names. We was cussed for so many bitches and sons of bitches and bloody bitches, and blood of bitches. We never heard our names scarcely at all." Slaves most likely used secret names among themselves to assert identity within their group, but whites seldom recognized such names.[2]

At emancipation, the adoption of official surnames and first names reflected and instilled self-pride and dignity and validated freedom. A name implied humanity, a unique personality, binding kinship ties, and a hint of immortality, as one's surname lived on in one's children. A name also cemented responsibilities as a citizen, father, or mother. The taking of a name momentously and existentially signified the creation of new identity.

Most freedpersons either incorporated their master's surname or maintained their father's last name. Freedmen who accepted their master's surname either indicated their sympathetic feelings toward the master or perhaps thought maintaining his last name would help in family reunions. On the other hand, choosing a new surname might be indicative of a rejection of the slave past and a desire to start all over. Most blacks used Anglo-American names or popular Biblical names. Pine Bluff and Hempstead County marriage records reveal that the most chosen male names were John, Richard, James, Samuel, and Stephen; freedwomen most frequently took Jane, Elizabeth, Sarah, Emily, Margaret, Hanna, Nancy, or Mary. Women also used state names such as Alabama or Florida. But not every freedperson willingly accepted English names, some choosing Hemptine, Narcissa, Nero, or Frederick Meshack Abednego. Whatever name they created, such naming reaffirmed to African Americans that this indeed was a new beginning, a time of new hopes and raised expectations. Names signified either an acceptance or rejection of past memories, with each individual dealing with the memories of the past and projections into the future in his or her own way.[3]

Family memories also sustained many freedpersons and crystallized identities. When struggling to answer Who am I?, freedpersons responded concretely with "Joe and Millie Smith's son" or "Ebenezer Hawkins' grandson." In a world devoid of many past guideposts, family connections, even if but a memory, encouraged many. Annie Hill of Nashville showed a WPA investigator in the 1930s a picture of her mother standing alongside her master's three children, promising that "anybody that bothered that picture would get in it with me." It is easy enough to imagine Annie Hill, in times of distress, gathering courage by returning to her mother's photograph for the thousandth time in the special place where she kept it. Elmira Hill of Pine Bluff treasured a letter from her mother. She kept it "for remembrance."

Cora Scroggins of Clarendon remembered, "My mother spoke of her one long journey [into Arkansas] on the steamboat and stagecoach. That was when she was brought to Arkansas. It made a memorable picture in her mind." Such family heirlooms created continuities as pasts penetrated the present.[4]

Freedpersons not only connected with relatives from the past, but also linked with new kin networks for support. As the industrial and scientific revolutions of the nineteenth century rocked European and American intellectual foundations, the family became for many *the* institution which sustained individuals and preserved values. In an age which magnified emotion, the family nourished and channeled heightened subjectivity into acceptable behavior. Freedpersons inculcated some of the Victorian, bourgeois family norms and added them to their long-standing devotion to and concern for the family. Family roles became clearer than in the tenuous connections under slavery, serving as emotional conduits which sustained and nourished an individual.[5]

Family control also gauged genuine freedom. Former masters reluctantly recognized blacks' kinship rights. Local bureau agents quickly recognized planter intransigence against newly sanctioned black families. General John Sprague, Freedmen's Bureau head in July 1865, reported, "Slaveholders still retain their [freedmen's] children contrary to law." Agent Lewis Carhart of Camden demanded that a Ouachita County planter "allow the bearer Sam [to] have his family. Wife and five children now on your place." He ordered another planter to allow Jesse Gattling "to remove his family and personal property from the premises." As late as 1867 bureau agents still pressed planters to free black children and allow freedpersons' families autonomy. Agent Fred Thibaut of Washington informed planter A. S. Justice that "the bearer Brown Bean (a freeman) claims that you have a minor Son belonging to him in your possession. He has a right to control and you will deliver the boy Isaiah to him upon receipt of this order." One of the major successes of the Freedmen's Bureau was its commitment to encouraging and sustaining the black family.[6]

Aided by the bureau, freedpersons at emancipation diligently searched for missing family members. Poignant inquiries for lost children and parents flooded bureau offices. Phillips Watts requested that the Little Rock office help him find his wife and son snatched from him and taken to Dangerfield, Texas, in the hectic days of 1863. In many instances, long distance separations had not weakened marital devotion, as evidenced by the thousands of husbands and wives who tried to reunite in the postwar world.[7]

Parents also anxiously searched for missing children. In October 1866 Diana Brown sought the assistance of the Freedmen's Bureau in regaining her ten-year-old child who had been taken from her in 1863 as her master fled from Pulaski County to southwestern Hempstead County. A Pine Bluff freedman yearned to be reunited with his five children in Alabama; unable to leave his crop in the crucial days of early summer, he requested and received aid to bring his children to Arkansas. Grandparents also demanded custody of their kin. Fort Smith freedwoman Lucinda Johnson insisted to Freedmen's Bureau agent Thomas Abel that she was "the nearest relative living and that she wants the child under her immediate control."[8]

The question of a child's "legitimacy" and the determination of parentage also perplexed bureau agents and freedpersons. Arkansas governor Isaac Murphy urged Freedmen's Bureau head General John Sprague to place children in two-parent homes as quickly as possible. Bureau agents often confronted paternity suits. In Jacksonport, for example, freedwoman Susan Seward testified that she never had sexual intercourse with any person other than George Owen, who she swore had fathered her child. Owen testified to fathering children with Milly Seward, Susan's sister, but denied he had ever been with Susan Seward. After Owen admitted to fathering two other children by another woman, the bureau agent determined that Owen was most likely the father of Susan Seward's child. But not every father shirked his responsibilities. Freedman Nickelson Taylor of Napoleon swore that he was the father of Airy Taylor's child and demanded custody, but Miss Taylor testified that the father was Knox Knowlton. The bureau agent believed Miss Taylor and granted her custody of the child. Napoleon agent J. C. Predmore eventually formulated a rule to guide him in custody cases: if the mother's labor contract contained a clause for child support, then she received custody of the child; if the mother had no child support clause in her contract, then the father took the child.[9]

Children joined in the search for lost loved ones. "After freedom,"

Lula Taylor of Brinkley remembered, "we kept writing till we got in tech with her. We finally got granny with us on the Jefferies place at Clarendon." A Hamburg bureau agent informed freedwoman Martha Bell of Texas that her "two boys are living in this county at or with B. T. Smith and are very desirous that the family be got together and would like to have you come here and they have sufficient money to pay all expenses."[10]

The family served as a crucial vortex for blacks confronting freedom. It taught values that supported African Americans as they faced a still harsh and unjust world and connected them to the past by linking them to kin who had endured. For the bureau, families inculcated order and conservatism by teaching black children the value of work and the importance of staying in one's "place." In extolling the family, bureau agents emphasized marriage, whether in solemnizing relationships shared in antebellum days or in joining males and females in monogamous relationships after emancipation. Marriage linked practical daily life to the bureau's ideology of preserving order in a revolutionary milieu, of keeping blacks in their assigned place, and of offering freedpersons the "good life" as perceived by Freedmen's Bureau agents. To achieve these goals, agents desired to persuade blacks to accept monogamy. Freedpersons assimilated these hopes and then chose how to behave and understand themselves sexually. When black and white values collided with blacks' sexuality, this crucially forged freedpersons' identity.

The wills of blacks and whites clashed in grappling with sexuality and gender. Sexuality offered additional choices for freedpersons and figured significantly in shaping their personality. To analyze black and white sexuality is to submerge into the crawl space of Southern history— a space filled with subterranean subconscious desires, suppressions, fears, and jealousies. Many Arkansas bureau agents unquestioningly accepted racial and sexual stereotypes from their past. Hampton agent John Scroggins believed that freedmen practiced "fornication and adultery" and "desperately needed education and moral training." William Dawes of Pine Bluff insisted, "Promiscuous cohabitation is the universal custom." Napoleon agent J. C. Predmore anxiously noted that "the freedmen seem to have but little idea of the sacred obligation of marriage and look upon it rather as a matter of convenience for the present, that is to be put aside whenever it becomes tiresome." He also worried that "the old practice of cohabitating without any ceremony whatever is carried on to a very great extent." "I have tried hard," he insisted, "to bring the evils of this system before the people." Agents worried that whites would become as sexually active as they thought blacks were, weakening the bonds of matrimony and of society.[11]

Enslaved African Americans had developed their own values and mores regarding sexuality and marriage. Rejecting Calvinistic sentiments of a tainted and sinful body, slaves engaged in premarital sexual intercourse as a matter of natural, biological instinct. Slaves followed certain guidelines, such as engaging with sexual partners for extended periods before marriage, staying with one partner monogamously until breaking the arrangement and going elsewhere. Elaborate courtship and marriage rituals developed, such as jumping over the broomstick or using certain floral bridal wreaths to symbolize the occasion's significance. These practices and values, emerging under the South's "peculiar institution" wherein a slave's relationship with family or any other person faced possible instantaneous disruption or degradation, reaffirmed a slave's dignity and humanity.[12]

White neuroses about black sexuality had a long and sordid history which has been brilliantly analyzed by historian Winthrop Jordan. He asserts that English racism was grounded in the English fear of the color black as indicative of evil, in their belief that Africans observed heretical religious practices and, in Africa, savage fighting practices. But even deeper worries perplexed Englishmen. The myth of the black male superpenis and of the insatiable sexual appetite of black women convinced Englishmen even further of the subhumanity of Africans. All these irrationalities grew even more dominant when Englishmen for the first time saw chimpanzees and equated them with African people.[13]

Bureau agents, along with Southern whites, mirrored their society's fear of interracial sexuality. Officials realistically worried that violence might erupt when white Southerners confronted this new order that allowed blacks and whites more sexual freedom. Many agents uneasily viewed a black and white couple, their racism overtly or covertly rejecting such liaisons. Colonel William Tallman, a white officer in Company A, 164th Colored Troops, lost his rank for "making a practice of hugging and kissing a negro woman in the presence of other officers and enlisted men." E. G. Barker, Monticello bureau agent, fined freedman John Parker eighty-three dollars and ordered him to leave the county for the crimes of idleness, theft, and being "too intimate with a white lady." General Sprague, bureau head, voided "all marriages of white persons with negroes or mulattoes." Washington and Alvin Lewis, freedmen, lived with two white women on the outskirts of Lewisburg when in December 1868 the Ku Klux Klan visited them with a brutal reproach for this "sexual violation." Washington was killed, Alvin escaped, and the violence feared by Freedmen's Bureau agents erupted in Conway County.[14]

Black prostitution also incensed bureau agents. J. L. Thorp of Camden believed hunger drove black women to sell their bodies as a last resort, but his sympathetic views were in a minority. Many agents and white Southerners considered black prostitution as confirmation of their notions of the subhumanity of African Americans in general. "Possum Hollow," east of the Little Rock freedmen's hospital, contained "a few cabins inhabited by colored prostitutes" who constantly annoyed bureau agents. Lewisville agent V. V. Smith dismissed Amy Ann Johnston after finding her pregnant and guilty of prostitution. Setting her up as an example of what happened to "licentious" people, Smith made Johnston a latter-day Hester Prynne. Two issues troubled Smith: Johnston's behavior reminded him of areas he could not control, and she, like other blacks, had made a sexual decision without consulting him. And, if every freedwoman became pregnant, could the plantation economy and white numerical superiority survive?[15]

In an effort to uphold the family and monogamy, bureau agents continually adjudicated black household disputes. Agents settled cases involving absentee fathers who had promised marriage to freedwomen and adultery conflicts which threatened to end in divorce. Freedwoman Mary Stewart claimed that the father of her unborn child abandoned her. Mary Reed, spouse of Washington Reed, swore that her husband forced her to sleep in another bed while replacing her in his bed with Margaret Jordan. Mrs. John Skearrer was charged with "cohabitating regularly with one Dr. Page who seems to have entirely superseded Skearrer as husband." Richard Harris accused his wife of adultery and petitioned the bureau for permission to leave her. Andrew Batteman, white, charged freedmen "Hal Pickett, Peter Hatchett, Tim Pickett, and John Pickett of living with women in a state of fornication to the detriment of the morale of the Freedmen." Bureau chief General Sprague encouraged local agents to inflict "severe punishment" on adulterers if grand juries ignored such activities. Like Puritan tribunals of the seventeenth and eighteenth centuries, Arkansas bureau agents attempted to force blacks to conform to their world view or be "harried out of the land." These conflicts also reflected the fluidity of sexual mores in the black and white communities during Reconstruction. Such choices only furthered black alternatives for identity.[16]

The case of freedwoman Martha Jane versus planter Daniel Stevenson illustrated the sexual morass in which Freedmen's Bureau agents, freedpersons, and Southern whites labored. Martha Jane, approximately forty years old, worked for Daniel Stevenson on a Desha County plantation. She gave birth in early 1866 to Stevenson's child. The birth created an uproar in the Stevenson home. Mrs. Stevenson forced her husband to expel Martha Jane and her two month old child and threatened to kill Martha Jane if she ever returned to the plantation. Stevenson eventually gave Martha Jane eight dollars and a steamboat ticket to Memphis, informing her that "you can't stay with me any more." In Memphis a crippling, festering infection on Martha Jane's leg incapacitated her and prevented her from working and earning enough money to purchase a ticket to Georgia, where relatives lived. She returned to Napoleon and sought aid from bureau agent J. C. Predmore, who ordered Stevenson to appear before him. Stevenson's daughter intercepted the summons, read it, and threw it into the fireplace. Martha Jane decided to entreat Stevenson personally for more aid, but he hustled her back on a flatboat and told her "to make do." Martha's infection worsened over time, and her health deteriorated. Agent Predmore again intervened and warned Stevenson, "It seems to me that it is only necessary for me to hint to you the consequences of the exposure of this affair to you for you to see that the child at least is well taken care of." No further mention of the case exists, so Stevenson probably agreed with Predmore and cared for the child and mother. The case reveals both the persistence of old practices and the revolutionary changes which rocked Arkansas in 1865. Planters still believed black women existed for their own pleasures, but now Freedmen's Bureau agents intervened in freedwomen's behalf.

That Martha asserted herself repeatedly by asking for bureau aid also reveals that black women openly sought remedies for injustices which they had suffered in silence during the antebellum years. And the child—what did he feel and think as he grew up? Did he become like William Faulkner's Joe Christmas from *Light in August,* wondering confusedly and maddeningly if he belonged in the white world, the black world, or some God awful no man's land in between?[17]

Blacks faced not only planters who still believed black women existed for their sexual enjoyment but also some bureau officials who embraced this antebellum notion. Arkansas County black and white citizens accused bureau agent Albert Coats of "improper conduct with nearly every colored girl he meets." Lewisville agent A. A. Wright "associated almost every night with lewd women both black and white." Although not every white perceived blacks as subhumans dominated by uncontrollable sexuality, many did, which made it necessary for freedpersons to encounter and reject images of themselves created earlier by people more powerful than they.[18]

Many blacks immediately and gratefully accepted white sanctions of monogamous relationships which some had nourished and cherished before emancipation. To receive whites' blessings in a church or civil procedure reaffirmed freedom, identity, and dignity among freedpersons. Wedding ceremonies symbolized to blacks that white men could no longer separate husbands and wives. Weddings also solemnized relationships by giving blacks a new appreciation for what it meant to be a father, mother, husband, or wife. They realized that relationships could now be permanent, that auction blocks no longer threatened lifelong commitment to another. Freedpersons could now answer the question Who am I? with a "good father, good mother, good husband, or good wife," and they could feel far more confident than under slavery that such answers were going to be more permanent responses.[19]

Weddings fueled individual and communal joy. Molly Horn of Holly Grove recalled, "We married at nights, borrowed lamps and had 'em settin' about. There was a large crowd. Ann Branch was the regular cake-cooker over the country. She cooked all my cakes. They had roast pork and goose and all sorer [sorts of] pies."[20]

Freedmen's Bureau marriage statistics reveal the perimeters of black marriage. Typical of nineteenth-century marriages, most unions con-

TABLE 3.1

Marriage Statistics: Age Analysis, 1865

Community	older husband	Marriages with ages equal	older wife
Madison	9 (90%)	1 (10%)	0 (0%)
Hempstead County	44 (81%)	2 (4%)	8 (15%)
Jacksonport	84 (76%)	5 (4%)	22 (20%)
Arkadelphia	187 (75%)	26 (10%)	36 (15%)
Pine Bluff	165 (76%)	11 (5%)	41 (19%)
TOTAL	489 (80%)	45 (7%)	80 (13%)

sisted of a husband older than his wife (see Table 3.1).[21] The average age at marriage was recorded for five Arkansas counties in 1865 (see Table 3.2).[22] In Pine Bluff, 236 newlyweds had married previously, but their marriages had been disrupted during the antebellum era for a variety of reasons (see Table 3.3).[23]

Freedwomen especially struggled in search of personal freedom and new identities. Degraded in numerous subtle as well as overt ways during slavery, freedwomen forged new personalities that demanded respect and enhanced self-worth. Most rejected the widely held white belief in black animalistic sexuality but also denied Calvinistic notions of the impurity of sexuality. Each chose her own way, undoubtedly pulled by the age's assumptions. Ellen Cragin of Little Rock testified, "My first baby was born to my husband. I didn't throw myself away." With each choice freedwomen controlled more of their destinies and lives.[24]

TABLE 3.2

Average Age at Marriage: 1865

Community	Average male age	Average female age
Madison	34	27
Hempstead County	32	25
Jacksonport	33	25
Arkadelphia	34	27
Pine Bluff	38	31

TABLE 3.3

Causes for Marriage Disruption

Reason for disruption	# of marriages disrupted
Quit	1
Deserted	6
Infidelity	7
Disagreement	9
No reason given	22
Power	45
Sale	64
Death of spouse	82
TOTAL	236

Black women often demanded new marital roles and voices. A Helena freedwoman requested and received bureau permission to stay with her contracted crop against the wishes of her husband who wanted her to move with him. Refusing to accept intolerable circumstances, women initiated many divorces and separations. Freedwomen also won new respect as wives and mothers when planters begrudgingly allowed them more time each morning away from the fields and in their homes to care for their households.[25]

Black females rejected their assigned "non-role" in the political arena. Although they agreed that a woman's place was in the home, they vehemently rejected the idea that this was her only place. At an Arkadelphia public forum on schools, black women asserted that "as the men had failed in their duty, they were determined to assist in the enterprise and accordingly organized themselves into an aid society." In Jacksonport, bureau agent William Brian reported that "as strange as it may appear," agitation for black voter registration seemed "confined to the females." Women often attended political mass rallies in large numbers, exemplified by a June 1867 constitutional convention rally where they made up a noticeable majority. Freedwomen engaged in political power struggles, either urging their male counterparts toward certain action or becoming actively involved themselves.[26]

But gargantuan dilemmas faced freedwomen as they struggled to fashion their freedom and new identities. Both their blackness and their femininity caused black and white males to view them as sexual objects, as subjects to master. Napoleon bureau agent J. C. Predmore complained that "the freedmen seem to think that they have a perfect right to whip their wives." Agent Sebastian Geisreiter of Pine Bluff concurred and noted that freedmen whipped their wives "unmercifully." Most agents grew incensed over such physical abuse. E. G. Barker of Marion warned a freedman: "Your wife Rebecca complains that you have been tampering with other women especially with Nancy Hamlin and that you have driven her from her home, abused her by whipping and cussing and she in a delicate condition. Such conduct will not be tolerated. I am determined to put a stop to this barbarous way of doing." But other agents grew less livid over such mistreatment. Betsy Johnson of Osceola charged her husband with physical abuse and sought redress before the bureau, but agent Eli Mix "found Betsy the most guilty" and lectured both husband and wife. That Mix found nothing wrong with a husband whipping a wife reveals what many bureau agents thought about black women, perhaps all women, and about females' expected marital subservience.[27]

In reconstructing personalities after the Civil War, black women not only faced physical abuse from their husbands, but also endured molestations. Although it occurred infrequently, black men raping black women troubled many bureau agents and blacks. Lewisville agent Smith heard a case brought by white Dr. L. G. Williams who accused freedman Harry Smith of illegally forcing his wife to leave him after she refused "to have criminal connection with him." William Brian, Jacksonport agent, arrested freedman James McMurty for attempted rape of young freedwoman Harriet Smith. Henry Johnson, Jacksonport freedman, raped "an idiotic but virtuous" freedwoman and was executed. Tom Jackman drugged his daughter after she resisted his seduction and "did violate her person." Such aberrant behavior, however rare, affirmed white racist beliefs about black sexuality and inferiority and made the climb to freedom even more arduous for freedpersons.[28]

Freedmen and freedwomen struggled with their identities as they responded to their sexual urges and to the expectations of their respective communities. When a black man stared at the reflection of himself in a pond in 1865, he undoubtedly saw an image clouded by his own sexual choices, by the desires and values of black women and men around him, and by what white women and white men thought of him and wanted from him. It was as though he viewed his reflection on a cold, December morning when the steam rising from the pond contorted and hid his face. Black men struggled to see themselves through their own eyes, black women's eyes, white men's eyes, and white women's eyes. The same could be said for black women, white men, and white women.

What the freedman mused over as he stared at himself in that same pond would grow even more complex if he puzzled over what the color of his face meant. Race and color has proven to be as treacherous as gender and sexuality for the historian dealing with the creation of freedpersons' new identities; and it equally troubled African Americans struggling to become free in 1865.

In 1865 both blacks and whites recognized they lived in a world which insisted that hidden and open meanings resided in the ideological construct of race. But they disagreed within themselves and with others as to what their color signaled. Meanings often blurred. James Oliver, an African American, escaped from slavery before the Civil War and resided in San Domingo. At the war's end he returned to Arkansas but adamantly refused to be labeled a freedman. Black barbers in Fort Smith who balked at cutting blacks' hair suggested that Reconstruction threatened their self-image or their economic livelihood which depended upon segregated barbering. By debating what to call themselves, freedpersons revealed the significance color played in their self-understanding. The nomenclature used in the mid-nineteenth century for freedpersons included "African, Ethiopian, Free African, people of color, free people of color, Colored Negro, Children of Africa, Sons of Africa, Colored American, black, Anglo-African, African-American, Afmerican, Aframerican, Africo-American, and Afro-Saxon." Such variety indicates the choices, confusions, and possibilities facing freedpersons who considered this aspect of identity. Whites and blacks derived their own skin color codes and internalized their meanings. Each freedperson had to either ignore, accept, or modify the colliding understandings of race that were being contested after the Civil War.[29]

Skin color established the perimeters of permitted and prohibited behavior. In a world so drastically altered by Yankees, by the destruction of chattel slavery, and by the death of the Confederacy, Southern whites desperately clung to precisely demarcated racial norms. Both blacks and whites responded to these "indiscretions." Bill Huiry, white, struck freedman Plymouth Hale of Lewisville twice with a pistol for violating the prevailing etiquette. When Hale failed to respond to Huiry's satisfaction, Huiry shouted, "God damn your soul and tell me where you were raised." "South Carolina," Hale replied. "God damn you," Huiry countered," don't you know I am a white man? God damn you when you meet me pull off your hat." Blacks behaved as defiantly as whites in this new world of colliding and nascent racial norms. Both black and white Arkansans and Freedmen's Bureau agents struggled to understand themselves anew by demanding that others abide by these newly created and disputed conceptions of race.[30]

Color not only provided pretext and context for defiance or submission, both responses adding to one's understanding of himself or herself, color also triggered memories of the past. Bureau marriage records listed the color of the bride, the groom, and their parents. In Pine Bluff, for example, agents recorded hues as "black, dark, brown, light, white, medium, and yellow." "Papa was a gingered color man," Laura Abramson remembered. Mary Peters of Little Rock insisted, "I couldn't help my color. My mother couldn't either." The "mulatto" population in Arkansas doubled between 1850 and 1860, increasing the color spectrum and complicating the task of those engaged in fashioning new identities.[31]

Bureau agents' understandings of slavery and of antebellum racial mores determined what they thought was possible to achieve in the South. The large presence of mulattoes in Arkansas revealed to agents that a rigid Southern caste system which prevented blacks and whites from interacting in numerous ways never existed. An 1861 will from Sevier County planter Orlando Jones, written before he went off to fight in the Civil War and placed in a Freedmen' Bureau agent's file, at first seems misplaced. In it, Jones established a trust fund for the house servant Mary Jane, for her children, and for children "born within nine months of my death." The local agent most likely filed the will to ensure fulfillment of its provisions, but he also sent it to Little Rock, where it was forwarded to Washington as a clue to the "real

South." Agents discovered and dealt with this "secret South" as they tried to facilitate black freedom.[32]

Miscegenation perplexed many Southern whites still championing white superiority and racial segregation. Freedpersons fashioned who they were by their attitudes toward marriages with whites. Did a "mixed marriage" symbolize equality, a forgetting of the past, or an assertion that the individual, not the race, was most important? Miscegenation acquired new intensity as the 1868 constitutional convention considered a resolution dealing with it. The *Weekly Arkansas Gazette* proclaimed in a bold headline on February 18, 1868:

RADICALISM THE PATRON OF MISCEGENATION
HOW NEGRO SUPREMACY IS TO BE ESTABLISHED

Bradley County white Methodist minister John Bradley raised the constitutional issue and proposed a resolution banning interracial marriages. Phillips County delegate William Grey, a black, eloquently opposed the prohibition, and eventually the convention decided to say nothing about miscegenation but strongly recommended that the Arkansas General Assembly enact legislation dealing with the issue. The *Weekly Arkansas Gazette* waxed especially vitriolic in editorials and features as it tried to taint the entire constitution with this single issue. For example, the *Gazette* reprinted an *Arkadelphia Standard* article about a black father who "whipped his two grown sons a few days since for advocating miscegenation." It never occurred to the *Gazette* that the father's behavior might be explained not by his desire for his sons to stay in their prescribed "place" but rather by his own hatred of a race that had enslaved him and by his determination that his sons would have no dealings with whites. Another *Gazette* story reprinted this speech:

> I will say that I am not, nor ever have been, in favor of making voters, or jurors of negroes, or of qualifying them to hold office, nor to intermarry with white people . . . that there is a physical difference between the white and black race, which, I believe will forever forbid the two races living together on terms of social and political equality.

The person speaking was Abraham Lincoln. In that same edition, *Gazette* editorialists hysterically warned white readers, "Your child will sit side by side with negroes in obedience to radical law, but the radical party encourages the latter to win the affections of your youthful child with a view to matrimonial alliance." The issue smouldered publicly throughout 1868 and forced blacks to confront it introspectively and existentially. Even in 1866, long before the first Jim Crow laws of the late nineteenth and early twentieth centuries, whether one viewed black-white social relations as amicable or hostile depended upon one's viewpoint and where one looked. How a freedperson ascertained his or her place in the new order through the lens of race and color influenced personality development and molded identity immensely.[33]

Blacks in Arkansas, regardless of complexion, also embraced Africans worldwide. Southern and Arkansas blacks felt deep affinity with the emancipated freedpersons of Central and South America. For example, Little Rock and Batesville blacks commemorated the emancipation of Caribbean slaves each year in August with parades, speeches, and large, communal dinners. Arkansas freedpersons enhanced their solidarity and racial pride by celebrating the achievements of blacks everywhere.[34]

Regarding color, Arkansas blacks responded to whites with either racial separatism or integration. Just as whites often espoused pro-white ideologies, so too did freedpersons often favor exclusion and separation. Magnolia black Baptists, worshiping with whites, wearied of segregated seating and of white aloofness. They formed their own all-black congregation, the Bethlehem Baptist Church, in 1868. As early as December 1865 blacks openly questioned white humanitarianism and demanded that black orphans be placed in African-American homes. Bureau agent Francis Springer grew chagrined when freedmen showed "an inclination to take children from white families merely because of color." Blacks often accepted racial stereotypes as readily as whites; an African Methodist Episcopal minister went so far as to describe Southern whites as having "long legs, short bodies, long necks, bullet heads, sway backs, flat breasts, and big bellies, long swinging arms, pendulous jaws, and a countenance in which ignorance and low cunning [seemed] to struggle by turns for mastery."[35]

Other blacks often opposed separatism and insisted the races work together. Over one hundred Hamburg citizens, blacks and whites, believed that all lived amicably together in their city and petitioned bureau head General Ord to disband the Freedmen's Bureau "for the benefit of all." In Lafayette County in 1868, from fifty to seventy-five poor blacks and whites shared their destitution while camping outside Lewisville in the woods. Beulah Hagg, North Little Rock freedwoman, "boarded with a white family" while working for the railroad after the war. The symbiotic, paternalistic relationship between whites and blacks lingered during Reconstruction as many freedpersons felt responsible for "their" whites. Matilda Hatchett, North Little Rock freedwoman, in the 1930s still longed to "get holt of some of my old white folks." Elda Johnson of Little Rock quizzed a WPA investigator, "Have you heard about the Grissoms down there [Helena]? Well, them is my white folks." Harriet Daniel, white Dallas County mistress, recognized that a symbiotic relationship between slaves and masters existed. "For slavery," she insisted, "had bonds of servitude and responsibility for white people as well as for Negroes."[36]

In December 1865 Camden freedpersons best revealed the precariousness which confronted Arkansans and the Freedmen's Bureau over color and race. A black man murdered a white girl and boy in Union County and fled to Bradley County. Racial fear and distrust soared. Bradley County blacks discovered and captured the murderer and, along with whites urged to join them, carried the culprit back to the place where he had hidden the murder weapon, a knife. Discovering the knife under a log and conducting what seemed like "a proper examination to both blacks and whites," white and black vigilantes convicted him and summarily burned him to death. "The old negroes and federal soldiers" even assisted "by bringing pine knots to make the fire." Did blacks so readily involve themselves in this lynching because they feared senseless and random vengeance? Did they believe the murderer restricted their freedom by his deeds? Did these vigilantes "follow him at a long distance to arrest him" to show that his action did not represent typical black behavior? Or was it rather that these blacks transcended whites' assertions of their inferiority and, with their attempts to bring the murderer to justice, declared themselves authentic members of the human race who would not condone murder?[37]

Freedpersons used whites—poor whites, wealthy planters, poor planters, merchants, upper-class white women, lower-class white women, and white children—to define themselves and to wonder about their own lives and their lives' meanings. Whites offered freedpersons values to accept, reject, or creatively synthesize. Whatever unique personality emerged from the rubble of Civil War in each of the 110,000 Arkansas freedpersons, each had to deal with "others"—whites—and with what it meant to be a black man or a black woman in a region so cognizant of race.

Blacks not only searched for identity signals personally and individually, but they also often looked for clues to their identity in groups created and convened for self-understanding. Although much identity formation occurred introspectively, group activities spurred blacks to consider and reconsider who they were and where they were going. Freedpersons not only wondered Who am I?, but they also puzzled over Who are my people? African Americans sought out and puzzled over their identity individually—through memory, kinship ties, sexuality, and racial self-concepts—and also often linked together to further self-understanding. No collective institution nourished black personal growth and quickened quests for identity more than did African-American religion. Churches became literal sanctuaries for freedpersons and provided spaces that blacks could totally control. All of the critical questions of the day about politics, economics, education, social standing, gender, and identity were debated, and answers were formulated, at the local church.

The creation of a permanent church edifice gave freedpersons a sense of permanency and order in an era and region lacking such security. Freedmen's Bureau head General John Sprague sensed that freedmen anxiously longed "to establish churches." African-American congregations favored building and owning their own churches to gain more freedom from whites. Freedman carpenter Joseph Nesley planned and built the Pine Bluff Methodist Church for black worship. In Pine Bluff and Magnolia, blacks funded impressive structures. Church members swelled with pride and joy as they watched their church emerge. Here stood a visible and tangible sign of freedom.[38]

Where freedpersons worshiped influenced their understanding of self and of others. Although bureau agent William Colby feared "a narrow sectarian feeling . . . among the freedmen," freedpersons reveled in such choices. Baptist and Methodist congregations attracted most Arkansas freedpersons, but numerous hybrids of each thrived: Free Will Baptist, Congregational Baptist, Methodist Episcopal South,

Methodist Episcopal North, African Methodist Episcopal (AME), African Methodist Episcopal Zion, Roman Catholic, and Northern Congregationalist.[39]

Local preachers molded much religious experience. As historian Carter G. Woodson observed, "Local churches sprang up here and there as Baptist preachers, a law unto themselves, went abroad seeking a following." Bureau agent Isaac Adair reported that *many* black evangelists "preached every Sunday" at Eunice, and many more opportunities appeared for black pastors and laymen in more populated areas. Little Rock bureau agent W. G. Sargent indicated that "preachers come and go." For many freedpersons, the black minister unraveled many of the mysteries of freedom.[40]

The strength or weakness of a local church depended on how well its pastor motivated members. The preacher, so significant a shaper of slave opinion in antebellum days, extended his power after emancipation. For young and old alike, the ministry proved personally satisfying to those with charisma. For a layperson, the minister became significant, someone who guided and shaped aspirations and dreams.[41]

Hierarchical bureaucracies demanded certain standards before licensing their ministers, and they disciplined misbehaving preachers. The Methodist Episcopal Church began appointing Arkansas pastors for freedmen in early 1866, and by July 1867 several Arkansas blacks had been ordained as full pastors for that church. But disciplinary measures weeded out other errant preachers from the Methodist Episcopal Church. It expelled Reverend William Millard, for example, in May 1866 for "licentiousness." Preachers without denominational affiliation had no hierarchical superior and were freer in a sense, but they often faced challenges officially ordained preachers did not. Black chaplain Coryden Millerd "encountered violent prejudice" as he brought his version of the good news to the streets of Pine Bluff; police ordered him to stop preaching and charged him with creating a public nuisance.[42]

Preachers sometimes exasperated school officials and patrons. A power struggle between preachers and school proponents occasionally flared. Some black ministers found William Colby, Freedmen's Bureau education director, most sinister. From Colby's viewpoint, many black pastors impeded black education as much as the Klan or unreconstructed Rebels. Calling black preachers "a bane both to the church and the school," Colby insisted that "the colored preachers seem to fear also that the effect of the teacher's work will be to weaken their own influence." He specifically reprimanded Greene, Craighead, and Poinsett Counties' ministers for "refusing to encourage education work." But not every clergyman opposed bringing schools to Arkansas. The Klan notified a white Methodist Episcopal minister of Jonesboro that if he spoke publicly in favor of black schools, "a coat of tar and feathers would be his reward." For some black preachers, schools seemed to threaten their power base and influence over the masses. But other black preachers perceived schools as another institution that enriched and brought true freedom to freedpersons. Whatever a minister said or did about education deeply influenced freedpersons' identities and the identities of future blacks.[43]

The theology expounded by black preachers and accepted by African-American congregations forged identity. Theologically, blacks focused on the "uplifting of the race" as a major tenet. Helping other blacks became a categorical imperative for many. Dardanelle freedpersons donated food, clothing, and shelter for a kinless, paralyzed woman. Churches found hundreds of homes for Arkansas orphans. Preachers also included practical, self-help information along with their sermons. At an African Methodist Episcopal rally, children sang tunes such as "Uncle Sam Is Rich Enough to Send Us All to School," "Who Is That Talking and Laughing in School," "Coming through the Rye," and "Downfall of Old King Alcohol," revealing the pragmatic, moral emphasis which hopefully proved to whites and blacks that African Americans deserved their freedom.[44]

Blacks not only grounded their theology in this world but apocalyptical thinking also naturally flourished in such a revolutionary era. Helena freedpersons excitedly heard a "prophet" who in May 1866 proclaimed "the end of the world was to be in a few days, and that God had sent him to tell them to prepare for it immediately." His promise to walk on water at Old Town Lake drew a large throng to witness his promised miracle. When he failed to walk on water, the crowd disbursed, disillusioned or perhaps bemused. It is easy to understand why freedpersons, having seen the miracle of choice and opportunity thrust upon them at the war's end, might believe further apocalypses possible.[45]

But most of the time black theology concentrated on earthly matters. African-American theology rejected a demarcation between church and state, religion and politics. The *Arkansas Gazette* reported at year's end in 1867 that "African churches in our western suburbs are strongly politically interested." Bureau agent Sebastian Geisreiter worried that Pine Bluff African Methodist Episcopal pastor George Rutherford spent most of his time "chiefly devoted to political matters." A Philadelphia AME bishop exhorted Arkansas blacks that "if they feared God they must carry him with them to the ballot box." An 1868 Little Rock Union League rally ended in a meeting at the "new African church." As election day 1868 dawned, many blacks gathered at black churches, to join in worship services there, then to parade down Markham Street, and finally to cast their votes. The day began in a church with hymns, prayers, and a sermon, revealing the importance of religion in black political behavior—a blending of the sacred and secular which still exists today.[46]

Many Freedmen's Bureau agents and white Arkansans supported black religion but favored one shaped in the image of a white God who kept blacks in their place. Pine Bluff agent William Dawes scathingly indicted "ignorant colored preachers" for "rapidly leading" freedmen "back to heathenism." "They can now be seen," Dawes's jeremiad continued, "upon occasions of religious ceremony dancing around piles of pieces of meat, fish, and lizards which they have thrown together in their blind infatuation." Monticello's agent Captain E. G. Barker feared that black religion was "often governed by a wild nervous excitement more than by pure religion."[47]

But not every bureau official wished to stifle black preachers or transform black worship into varieties of white religious experience. Agent J. C. Predmore of Napoleon advised freedpersons threatened with death for their religion to "select some quiet place and go on with their preaching and prayer meetings." Agent E. G. Barker of Fort Smith requested aid from New York City's First Baptist Church for a Colored Missionary Baptist Church "struggling for life" in Fort Smith. Helena agent Henry Sweeney perceived "the need of a minister of religion is sorely felt." "A good earnest man that will preach good practical truths and not," he insisted, "spend all his time in teaching the people that *they* should, *of right*, own every foot of the soil; but one who will explain in plain language that they can understand who God is and the enormity of sin."[48]

Although black congregations received aid from some bureau

agents, they faced enormous hostilities from many white Arkansans. Napoleon freedmen received death threats warning against continued religious meetings. De Valls Bluff whites viciously whipped blacks engaged in a prayer meeting in 1866. Whites not only assaulted black worshipers, but also destroyed black places of worship. Whites burned three freedmen's churches in Camden in 1868. In Osceola, freedpersons reverted to brush arbor meetings after arsonists ravaged their church in June 1868. After smashing the windows of Helena's First Baptist Church for freedpersons in January 1867, culprits swore "at the time that they would burn the church down" if blacks continued meeting.[49]

African-American religious organizations offered Arkansas blacks a place for public meetings which furthered community and individual identity formation. The construction of a church building gave freedpersons a sense of permanency and order in a time and place lacking much that even hinted at stability. A church reflected a place in the community, enhancing black pride and self-dignity. For many whites, these sanctuaries seemed like never-healing cankers that constantly reminded them of the changes spawned from the Civil War. As indicative of the New South as the statues of Robert E. Lee and Stonewall Jackson that rose from Southern soil after the Civil War, these churches powerfully rebutted the lost cause of the antebellum South.

Blacks not only turned to churches for new insights into their identity, but they also created new understandings of themselves through their political organizations. Just as a steeple and church bell symbolized the revolutionary changes brought about during Reconstruction, so, too, did political rallies and elections signal to Arkansas blacks the reality and opportunities of freedom.

The public engaged in political activity at an extraordinary rate in the nineteenth century, as exemplified by the 1860 election, where over 80 percent of those eligible voted. Citizens voted in unprecedented numbers because they believed their votes made a difference. Tariffs, extensions of slavery into the territories, the monetary system, immigration quotas, the national bank, and other complex issues captured the minds and spirits of an amazing number of Americans. Politics also provided citizens with much needed communities, centers where isolated individuals joined together not only to discuss the issues of the day but also to compare their suit or dress to a neighbor's clothing, laugh, dance, drink, eat, tell dirty jokes, and have a good time.[50]

The political arena was so much more than electoral colleges, cultural symbols, and election days; rather, it became a forum where individuals tested their new identities to see whether or not they could communicate with the masses, shaped their identities by joining Republicans or Democrats, and decided whom to listen to and whom to follow. The Military Reconstruction Act of 1867 and the Fifteenth Amendment to the Constitution guaranteed black male enfranchisement. African Americans embraced their new political privileges. Bureau agents in Arkansas County, Lewisville, Fountain Hill, Magnolia, Princeton, Hamburg, and Jonesboro all agreed that freedmen "grew quite elated with the idea of getting to vote." Thomas Williams, Madison bureau agent, condescendingly reported that, "The Freedman shows a disposition for and an aptitude in engaging in political discussion and heated arguments, imitating his 'white brother' as nearly as his untutored mind renders it possible for him to do so."[51]

Political paraphernalia kindled political excitement in Arkansas in 1867 and 1868. Caroline Matthews remembered wearing "Grant and Colfax" buttons in the 1868 presidential campaign. Posters dotting the urban landscape alerted freedmen to registration and voting procedures. Buttons and posters seem insignificant to modern consumers inundated with a dazzling array of political campaign artifacts, but the material world was far less cluttered in the nineteenth century. Posters and campaign buttons were novelties that drew attention to politics. A newspaper geared to encouraging Arkansas blacks' political involvement, the *Arkansas Freeman*, emerged in August 1869. It offered blacks political and economic advice, advertised rallies and public meetings which facilitated community formation, and fostered black pride by its very existence.[52]

Many bureau agents sympathized with newly empowered blacks and encouraged them to engage in politics. Lewisburg agent William Morgan insisted to freedmen "that their future welfare depends in a great measure upon their registering to vote and the manner in which they vote at the coming elections." Madison agent Thomas C. Williams distributed the *Weekly Republican* so "that the 'Gospel of Reconstruction' may be spread abroad into every corner and domain."[53]

Freedpersons took such encouragement to heart and joined a rich array of political clubs. When agent Fred Thibaut of Washington, Arkansas, grew too sick to disseminate registration information, blacks themselves organized committees to spread the word of approaching elections. In urban areas such as Little Rock, neighborhood clubs formed, where freedpersons debated and discussed the issues of the day in small, informal groups. One such group met three times in one day in the intense political climate of 1867. Such fervent political activism troubled some planters and bureau agents. Sebastian Geisreiter, Pine Bluff agent, recognized that "freedmen are frequently holding meetings of a secret character, sometimes protracting them until two or three o'clock in the morning. As these negroes are all armed, the planters are becoming fearful."[54]

African Americans also became involved in a more formal organization, the national Union League. The Union League in Arkansas and in most other Southern states considered the raising of black political consciousness as a primary function. Lured by a desire to investigate political issues and candidates and by wishes to belong to a large and powerful group, freedpersons also found the group rituals mysterious and appealing. A leadership hierarchy, sanctioned by national headquarters, had "full authority to initiate proper persons into the secrets of the Union League of America." In Helena, over 2,000 blacks attended a May 1867 Union League rally. The league primarily encouraged black men to register to vote. In Magnolia, over 400 freedpersons persuaded over 740 black men in Columbia County to register. In Little Rock the league raised over $1,775 for forthcoming elections.[55]

Long-time residents and recent arrivals from out of state (black carpetbaggers) constituted the leadership of the Union League, which included both former slaves and free persons of color. Edward Gantt, a national Union League official, became the primary liaison between the national organization and the Arkansas chapters. He worked from Little Rock to implement league goals and to build a strong pro-Republican political machine. Local law enforcement officials sometimes assumed leadership positions. A Jefferson County deputy sheriff counseled blacks "in secret" during league meetings. L. Meyer, an El Dorado freedman, wrote to the *Little Rock Evening Republican*, "I think every colored person ought to take an interest in this [Union League meeting] and vote for a convention."[56]

But not everyone favored the Union League. The *Arkansas Gazette* protested that the league "deluded" freedmen, insisting that "the enfranchisement of the negro has stirred the slimy sediments of society." Chicot County whites disgustedly noted the arrivals of two black Union League leaders and refused them public accommodations. They finally bedded at the provost's residence, where shots from unknown assailants ripped through their lodgings but, according to the *Chicot Press*, "did no real damage."[57]

Mass political rallies, spawned from the Union League and local political clubs, increased black opportunities for political involvement, leadership, and group solidarity. A Jefferson County correspondent wrote to bureau agent Major J. W. Dawes, "The great event of the day is the convention . . . You should have seen the crowds of negroes in town yesterday. It is safe to say that there were over a thousand in the state house yard at the assembling of the convention." Freedpersons in Little Rock, Batesville, Camden, Fort Smith, and Pine Bluff held annual rallies on the Fourth of July. Their large numbers always impressed both blacks and whites. The *Arkansas Gazette* described an April 1867 mass meeting "composed in the main of negroes, who from distant plantations had rocked into town, dressed in every conceivable style, bedizened with tinsel and decked out in assorted colors." Many whites worried when only two or three blacks gathered together; their fears intensified when glimpsing or reading about rallies of black multitudes. For freedpersons, however, such large numbers only emboldened their political commitments. Political rallies deeply shaped black personalities and influenced identities.[58]

Freedpersons gained valuable political and organizational skills when planning these mass rallies. The Little Rock Republican Club designated ten members to "superintend the barbecue" planned for January 1, 1868, and encouraged them "to invite the different societies and schools friendly to the cause to take part in the proceedings." Publicizing an event, providing food and speakers, and locating meeting places offered freedpersons valuable experience in crowd control and prepared them for mass political participation.[59]

Thorough preparation produced well-run meetings that impressed both blacks and whites, opponents no less than loyal supporters. In Hot Springs on July 4, 1867, for example, a parade began the day's festivities; the lines of freedwomen, promenading two by two "wearing dresses of white and ribbons of blue," indelibly stirred many. Carrying banners proclaiming "We Trust in God" and "The Best Government the World Ever Saw," marchers whose complexions ranged in color "from a new saddle to a pair of boots" wound through Hot Springs streets, concluding their parade with a speech from Indiana governor Oliver Morton. But then the usually vitriolic *Arkansas Gazette* described a public night rally of blacks which weaved down East Main to Markham Street where freedpersons waved banners proclaiming "We Are the Republican Party." This caused the *Gazette* to return to its hysteria. It wailed "Nothing for the country—all nigger. Nigger first, nigger last—nigger all the time." As revealed by this outburst, black mass rallies unhinged many whites who interpreted them as threats to their power, status, and identity.[60]

Most rallies culminated in the sort of political oratory cherished by nineteenth-century citizens. Bishop Jabez P. Campbell of the African Methodist Episcopal Church addressed a crowd at the Little Rock State House in typical fashion. Campbell asserted, "There were black men and white men that he would not associate with—all he wanted for the negro was an equal chance in the great race of life." Urging blacks to work diligently and save their money for school construction and farm purchases, the bishop concluded by promising that "he wanted no one's lands, silver or gold, but only an equal opportunity of accumulating them for himself." Through these rallies and speeches, blacks fashioned a politically involved, self-help ideology that opened up rich, new opportunities for personal growth through political activism.[61]

Since freedpersons presented no monolithic, homogeneous front in facing Southern, unreconstructed Rebels, factions inevitably emerged. Such options as opposing the Republican Party or opposing powerful black Republican elites offered freedpersons even greater choices. Most accepted Republicanism and supported the party of Lincoln, but many blacks tenaciously fought against whites and among themselves for political power and control in the Republican Party. Most black Republican factions split over personalities and personal power struggles, which were camouflaged in rhetoric emphasizing ideology or issues, just as happened in white factions; such divisions offered freedpersons even more complexities and alternatives to decipher. Factions erupted from sparsely populated villages to the larger towns of Arkansas. In Lewisburgh (a population of 199 whites and 40 blacks), much factionalism among blacks appeared. William Colby discovered similar fissures in Little Rock and sensed "a disposition of jealousy on the part of some of the leaders of the colored people." Washington freedpersons split into pro– and anti–Mary Stuart camps in a controversy over Mrs. Stuart, who was a white Northern teacher opposed by a minister of a rival denomination. In Pine Bluff, blacks initially divided over whether to support calls for a new constitution. Eventually deeming a new constitution necessary, many Pine Bluff blacks "tore off their tickets the name of Moses Bell, the radical candidate for delegate to the Convention and voted only for a convention." Factional struggles reveal that blacks never acted as a political monolith: issues and personalities divided them just as they did whites. Factions offered freedpersons greater choice.[62]

Blacks were free to leave the Republican camp, and a vocal minority worked in and supported the Democratic Party in Arkansas, thus furthering alternatives for freedpersons. Democrats initially accentuated the uneasiness, strains, and terror of the moment and urged freedmen to remember the "security of slavery" compared to the uncertainty and angst they now experienced. When this appeal failed, black Democrats warned that Republican promises for black aid would disappear. These conservative black Democrats believed Republicans courted freedmen for their votes and would ignore them after the election. John Harris, a Tennessee black conservative touring Arkansas for the Democratic Party, warned Arkansas freedpersons, "If the colored people waited for them [radicals] to carry out their promise they would die waiting." Applauding a Harris speech given at Dardanelle, the pro-Democrat *Arkansas Gazette* agreed that freedpersons had "been blinded and deceived by bureaus and villainous office-seekers."[63]

Republicans effectively used political clubs and rallies to mobilize freedpersons' support; so, too, did Democrats woo adherents. Freedpersons organized Democratic clubs in Hamburg, Marion, Jonesboro, Pine Bluff, Searcy, and Marion. Although pro-Republican bureau agents disdained these black Democrats either as "the most ignorant black men" or as desperate men who joined "to escape the imputations of their employers," ignorance or fear explained only marginally why blacks supported Democrats in 1868. Bureau agents, carpetbaggers, and many traveling Northern journalists often slipped into the erroneous habit of viewing freedpersons or blacks monolithically, but such was never the case. Some blacks joined the Democratic

Party because they were concerned that Republican Party black leadership roles were all filled and the acquisition of personal power required working in another party. There also was a strain of black conservatism which sincerely believed the Freedmen's Bureau and Republican promises would reenslave blacks just as Southern white planters had previously done. Blacks in newly formed Little River County met in early 1869 and signed petitions that insisted they were "totally capable of governing themselves." This declaration revealed the self-help emphasis and distrust of government which lured some freedpersons to the Democratic Party.[64]

Black Democrats also joined white Democrats in public rallies for Horatio Seymour in 1868, and they occasionally held all-black gatherings. Integrated mass rallies occurred at Little Rock, Batesville, Camden, Fort Smith, Pine Bluff, and in Phillips County, and usually included both black and white speakers in the ceremonies. Democrats launched a large balloon during a September 1868 Fort Smith rally to photograph the occasion. The hearts of children and adults thrilled as they saw such a feat. Over three thousand attended, blacks and whites, children and elderly, men and women. For black identity formation, a viable two-party system offered blacks choices and allowed the development of political identity within a context of real alternatives.[65]

Although some bureau agents rejoiced at this raising of black political consciousness, other agents feared that too much political activism jeopardized order and the plantation economy. Their responses reflected their individual world views, personal ambitions, and the extent to which they agreed with or had been co-opted by local white elites. General C. H. Smith, Freedmen's Bureau head, warned freedmen "against undue excitement growing out of local political conventions." He feared that such excitement filled freedmen "with expectancy" and "unsettled their minds," making them "unlikely to return to their labor afterward." Madison agent Thomas Williams advised freedmen to "abstain from attending any political meetings, to refrain from discussing any political questions, to apply themselves to the labor of their crops." Jonesboro agent William Inman concurred and advised blacks to boycott political meetings and "remain quietly at work." Agent William Brian of Jacksonport agreed and implored freedpersons to "keep quiet, have little to say, remain at home, and attend to their own business."[66]

Many whites appreciated agents who kept blacks politically mute and joined them in suppressing black political activity. Whites at first used rumor and innuendo, warnings and threats, to maintain an all-white political domain. For example, rumors blanketed Napoleon that voting registration files would be used for future enslavement of all black voters. Whites also created rumors that blacks who voted would be enlisted in the army and would lose a week's wages. Bureau head General Smith reported, "Efforts were made to influence the colored people in the way of giving of or discharging from employment according as they voted at the election." At Helena, planters warned freedmen, "Vote like we say or we'll drive you from the country." Republican posters in Little Rock advertising an October 1868 political rally were mysteriously defaced, someone penciling in: "Come, come, come all; And bring your arms." Blacks puzzled over this cryptic addition. Were Democrats challenging Republicans to a fight or were they pushing Republicans into starting one? Uneasiness and discord reigned, just as the culprits wished.[67]

Threats turned more violent as registration and elections approached. Ellen Vaden of De Valls Bluff remembered that the Ku Klux Klan "whipped you if you a Republican; ok if you a Democrat." Ex-Confederate E. A. Warren warned Washington blacks that if they voted for a new constitution "their throats would be cut." An anonymously written note threatened a Drew County black: "If you vote the radical ticket you will not live twenty-four hours, we will kill you as shor as Hell." Planters in Jonesboro, Marion, and Napoleon warned freedmen that to vote would ensure that "throats would be cut."[68]

A contemporary newspaper editorial, published in the *Washington Telegraph,* reveals the apoplexy and terror inundating the region. The editor warned:

> Mask it before it hatches! Out of it will come vipers, and loathsome slimy reptiles, which will infest the State, until you will fly the land. Drop your ploughs and your planes, and your pens, and your pill boxes and your bibles! Your wives are pale with terror! Its progeny will coil about your children until they turn black in heart and face. The hateful blood will eat up your substance. Run from your farms, and your shops, and your pulpit. Put your heart upon it, and clinch your teeth, and grind it into the earth! Shout to

your neighbor! Shake him if he sleeps, and tell him for God's sake to jump on it at once! Never mind its stench! Bury your clothes afterward![69]

As elections approached, bureau agents' actions became more crucial. Some personnel recognized that political power furthered the economic and social power that could make freedpersons really free. Lewisburg agent William Morgan, urging freedpersons to become politically active, tried "to impress upon their minds that their future welfare depends in a great measure upon their registering and the manner in which they vote at the upcoming elections." General O. O. Greene, hoping to dispel rumors, issued General Order Number 7 to assure freedmen that no connection linked voting and mandatory military service. Thomas C. Williams, Madison agent, received copies of the *Weekly Republican* and distributed them so "that the 'Gospel of Reconstruction' may be spread abroad into every corner and domain." An August 3, 1867, circular issued from Little Rock headquarters ordered Freedmen's Bureau agents to cooperate with registrars to insure black political participation.[70]

Late in 1867, with political fervor unabated, General C. H. Smith tried to stifle political debate by ordering his subordinates, "Send me the name or names of any official or other person who has been or may make inflammatory speeches to freedmen, or endanger the public peace by exciting one class or color against another." Lieutenant S. M. Mills, assistant superintendent of education at the Freedmen's Bureau, advised Pine Bluff agent Geisreiter, "It is better for agents to avoid politics altogether than to make enemies thereby."[71]

Undaunted by such delirium, most Arkansas blacks participated in postwar elections for a new constitution, the presidency, and state officers. Eight Arkansas counties registered a majority of black voters, and in seven other counties black and white registered voters came within 5 percent of each other. In 1867 there were 49,722 (74 percent) Arkansas whites and 17,109 (26 percent) blacks registered to vote.[72]

The failure to deter black voter registration intensified white anxiety. Increased violence accompanied elections. Intimidation and fraud frequently occurred at polling places. At Bright Star in southwestern Arkansas, Cullen Parker, "a notorious Texas hooligan," entered Arkansas and threatened Bright Star black voters with torture and death if they voted. In Marion, whites "bullied off" many freedmen. In Columbia

County, a Rebel sympathizer held "tickets against the constitution in one hand and a revolver in the other" to threaten freedmen with death if they supported the constitution. F. H. Brown of North Little Rock remembered that the Klan posted signs prior to an election that warned: "No niggers to come out to the polls tomorrow." An Augusta newspaper sent poll watchers to record anyone not casting a yellow, anti-constitution ticket and threatened to publish their names for future retribution. At Magnolia, those opposing black enfranchisement feared that violence and intimidation would not prevent blacks from voting, so they printed counterfeit tickets for use in manipulating the election. These fraudulent tickets, however, stored in old candle boxes, became easily detectable as the tickets absorbed candle grease.[73]

In some areas, coercion worked and few blacks voted; in others "nearly every freedman voted." At Napoleon, for example, agent J. C. Predmore reported that most freedmen did not vote and gratefully reported "all quiet now." Other areas experienced just the opposite and recorded high voter-turnout. Agents breathed a sigh of relief in Little River and Mississippi Counties when the election prompted no disorder despite the high black-voter participation. Freedmen vividly remembered their first votes. Charles Anderson of Helena recalled voting "the Republican ticket. We would go to Jackson to vote. There would be a crowd." Beulah Hagg of North Little Rock recalled, "Army men come around and registered you before voting time. It wasn't no trouble to vote them days; white and black all voted together." John Johnson chronicled election days fondly, recalling, "Of course I did vote. I used to have a heap of fun on election day. They give you a drink. It was plentiful I tell you."[74]

In large communities, blacks gathered on election morning and marched en masse to vote. Freedmen in Little Rock in March 1868, "carrying clubs and wearing red sashes," marched to the polls and helped ratify the new Arkansas Constitution. Typical of American election rituals throughout the United States, freedpersons met after voting for a celebration which included plenty to eat and drink. The *Arkansas Gazette*, bitterly opposed to the constitution and even more opposed to black suffrage, perceived the event as more of a dirge than a celebration. It moaned, "The surrounding country had evidently vomited its black hordes upon us."[75]

In some areas, blacks paid dearly for the voting privilege. In Washington, for example, justices of the peace issued frivolous warrants for freedmen who voted and refused to allow the accused to call witnesses in their defense. But blacks reaped large dividends as isolated, individual blacks bonded together in meaningful groups. In 1867 and 1868, answering the question Who am I? with Republican or Democrat offered a freedman a real sense of place and purpose. Political activism also gave freedpersons a definite sense of power and affirmed their belief that working together in groups brought about many beneficial changes.[76]

Politics furnished blacks who had leadership talents with an arena in which to utilize their skills. These new African-American political leaders served as role models for young blacks and encouraged both young and old blacks by publicly affirming African-American achievement. State and local black leaders, mobilizing black masses for a political party's candidate or for a certain issue, became power brokers on the national level and therefore bargained for advantageous legislation. Black republican ideology also emerged from this early political experience. Blacks believed, even though facing violence and intimidation, that to persevere was important. They insisted that voting and political activism were prerequisites for full, rich citizenship and humanity. In turn, individuals in Arkansas during Reconstruction found their identity richly transformed by politics.[77]

Although many black elites remain largely invisible in the historical record, the eight blacks elected to the 1868 constitutional convention reveal at least some characteristics of the black elite. Biographical details of these eight reveal a diversity of background, age, and occupational skills (see Table 3,4).[78]

Of these eight delegates, the most is known about James Mason. Fathered by wealthy Chicot County planter Elisha Worthington, Mason received his education from Oberlin College in Ohio and studied in France until 1860. Mason and his sister, Martha, ran their father's plantation from 1862 to 1865 after their father had fled to Texas at the approach of Union troops. During Reconstruction, Mason emerged as the Republican "boss of Chicot County" and was elected state senator and county sheriff. He died as Reconstruction was ending in Arkansas in 1874.[79]

To defend these newly gained political rights, blacks often formed paramilitary organizations to oppose whites. In response to the violence of the white Ku Klux Klan, blacks first formed paramilitary organizations in the autumn of 1867 and drilled in preparation for the upcoming elections. Texarkana freedman Doc Quinn recalled, "We would ride up to a negro settlement, and tell de niggers we wuz organizing a colored militia . . . Most ob de negroes would join." Blacks marched in Little Rock, Marion, Rocky Comfort, Pine Bluff, and Washington to preserve their new opportunities. Many black families left their homes on Friday to arrive at a Saturday rendezvous. They returned home by walking on Sunday and recuperated from the arduous weekend on Monday. Such priorities disconcerted many planters and bureau agents, but seemed mandatory to blacks who intended to maintain their freedom at all costs.[80]

TABLE 3.4

Black Constitutional Convention Delegates: Biographical Details

Name Home county	Birth	Occupation	Slave
William Grey Phillips Co.	1830 Washington, D.C.	Minister Teacher	No
Monroe Hawkins Lafayette Co.	1832 North Carolina	Minister Farmer	Yes
Thomas Johnson Pulaski Co.	1813 North Carolina	Minister	Yes
James Mason Chicot Co.	1842 Arkansas	Postmaster	Yes
William Murphy Jefferson Co.	1810 Kentucky	Minister Farmer	Yes
Henry Rector Pulaski Co.	1846	–	Yes
Richard Samuels Sevier Co.	–	Farmer	Yes
James T. White Phillips Co.	1840 Indiana	Minister	No

African Americans struggled fiercely for the right to possess guns, and they used such arms to defend themselves. Although planters tried from 1865 to 1868 to disarm blacks, bureau chief General Sprague insisted that "Negroes have the same right to carry arms that white men have and will be protected in it." Napoleon agent J. C. Predmore observed the "practice of carrying pistols is almost universal." Freedmen carried guns to the fields where they worked and to political meetings which they feared might be disrupted. Little Rock blacks created a communication network that allowed large numbers to mobilize and arm quickly when necessary. Providing self-defense and fostering self-worth and a sense of power, these informal or extralegal militias enabled freedpersons to express their determination to care for themselves.[81]

Blacks bonded in a variety of organizations other than churches, political parties, clubs, or militias. Freedpersons gathered together for many different reasons, with each group or club offering new opportunities to enrich life. Blacks organized "burial societies, debating clubs, Masonic lodges, fire companies, drama societies, trade associations, temperance clubs, and equal rights leagues" throughout the South. Each new institution furnished blacks with places for thought, fellowship, and camaraderie.[82]

Among these institutions, temperance clubs were most enthusiastically promoted by Freedmen's Bureau agents who hoped that such organizations would foster alcohol abstinence and encourage a disciplined, hard-working, sober agrarian work force. Urged to begin temperance societies by national bureau head General O. O. Howard, local agents responded positively and built on precedents enforced during slavery which controlled black use of alcohol. They even established clubs and provided speakers for weekly meetings. Agents and freedpersons established temperance societies in Lewisville, Washington, Little Rock, and Camden. Most of these societies experienced phenomenal growth, as illustrated by Helena's society which increased from 288 members at its inception in June 1867 to over 600 members by the end of the next month. Some freedpersons obviously attended simply for the fellowship, for the pleasure of getting together with kindred spirits. Others probably thought it best to stay in the good graces of Freedmen's Bureau agents, cultivating their friendship for some future favor. But others probably believed that keeping their fellow freedmen sober would be beneficial. Realizing that many whites believed blacks incapable of self-discipline and perceived drunkenness, along with sexual licentiousness, as immutable black attributes, black leaders urged moderation and self-discipline and promoted temperance societies to disprove white stereotypes about blacks. Ever trying to prove that they deserved freedom, freedpersons joined temperance societies hoping to change white attitudes about blacks.[83]

Bureau agents promoted youth organizations that encouraged education, sobriety, charity, and discipline—all those bourgeois virtues thought necessary for a stable work force. William Colby, Arkansas Freedmen's Bureau superintendent of education, established a "Vanguard of Freedom" in Little Rock where young blacks sang, participated in group rituals, heard pedantic sermonettes on duty, honor, and other ideals, and shared in games and refreshments. Colby also created juvenile temperance schools, which met on Sundays after church services for temperance education. Struggling to maintain these schools, Colby was shocked and dismayed to learn that one Little Rock church allowed eggnog *"at a festival held within the church."*[84]

Freedpersons also thronged to literary societies which encouraged and stimulated literacy and provided newly literate blacks with reading material. Helena's bureau agent Henry Sweeney, ever sensitive to freedperson's needs, encouraged the formation of a Literary League in Helena. At Camden, African Americans organized a reading club and purchased subscriptions to several Northern newspapers. Blacks came into town from the nearby farms and listened to accounts of life in Mobile, New York City, Washington, Chicago, or Little Rock.[85]

Blacks also gained new perspectives on their identity during leisure hours. Unsupervised by whites, freedpersons engaged in leisure activities that made life richer and more enjoyable and that cemented group ties through bonds of affection and well-wishes. Freedpersons exuberantly celebrated Christmas, not only as a religious holiday but also as a commemoration of the end of cotton-picking season and the year-end "settling up" at the local store. Many rural blacks journeyed to a nearby town or city to buy Christmas gifts and holiday food and to see friends and kin. Pine Bluff agent Major William Dawes feared that a Pine Bluff congested with blacks and whites might spark "racial trouble." He prayed for an arctic blast that would keep Jefferson County farm families huddled in their cabins instead of thronging the streets of Pine Bluff.[86]

Freedpersons also observed special events such as Easter or the Fourth of July with large balls where they wore their finest clothes, polished their appearances, and enjoyed themselves immensely. The Klan thought blacks enjoyed themselves too much at these festivities. Rachel Harris, Pine Bluff freedwoman, remembered, "Once we had a big ball. We was cuttin' a dash that night. The Ku Klux came and made out they were dead. Some of the folks run they was so scared." Although momentarily frightened, blacks refused to let whites intimidate them and hold them hostage inside their own cabins. Molly Horn of Holly Grove fondly remembered group candy-pullings and "colored fiddlers." "We had something every week," she recalled. Freedpersons shaped much of their attitudes about life and other people during these after-work experiences.[87]

In each of these group actions, an individual's responses critically shaped personality. What church one joined, what political party one supported, how actively one participated in political rallies and demonstrations, and what civic and social groups one joined all added to new dimensions of identity for Arkansas freedpersons.

African Americans struggled from 1865 to 1868 with the burdens entailed in freedom that all humans endure. Their struggles, however, took place in a context where freedom had been denied to them for so long and where they were often assumed to be inferior and subhuman. They courageously defended their families, their new understandings and definitions of themselves, their churches, their right to vote, and the privilege to peacefully assemble either for political or celebrative purposes. But economics remained the real foundation which would guarantee whether these newly created identities and institutions would endure. If blacks became truly free, they had to possess the means to care for themselves and their families economically, unfettered by any bonds to whites. The economic grounds of freedom played a major role in the world fashioned by blacks, Freedmen's Bureau agents, and white Arkansans in the world after the Civil War.

CHAPTER 4

SEARCHING FOR ECONOMIC FREEDOM, 1865–1868

Freedom is the most significant economic, philosophical, political, and social concept that fashioned modernity in the Western world; yet it remains a most perilous essence to analyze, understand, or communicate. Although freedom transcends economic reductionism, economics obviously played a crucial role in genuine freedom. In the West, economic standings conditioned viable alternatives. Although no formula exists that adequately explains the complexity of the relationship between economic standing and authentic choices, in the United States in the nineteenth century most people unthinkingly assumed more money meant more choices. Economic success or failure shaped an individual's identity. Americans, "people of plenty," to use David Potter's brilliant insight, historically defined themselves and their freedom in materialistic terms. Post–Civil War blacks were expected to embrace the materialistic notions that dominated Victorian America and join in the march of progress for higher standards of living, increased consumption, more material possessions. Clearly, freedom had a materialistic grounding: fewer choices appeared for freedpersons devoured by hunger and poverty. Freedpersons also confronted psychological levels of freedom: once bread was assured, would they be immobilized by freedom, desperately wanting someone, anyone, to take away the burdens of self-responsibility? Who Arkansas blacks became during Reconstruction depended largely on the economic livelihoods they eventually worked out. In 1865 the fluidity of the moment made many different dreams about one's economic future seem possible.

Arkansas, an agrarian state with lingering frontier vestiges, offered a promising future for farmers and entrepreneurs. High cotton prices in 1865 encouraged Arkansans to cling to the cotton kingdom. An absence of railroads made industrial development unlikely or at least not soon realizable. Freedpersons were most experienced with digging potatoes, chopping cotton, and hoeing corn, skills which encouraged them to stay with what they knew best, farming. But economies are more than material realities. Social constructions—the perceptions, values, and beliefs of humans—mold the effects of the cold, hard economic facts.

Arkansas blacks would either embrace or lose, to varying degrees, their economic freedom in the days after the Civil War. The Southern economy mirrored societal and cultural cleavages which rocked Arkansas. Historian Pete Daniel evocatively captured the moment's angst by noting, "Like a patchwork quilt, the new labor system in the South was varied and complex, an unpatterned blend of illiteracy, law, contracts, and violence, confusing, if not incomprehensible, even to those closest to it." A Pine Bluff planter told Yankee traveler J. T. Trowbridge in 1865, "On twenty plantations around me, there are ten different styles of contracts. Niggers are working well; but you can't get only about ⅔ as much out of 'em now as you could when they were slaves."[1]

Many problems threatened to unravel what Daniel described as the patchwork quilt. Planters constantly complained to Freedmen's Bureau agents about absent or lethargic laborers. In many areas in Arkansas, as in other Southern states, planters covertly reinstituted slavery. Lewis Carhart, Camden agent, found "slaves still in bondage" upon arriving in Ouachita County. William Tisdale of Jacksonport insisted, "Slavery is to all intents and purposes just as strong as ever in those sections in which our troops have not penetrated." Arkansas bureau chief General Oliver Otis Howard stated, "In some parts of Arkansas remote from such officers, the Freedmen are still treated as slaves, and the belief among the former slave owners is gaining ground of late—that slavery under some new name or guise can be maintained." He later warned agents to beware of bribes offered by planters for approval of favorable labor arrangements. Augusta sheriff John Thorp promulgated a county black code which required blacks "to go to bed early" except "on special occasions." Rule Number 13 required church attendance, and Rule Number 20 prohibited drunkenness. Although later discarded, the rules reveal that many still believed slavery had not ended.[2]

Even if bureau agents stymied planters' attempts to reenslave African Americans, the ravages of war further hindered the bureau's efforts to help freedpersons become economically independent. A currency shortage bedeviled bureau operations and hampered the introduction of wage labor. "There is no money here," lamented agent A. W. Ballard of Paraclifta. A shortage of farm implements and livestock retarded farming. Timing of the bureau's entrance into Southern life also hindered success, since agents arrived months after the cotton crop for 1865 had been planted. This seriously restricted alternatives for both freedpersons and agents. General Order Number 68 recommended, "The season is now so far advanced that freed people are advised to remain where they now are for the remainder of the year."[3]

Regardless of the problems faced, bureau agents' ideologies dictated that they encourage blacks to work. Bureau head O. O. Howard reminded state officials that all freedpersons should "choose their own employers," but he also warned agents that blacks should not remain unemployed. General Sprague urged Augusta agent John Thorp to "teach freedmen to keep contracts" and to "enforce vagrant laws" in order to inculcate the proper work ethic in freedpersons. Major J. J. Reynolds ordered the army to encourage freedpersons "to work for their living." "Freed people," he warned, "will not be allowed to congregate in towns, and about military camps, or to waste their time in idleness. Commanding officers will be held responsible for acts of vagrancy."[4]

Local bureau agents took such advice to heart and served as a gigantic labor agency, moving freedpersons into areas needing workers. General Order Number 138, issued in September 1865, authorized bureau expenditures for transporting blacks to critical regions. Agents issued rail and river passes primarily to Little Rock and Memphis, ports of entry into rich Mississippi and Arkansas valley farmland. Officials often encouraged freedpersons to move to areas offering greater economic opportunities. Lewis Carhart of Camden, for example, encouraged blacks to move to Little Rock after agent D. H. Williams requested "one-hundred to one-hundred and fifty good plantation hands." Historian William Cohen overstates the case when he likens bureau agents to antebellum slave traders, but for some agents, winning planters' approval clearly became more important than helping blacks gain economic freedom.[5]

Apprenticing black children proved to be an especially troublesome issue to bureau agents. Captain John Montgomery of Washington and A. W. Ballard of Paraclifta queried superiors whether parentless and friendless orphans could "be bound until age?" Still unsure and unfocused regarding its mission, the bureau in 1865 indentured young blacks to planters desperately needing workers. Agents' motives ranged from wooing planters to practically providing food, clothing, and shelter for hundreds of homeless black children. But to many it smacked of slavery and gnawed at their conscience. Chaplain E. O'Brien insisted, "All this amounts to practical slavery and keeps those families [of freedmen] broken up and scattered."[6]

The agreement between planter W. C. Draper of Arkadelphia and the bureau acting in proxy for the orphans Ann Jones, age twelve, and four-year-old Willie Jones typified apprenticeships. Draper guaranteed that one-fourth of their time would be allotted for school and that food, medical supplies, clothing, and housing would be provided. At the age of twenty-one each orphan would receive fifty dollars and a horse, saddle, and bridle. In return for such "beneficence," planter Draper received ten years labor from Ann and seventeen years from Willie. In 1867 the United States Supreme Court nullified such contracts.[7]

Agents not only supervised children's apprenticeships, but they also guided adults in their first days as free workers. Planters urged bureau agents to accept wages for blacks of five to six dollars a month for tasks that white men received seventy dollars to perform, but most officials rejected such paltry sums. Although planters uniformly clamored for low wages, each bureau agent had his own opinion regarding the best kind of contract for freedpersons. One advantage of wage-labor arrangements was that blacks were less likely to become mired in debt, especially if they purchased merchandise with cash. Also, such wages did not hinge on the wildly erratic and unstable cotton market. If a laborer hired for ten dollars a month, as did many, he received ten dollars a month, regardless of the price of cotton. Disadvantages of the wage system included a critical lack of currency in the South. If planters declared bankruptcy, as many did, freedpersons forfeited their earned wages. On the other hand, if one labored for shares (a share of the crop), a bale of cotton could be confiscated by authorities. But, if the price of cotton skyrocketed, as during the war and as planters expected after the war, then freedpersons would benefit by shares more than by wages. Any system an agent proposed had both advantages and disadvantages for freedpersons.[8]

Agents received no bureaucratized forms or guidelines from Washington on the type of contract most advantageous to freedpersons. Diversity ruled in 1865 as local agents approved a wide variety of contracts. Some contracts reestablished slavery, as did the agreement approved in Arkadelphia where landowner Newton Bridges hired thirty-four-year-old Israel Malcom, his seventeen-year-old wife, Julia, and their child for "food, two suits of clothing, one pair of shoes each, and medical aid," but no wages or share of the crop.[9]

But most agents rejected such reenslavement and suggested either wages or shares. The provisions of wage contracts at De Valls Bluff in 1865 reveal a wide variety. Males received from $5.00 to $60.00 per month, while female wages ranged from $5.00 to $40.00 per month. Most men contracted to work in planters' fields, while most women labored as house servants or farm laborers. Men earned an average $17.25 per month, and women earned an average $12.00 per month. Many men supplemented their income by cutting wood in the spring for $1.50 per cord. Interestingly, 42 men and 50 women of the 333 registered at the De Valls Bluff Freedmen's Bureau office, nearly 28 percent of the total, declared themselves self-employed as seamstresses, laundresses, draymen, carpenters, teamsters, and cooks.[10]

Other areas utilized sharecropping contracts. Cora Gillam, Little Rock freedperson, recalled that "the colored people were turned loose with nothing, and there wasn't nothing to do but for them to work on shares. They would work all the year and get nothing out of it but something to eat. At the end of the year, the white folks would say to them, 'you'll do better next year.' But the next year it would be the same thing over again."[11]

Uncertain income for both landowners and croppers characterized sharecropping. Both parties had to modify and adjust expectations with market fluctuations. The tentativeness of sharecropping in 1865 flawed a system already weakened by the "absence of relevant law and custom." Arkadelphia agent William A. Stuart perceived a basic defect that would hamper sharecropping from the beginning—debt. He worried that freedmen would buy needed provisions for planting crops at exorbitant prices and then be unable to pay their debts at harvest. He also feared that freedpersons would fall into "the power of the white man when he keeps a running account against them for a whole year's expense."[12]

Other freedpersons rented land and continued the work they knew best while gaining some independence in controlling their time and labor. General Sprague rented abandoned lands in Arkansas on one-eighth shares, with use of the land contractually guaranteed until January 1, 1866. Some blacks tried not to work at all. A Little Rock agent noticed that freedpersons often "refused to work" to gain "a more tangible form to the fact that they are free." But a withdrawal of bureau rations and concern for self and family sustenance required idle freedpersons to pursue other choices.[13]

Bureau agents mediated between freedpersons and planters during the 1865 harvest. John R. Montgomery of Washington warned planters not to throw freedpersons off of their land when the crop seemed to be failing. Arkadelphia agent William Stuart forced a Ouachita County planter to give blacks two bushels of wheat and two sacks of corn for work rendered. Bureau agent E. G. Barker reprimanded labor agent J. D. Taylor of Arkansas County for "practicing deception with freedpersons." Blacks often presented agents with intractable problems to solve, as when a male argued that his wife, Hanna, worked better "than Juda and deserved wages." Bureau agents labored, some diligently and others deviously, in some cases for themselves but often to realize their economic visions for Arkansas.[14]

Each freedperson responded differently to these many new possibilities. Some people stayed on the land they knew best and maintained relationships with the people they knew best, their former masters. In southern Arkansas, agents reported "thousands of blacks are remaining and expect to remain with their former owners until Christmas." Iran Nelson of Pine Bluff remembered that "after Mama was free, she stayed right there on the place and made a crop. Raised 800 bales and the average was nine. Mama plowed and hoed too. I had to work right with her too."[15]

Others moved, seeking either psychological distance from painful memories, tangible evidence of freedom, or improved economic conditions. "A considerable number of colored people are coming up from Texas," reported Freedmen's Bureau agent Francis Springer of Fort Smith. Bill Rector, a Washington freedman under contract, drove a team to Little Rock, saw the higher wages there, and refused to return home. Jacksonport blacks, like Bill Rector, discovered wages were higher along the bottomland and moved to those more profitable areas.[16]

Especially on large antebellum plantations, slaves labored together in gangs to maximize plantation efficiency. At emancipation, freedpersons jettisoned gang labor in preference for smaller squads that enhanced autonomy and self-control. Cliometricians Roger Ransom and Richard Sutch estimate that the actual number of hours of labor by freedpersons declined from between 28 percent to 37 percent after emancipation. They believe this became the major factor for plummeting cotton production after the Civil War. Freedmen precipitated such productivity decline by using their wives less in the fields and more in their homes and demanding more time off than they had under slavery. Postwar labor scarcity in the South in 1865 and 1866 forced planters to turn to labor systems other than the gang labor of the old plantation system. These new work patterns reenforced new African-American identities and empowered blacks in their self-concepts.[17]

In interviews granted in the 1930s, freedpersons remembered these economic changes. Henry Pettus of Marianna recalled that his landlord allowed "a melon patch, and a cotton patch [of] our own to work." Lula Taylor of Brinkley recollected, "Master Wade Deal at freedom gave papa a pair of chickens, goats, sheep, turkeys, a cow; and papa cleared ten acres of ground to pay for his first mule." Cora Gillam of Little Rock remembered that all freedpersons worked "using the white people's things." J. M. Parker, Little Rock sharecropper, recalled "that potatoes and things like that went free. All women got an acre free." He concluded, "War doesn't always make things better. It didn't after the Civil War."[18]

In 1865, and throughout the bureau's tenure in Arkansas, many

Northerners, freedmen, Southern planters, and bureau agents believed that land would be *the* palliative which would alleviate freedpersons' poverty and eliminate the shackles of paternalism that made freedom unrealizable for most Arkansas blacks. "Forty acres and a mule" became for freedpersons as magical a phrase as "independent yeomen farmer" was for Thomas Jefferson. The black desire for land fit in nicely with remnants of Jeffersonian republican ideology, which still lingered in the South and West and insisted that the individual and the republic were best sustained in a society where each individual possessed his own inviolable domain. Also, according to this ideology, virtue, so vital in preventing the republic's decay and degeneracy, was best nourished in agrarian endeavors far from cities. Land was to be the magic carpet which transported freedmen from bondage into freedom.[19]

Freedpersons tirelessly pushed bureau agents for land. An Ohioborn physician overheard General John B. Sanborn and a freedman discussing the need for land in Fort Smith in 1865:

> Freedman: Sir, I want you to help me in a personal matter.
> General: Where is your family?
> Freedman: On Red River.
> General: Have you everything you want?
> Freedman: No, sir.
> General: You are free!
> Freedman: Yes sir, you set me free, but you left me there.
> General: What do you want?
> Freedman: I want some land; I am helpless; you do nothing for me but give me freedom.
> General: Is that not enough?
> Freedman: It is enough for the present; but I cannot help myself unless I get some land, then I can take care of myself and family; otherwise, I cannot do it.[20]

Both black political elites and many Freedmen's Bureau officials labored to assist freedpersons in their acquisition of land. A conference of twenty black Southern leaders met with Secretary of War Edwin Stanton and General William T. Sherman at war's end and insisted, "The way we can best take care of ourselves is to have land, and till it by our own labor." Bureau officials agreed. Oliver Otis Howard, bureau leader, observed that "nothing excited higher hopes" than blacks' visions of landownership. Helena agent Henry Sweeney recognized that freedpersons who obtained even small parcels of land for themselves worked "with far more satisfaction and contentment" than those who worked for wages or shares. Lieutenant S. H. Rains of Little Rock reported, "The freedmen of this district are very anxious to get lands of their own to work next year." General James S. Brisbin, touring Arkansas in 1865, testified to the Joint Committee on Reconstruction that freedmen seemed "very anxious to acquire property." Both freedpersons and many bureau agents insisted ownership of land was a prerequisite of real freedom.[21]

This dream for land confiscation and distribution to freedpersons was not chimerical; various schemes for redistribution had been approved by President Lincoln and Congress and implemented by the army during the Civil War. As early as August 6, 1861, Congress authorized the president to seize property used for Rebel support. The army confiscated forty thousand acres of South Carolina Sea Island property in 1862 for delinquent taxes and made it available for purchase by blacks. Freedpersons received much of that land in forty-acre segments in 1865. Confiscation and distribution to freedpersons of Davis Bend Plantation in Mississippi, which had belonged to Confederate president Jefferson Davis and his brother Joseph, proved highly successful. Laborers raised nearly two thousand bales of cotton in 1865 and earned $160,000. The army preempted land, and freedpersons worked many abandoned plantations in Arkansas and throughout the Mississippi Valley during the war. Precedents definitely existed for land confiscation and distribution.[22]

The most vociferous congressional champions of land distribution were Thaddeus Stevens and George Washington Julian. Stevens has been called by a biographer "the greatest dictator Congress ever had." Motivated entirely by self-interest, Stevens championed throughout his career anti-Masonry, the Bank of the United States, westward expansion of the railroad, a high protective tariff (especially favorable to his Caledonia Iron Works), Free Soil, prohibition, and radical Republicanism. Believing that Lincoln and his successor Andrew Johnson dealt far too leniently with the defeated South, Pennsylvania congressman Stevens clamored for redistribution which would include Southern land confiscation. In a September 1865 address, Stevens insisted "that the property of the chief rebels should be seized and appropriated" and given to freedmen in forty-acre segments. Stevens believed land distribution would bring freedpersons into the ranks of the Republican Party and cripple the Democratic Party of Southern planters. Freedpersons were not nearly as interested in Stevens' motivation as they were in getting their forty acres.[23]

George Washington Julian, Indiana representative, similarly championed land for freedpersons by insisting, "Real liberty must ever be an outlaw where one man only in 300 or 500 is an owner of the soil." He contended that the South must be made "safe for the freedmen" and that a "Christian civilization and a living democracy amid the ruins of the past" should be constructed.[24]

The original version of the Freedmen's Bureau bill provided "to every male citizen, whether refugee or freedmen," forty acres of land for three years' rental, followed by the opportunity for land purchase; but that version never exited a congressional conference committee. In July 1865 General Howard recommended dividing abandoned land into forty-acre segments and renting them to freedmen; but many doubted the constitutionality of such a scheme. Local agents therefore had some freedom in the disposition of land. Henry Sweeney, for example, divided abandoned land in Phillips County into twenty- to fifty-acre plots and rented them to freedpersons.[25]

General John Sprague, Arkansas bureau chief, notified his superior that "there is very much land in the state that is 'abandoned' and much that ought to be confiscated." Bureau records indicate over 106,000 abandoned acres in Missouri and Arkansas in the summer of 1865. Agents reported that planters had fled from over 350 plantations in Arkansas for reasons as diverse as "Gone to Texas" and "Killed at Shiloh battle." For freedpersons, such land promised hope and raised great expectations.[26]

But the hopes for desired land fizzled in 1865, primarily silenced by President Andrew Johnson. The successor of Lincoln proclaimed at the beginning of his administration that Southern plantations "must be seized and divided into small farms and sold to honest, industrious men." But the presidency metamorphoses individuals. One day Andrew Johnson awoke after a night of uneasy sleep and found himself a planter sympathizer. A May 1865 Proclamation of Amnesty liberally granted pardons to planters. By the end of 1865, the Freedmen's

Bureau controlled only ⅕ of 1 percent of Southern land. Whatever motivated Johnson—racism, sanctity of property ownership, political self-interest, or class consciousness—his liberal pardon policies jettisoned blacks' dreams for their own land in 1865.[27]

Freedpersons, facilitated by Freedmen's Bureau agents, moved toward economic freedom in 1865. But 1866 would be the first full year of freedom, in which more rationalized economic patterns would emerge. No black sighed with Macbeth of the sameness of "tomorrow, and tomorrow, and tomorrow," for no one yet knew what would occur in 1866.

Bureau agents discovered and freed blacks who were still enslaved throughout 1866 and 1867. Simpson Mason, Fulton County agent, reported in March 1867, "One [Rebel captain] Matthews still retains two freedmen in abject slavery." Jacksonport agent A. S. Dyer observed a planter who used blacks "as much his slaves now as ever." "He allows them to see no other freedmen or leave the plantation at any time," continued Dyer, "and says that they do not know that they are free." Lawrence County registrars in northeastern Arkansas in November 1867 discovered "several freedmen were held as slaves, and cruelly treated on the East Side of the Black River." The compulsion to whip blacks to force them into obeying planters remained as alive as in antebellum days. Lewisville agent V. V. Smith chronicled, "Men in this county have been allowed to whip, swindle, discharge, and fine their employees whenever they saw fit to do so." Captain J. M. Cain of Camden despaired that whites still whipped blacks "as formerly."[28]

Planters also invoked newer forms of submission. They often drove freedmen from their lands after the cotton crop had been gathered. V. V. Smith reported that landowners forced over one hundred freedmen from the county in 1867 and conceded that little had really changed for Arkansas blacks. "When I send freedmen back to a plantation from which they have been discharged," Smith reported, "they are once again driven off and word sent to me that it is 'none of my damned business.'" A Chicot County planter complained of blacks "turned adrift without a dollar. Starvation will be upon them." Planters also picked quarrels with freedmen "just as crops approached maturity" to induce them to leave. Often law enforcement officials aided planters in limiting freedperson's freedom. W. V. Steel, Columbia County sheriff, "persuaded" no one to bid on the cotton raised by freedman Russell

Latter, thus forcing the price to a ridiculously low level. Planters and white conservative politicians, biding their time as radicals controlled political power for a season, slowly but surely forged new fetters to reenslave Arkansas blacks, thereby making the bureau's job even more arduous.[29]

Precise contract terms still perplexed many bureau agents and freedmen. The Camden agent resolved a case in which a thirteen-year-old "house servant" protested that she had been turned into a "field servant." Thomas Abel repeatedly instructed Chicot County planters on the proper content of rations guaranteed contractually. Liens also perplexed many agents. Lieutenant John Bennett of Madison wondered what to do when "a doctor and a merchant gives claim for payment simultaneously?" The state legislature eventually clarified liens by granting state courts adjudication when several liens existed simultaneously on land or on a crop and by instructing courts to use a pro rata formula.[30]

Constant disagreements about mules and cows reveal the rural environment in which bureau agents worked. Little Rock overseer T. J. Churchill of Thibaut Plantation stopped issuing contracted rations in the autumn of 1867 as punishment over a dispute concerning who killed a mule. Unable to find the guilty party, Churchill hoped to punish all by withdrawing rations until he exposed the culprit, but the local bureau agent ordered the rations restored. Someone shot a cow in October 1867 in the village of Solitude. The event was minutely detailed in a four-page letter to the Marion County bureau agent. Mules and cows, which provided labor savings, milk, and future animals, were crucial to an agrarian economy and, therefore, the cause of many important bureau investigations.[31]

Bureau agents increasingly mistrusted planters and monitored them more carefully. They stood up for freedpersons' rights in a land swamped with bitterness and hate. Agents spent much time on contractual arbitration as they tried to balance equitably both planters' and freedmen's claims. The cases reaching Lewisville's V. V. Smith in July 1867 indicate the quagmire agents worked in regarding contracts. Freedman A. N. Lee discharged his wife, Hesley Rhodes, without annulling their contract. Smith ordered Rhodes back to work where she would "receive justice at the final settlement." Amy Ann Johnston was charged with prostitution and demoralizing the plantation work force. Smith voided her contract and discharged her from the estate. Planter W. B. Merriman whipped employee Easter Merriman. Smith annulled the contract and guaranteed a final harvest settlement. Planter F. M. Cole dismissed freedman Eli Chapman for missing work while registering to vote, but Smith favored Chapman. Both parties agreed to annul the contract and reached a mutually acceptable settlement. R. N. Williams held down and whipped freedperson Nancy Wiley. Smith determined such violence had breached the contract and awarded Wiley payment for services rendered as well as money for a new dress and pair of shoes. Napoleon's J. C. Predmore attempted to delegate authority in contract arbitration by proposing that litigation be decided by a committee of three: a planter's representative, freedmen's representative, and Freedmen's Bureau representative. But the rule by committee never caught on, and individual bureau agents continued to deal with most disagreements alone.[32]

Disputes over time and schedules besieged bureau agents. Freedman A. Thurman refused to eat lunch in the fields as his employer insisted. Did any of the hours contracted to working in the cotton fields belong to him? Agent Charles Banzhoff ruled against Thurman who "agreed to take his meals in the field." "Lost time" complaints inundated bureau officials. State headquarters eventually decided that planters could not deduct wages or rations due to bad weather. Bureau officials worried over what planters could force freedmen to do while under contract to them. Agents eventually defined permissible work as "cultivating the crop, keeping fences and gates repaired, harvesting the crop, and readying the crop for market," guidelines that were still extremely ambiguous.[33]

Bureau agents often intervened in crop and cotton disputes between planters and freedpersons. Agents frequently ordered planters to allow blacks to gather crops unmolested. A. S. Dyer of Jacksonport, for example, commanded planter Trumer Perry to "allow Robert Wilkinson (colored) until the 17th to finish picking his cotton" on Perry's land. E. G. Barker's warning to a Marion planter was typical: "You will not remove any portion of your present crop or in any manner dispose of it till you have settled with and paid the Freedmen for their services for the year 1866 and 1867."[34]

Other agents' missives dealt with broader concerns. Agents in South Bend and Monticello blockaded all cotton shipments until freedmen received their fair share of the crop. Helena agent Henry Sweeney implemented a program that required freedpersons to obtain coupons from him before selling their cotton. Sweeney feared that planters swindled blacks by buying crops auctioned at "unreasonable hours" and hoped that his supervision would benefit freedpersons.[35]

Contracts in 1866 and 1867 continued to reveal a lack of uniformity. Rocky Comfort agent H. F. Willis reported, "Freedmen have different ideas as to what system is best." He observed that two-thirds of the freedmen worked for shares, while one-third labored for wages. Diversity and confusion regarding contracts prevailed throughout these years.[36]

Time stipulations became more prevalent and precise by 1866. Lewisburg blacks contractually agreed to labor twenty-six days per month, ten hours per day. W. D. Cotley, Ouachita County planter, granted freedmen two hours off at noon in the summer, with only a one-hour lunch during spring, autumn, and winter. Freedmen worked half-days on Saturdays except in cotton chopping and picking time. H. W. Ratcliff of Pocahantas promised forty-year-old freedwoman Mary "one day each week and a piece of land to raise as much cotton as she can attend to." Samuel McKaye of Lafayette County charted minimum daily work hours for his laborers. All employees, he contended, must "arrive at day break." They must then work nine hours per day in January and February, ten hours per day in March, April, November, and December, and eleven hours per day May through October. He also bound workers to "perform all important or necessary duties even on Saturday, evenings, and during holidays."[37]

Finely tuned and detailed work stipulations were included in many contracts. Sytle and Dumas, Madison planters, required in 1867 that freedpersons agree to work for "quarters, fuel, ½ pound pork, and one peck of meal per day." They provided plots for vegetable gardens and all necessary implements. Workers, in return, gave planters one-half of the cash valuation of staves and shingles manufactured and one-half of the cotton and corn produced on the plantation.[38]

Many contracts detailed food distribution. Ouachita County planter W. C. Cotley specified rations of "182 ½ pounds of bacon meat without bone or 208 pounds of bacon meat with bone plus thirteen bushels of good corn meal." The Steele brothers, Conway County planters, provided two hundred pounds of bacon and thirteen bushels of meal or flour per person per year; smaller boys received only one hundred pounds of bacon and one-half of a bushel of meal or flour.[39]

Planters often tried to modify behavior contractually. Dallas County planters G. S. Dunn and S. L. Nupell required deference, stipulating that freedmen "be respectful in their deportment to said employer and his family and obedient to his orders." Samuel McKaye of Lafayette County prohibited "quarrelling, thievery, or stealing," and punished robbery with a fine that was double the value of the stolen item.[40]

Contracts often recognized the new role for black women demanded by blacks of both sexes. In a deal with John James, freedman Charles Hick agreed that his wife would "do all the housework such as cooking, working, and scouring after which she is to make a hand in the field." Mrs. Charles Taylor promised to cook, wash, iron, milk, and sew on the Dunn and Nupell estates. Freedpersons demanded contractual recognition from planters for the new status of women and family. Such insistence allowed freedpersons to solidify their new self-concepts.[41]

Statistics reveal the dimensions of the Arkansas labor force. In Hamburg in 1867, for example, male workers outnumbered females 314 to 260. An average of 7.5 children worked on each Ashley County area plantation. At Big Rock, 20 men and 17 women labored under bureau supervised contracts. The average male worker earned $17.60 per month and was twenty-two years old; the average female earned $15.60 and was twenty-three years old.[42]

The number of workers who contracted in any given area greatly influenced the quality of life there. Many freedpersons continued to choose to work in squads of 2 to 4 laborers. In Lewisburg, 2.7 workers on average labored on each plantation. But not every freedperson worked on such a small scale. Sixteen Chicot County planters contracted for 789 workers in 1867, averaging 49.3 laborers per plantation. Such numbers seem impersonal, but when one remembers that the quality of existence was determined by where blacks worked and the size of their work squads, one recognizes the significance of these economic rhythms and demands.[43]

County statistics revealed the broader dimensions of Arkansas

TABLE 4.1

Family Farming Units: 1867

County	# of families employed in March 1867	Male	Workers Female	Children
Ashley	120	135	161	256
Arkansas	252	351	317	440
Chicot	155	366	374	381
Calhoun	163	258	216	456
Clark	65	84	84	167
Desha	225	327	351	315
Dallas	29	44	44	43
Fulton	35	15	45	65
Mississippi	261	603	380	320
Pulaski	269	367	317	374
Phillips	254	477	459	602
Sebastian	59	73	53	140

employment in 1867 (see Table 4.1). Bureau agents viewed working units as family units, suggesting the significance and viability of the black family by 1867. This attitude also implied that agents recognized families—parents and children—as an integral work force component. Men outnumbered women workers in six counties, while more women than men contracted in four counties, but in only two of these ten counties were the differences substantial. Fulton County, in northern Arkansas, recorded contracts at a three-to-one ratio for women and men, while Mississippi County contracts for eastern Arkansas reveal a three-to-two ratio in favor of men. Each family unit averaged two children. Mortality statistics reveal the precariousness of life, especially among the young, as children made up 56 percent of the total deaths.[44]

Gender-based wage differentials strengthened the new understandings which emerged regarding what it meant to be a black man or a black woman. The male to female ratio was 314 to 260 in Hamburg in 1867. There were 7.5 children per plantation if one counts all twenty-four plantations, and 10 children per plantation if one counts only the eighteen plantations where children actually lived (see Table

TABLE 4.2

Gender and Age Distribution of Farm Workers
Ashley County: 1867

Employer	# of males	Employees # of females	# of children
Alford Hill	7	8	5
J. H. Bell	26	19	–
S. S. Bell	8	11	11
M. L. Butler	15	13	–
E. L. Crocker	5	5	3
T. Carter	25	14	13
N. T. Commack	23	12	–
N. B. D. Yambert	6	4	1
J. L. D. Yampert	15	5	4
Donaldson & Bell	4	6	3
N. P. & Jill Fisher	14	16	10
Thomas Headley	16	7	18
Herod & Tigman	22	22	–
J. P. & P. F. Harlianson	15	18	–
W. E. Kettrell	17	7	29
G. R. King	8	9	17
R. A. Pugh	8	12	6
John Robinson	12	6	4
John Simn Jr.	20	21	–
Tunstall & Scott	9	4	16
P. A. Thompson	4	5	4
Joel Millios	14	13	14
Wigins & McCurdy	10	17	16
T. P. Womack	11	6	6

4.2). At Big Rock in Pulaski County, age, sex, and pay statistics were documented on the Hobbs' Plantation. Twenty men and 17 women labored at Big Rock. The average age for male laborers was twenty-two, for female laborers, twenty-three. Men earned, on average, $17.60 per month; female workers, on average, made $15.60 (see Table 4.3).[45]

TABLE 4.3

Gender Wage Differentials: 1866
Big Rock, Pulaski County

Age	Male Pay per month	#	Age	Female Pay per month	#
10–14	$4	1	10–15	–	0
	$10	1			
	$12	1			
	$14	1			
16–20	$15	1	16–20	$15	3
	$16	2		$16	5
	$20	5			
21–29	$20	5	21–29	$15	2
	$16	4			
30–39	$20	2	30–39	$15	2
	$16	1			
40+	$25	1			

Lost time statistics—the phraseology revealing the bias of the planter keeping the record—indicated freedpersons' work habits and leisure ethic (see Table 4.4). To a large degree, freedpersons asserted their own work ethic and worked when they wished. Such decisions reaffirmed new understandings of identity.[46]

Extant Dallas County records indicate that the contract process grew more rationalized over time. A chart reveals the maze of contracts agreed to in 1866, as compared to those in 1868 which were far more homogeneous (see Tables 4.5 and 4.6). The drastic decline from forty-one in 1866 to one in 1868 in the number of freedmen contracting for a year's supply of rations, food, clothing, medicine, and quarters—which constituted but another form of slavery—is immediately striking. By 1868 shares coalesced to one-fourth, one-third, or one-half shares, but in 1866 one senses the newness and tentativeness of the contracts in which shares are in fifths, sixths, and sevenths.[47]

An overseer's ledger from the Bayner Plantation in Jefferson

TABLE 4.4

Monthly Work Statistics: 1866–1867

Planter	County	# Working	Average days worked	Average days lost
Burt & Cox	Hempstead	8	20.9	4.9
Wood Co.	Pulaski	19	20.4	7.0
C. E. Moore	Calhoun	20	17.8	8.0
Wm. Murphy	Ashley	15	22.0	4.0
J. H. Bale	Ashley	21	24.9	1.0
McFadden & Black	Hempstead	8	20.2	5.6
M. V. Cheatham	Hempstead	15	20.5	5.5
W. L. Cabell	Franklin	8	19.0	9.0
H. H. Carrigan	Hempstead	10	29.4	2.0
James Henderson	Jackson	42	21.4	4.1
I. P. Harbison	Ashley	14	26.0	4.0
John Nelson	Hempstead	9	24.3	1.6
C. O. Pumphrey	Pulaski	23	24.3	1.6
S. J. Robinson	Jefferson	51	20.0	7.0
D. B. Smith	Jefferson	12	22.0	5.0
W. H. & D. B. Tibbs	Ashley	17	22.0	4.0
Allen & Beson	Hempstead	12	21.6	4.4

County underscores the perimeters of work and freedom of blacks in 1867. Over sixty-two workers, supervised by an unnamed but exasperated white foreman, raised cotton in the Arkansas Valley during 1867. The plantation contained only eight mules, "two waggons —one very sorry," two sets of wagon gears, three spades, three shovels, and one cram-cut saw. Even more scarce than farm tools were amicable relations between laborers and employers.[48]

Freedpersons' work never suited their taskmaster. During the week of February 25 to March 3, for example, nearly one-half of the field hands on the Bayner Plantation missed work on one or more days for many varied reasons (see Table 4.7). "Damned sorry work week," the overseer scribbled in the plantation ledger.[49]

Other account-book comments reveal that blacks often worked

TABLE 4.5

1866–1868 Contract Provisions: Dallas County

Contract provisions	Number of contracts in		
	1866	1867	1868
⅛ of crop	2	–	–
⅐ of crop	1	–	–
⅙ of crop	3	–	–
⅕ of crop	7	2	–
¼ of crop	2	4	5
⅓ of crop	30	3	5
½ of crop	27	28	17
⅝ of crop	1	–	–
⅔ of crop	1	–	–
¾ of crop	1	–	–
Rations, fuel & clothing, medicine, quarters	41	4	1
1 mule, 40 bu. corn	1	–	–
1 bale of cotton	1	–	–
1 acre of cotton	1	–	–
100 rails @$1	1	–	–
2½ acres of cotton	–	–	–

TABLE 4.6

1866–1868 Contract Provisions: Dallas County

Contract provisions	Number of contracts in		
	1866	1867	1868
$5	1	–	–
$10	3	–	–
$12	2	1	–
$15	1	–	–
$18	–	2	–
$20	5	1	–
$24	2	–	–
$25	7	2	1
$30	8	1	1

TABLE 4.6 (CONTINUED)

Contract provisions	Number of contracts in		
	1866	*1867*	*1868*
$36	3	–	–
$40	10	2	3
$45	–	–	2
$50	14	10	5
$60	17	9	3
$70	1	–	–
$72	2	1	–
$75	4	1	2
$78	1	–	–
$80	2	–	–
$85	–	–	1
$96	1	–	–
$100	9	3	2
$105	1	–	–
$110	1	–	–
$120	–	10	1
$125	2	–	–
$130	2	–	–
$140	1	–	–
$144	1	–	–
$150	9	6	2
$175	2	1	–
$180	–	1	–
$192	1	–	–
$200	3	–	1

when, where, and how they wished. Some February entries indicated the overseer's discontent:

> 20: No better I talked to sum this morning about getting out so late.
> 21: No difrance.
> 22: I told Alfred that they would have to loose all the extra hours made them mad.

TABLE 4.7

Bayner Plantation Work Absences:
February 25–March 3, 1867

Reason for missing work	# Workers
In Memphis	1
Hunting	6
Pneumonia	6
Went to lake	1
Went off in AM	2
Child sick: stayed home to nurse it	7
Cooking	1
Confined	1
Sick	3
Not out at all	1

The manager still fumed in a later entry, "I have talked and talked it does no good about getting out of mornings it does no good." On a spring Saturday when, according to the overseer, cotton and corn should have been hoed, the "men lost all day on the account of wedding of Edmon Summers and June Jane was married." In May, the ledger keeper sighed, "There is no use in trying to get them to work on Saturday evening for tis plum folly." Apoplectic again in July, the overseer noted, "Rained on the evening of the 30th of June and none went to work on the lst. Hilliards hands all ploughing and at work mine fishing and loafering." Probably the most telling entry is from April 25:

> My patience worn plum out with Negroes and mules
> Old Joe or some of his clan drove two of my mules in the
> river today
> One of them I think is drowned as I can't see or hear anything of her.

That the manager equated "Negroes and mules" indicates his distaste for the new world ushered in by Reconstruction.[50]

Bayner Plantation blacks occasionally resorted to more than substituting a dropped hoe with a fishing pole. In two instances in May

1867, freedpersons openly rebelled by refusing to work further until the overseer resolved difficulties. On May 2, the manager "had a big fuss today with all of the men Sim reported that they refused to work under me any longer." Talk defused the confrontation, but two weeks later on May 18 another labor revolt erupted. "A perfect rebellion amongst the Hands," the overseer penned, undoubtedly after he had averted the crisis and steadied his nerves. "All came up," he continued, "and said that if I killed or discharged Alfred that they was not going to work on the place any longer." What Alfred did to make his fellow workers fear for his life is unknown; but that they so brazenly supported him clearly reveals the assertiveness of these African Americans. But as so often happened in labor disputes in the Gilded Age, the manager refused to yield, and the expediency of having no alternative for family care forced freedpersons to watch a dismissed Alfred walk down the Jefferson County lane as they returned to their hoes. They had spoken up and done all they could for Alfred; they had reinforced their dignity. But Alfred must not be forgotten in the celebration of workers' assertiveness. He now had no job, which indicated the real limitations of freedpersons' freedom. The laborers' work stoppage also, in the end, showed freedmen their impotence. It changed nothing. Brute power, unaffected by dignity, remained for freedmen to confront as they attempted to forge freedom and new identities for themselves and for their children.[51]

Sometimes freedom drove freedpersons toward conflict. If an individual proved his or her freedom by colliding by choice with the powers that sought to hedge genuine options, then the contract negotiations, work slowdowns, and talking to the boss as an equal constituted tangible evidence of the dialectic of freedom that blacks engaged in. But although such assertiveness boosted the spirit of most freedpersons and of many bureau agents, fears also began to surface that blacks could soon lose their newly gained independence, shackled once again, this time by debt.

By 1866 serious problems began to plague blacks who struggled to gain economic independence. Whether freedpersons labored for wages or shares, they suffered from a shortage of farm tools, animals, and seeds. Many quickly became mired in debt to plantation-owned stores or local merchants. Such obligations often shackled them to work in the same location, ever struggling to free themselves. Many blacks became landlocked, forever destined to grow cotton as dictated by a European and American oligarchy.

Historians view these country stores and their accompanying systems of credit as both a blessing and a curse. Cliometricians Roger Ransom and Richard Sutch believe merchants dictated that Southern farmers turn from subsistence to cotton farming, a shift that caused a 50 percent decline in food production and necessitated the purchase of food on credit from merchants. Other scholars evaluate the stores' impact much more positively. Lawrence Powell believes plantation stores dispensing material goods to freedpersons dangled capitalistic incentives before them in the forms of clothing, foodstuffs, or fiddles. Henry L. Swint contends that a major goal of Reconstruction was to flood the South with Northern goods, thereby expanding Northern industrial markets and profits. Country stores served, therefore, as capitalism's missionary outposts, ever spreading its materialistic salvation. Thomas Clark argues that these stores provided freedpersons with real choices and richly added to the material aspects of their daily lives. "Now the freedom of going into a country store and looking over its crowded shelves," Clark writes, "was for him [freedmen] nothing short of a trip to heaven."[52]

But to many Freedmen's Bureau agents, the "heaven" Clark discusses was illusory, gild, ersatz—a deceptive entrance into a never-ending hell. Few were as perceptive as Arkadelphia's bureau agent William Stuart, who in 1865 denounced the indebtedness to planters and merchants. Freedpersons, he insisted, "are in the *power* of the white man when he keeps a running account against them for a whole year's expenses . . . This doubtful policy—so pregnant with disputes, and misfortunes to the freedmen, I now discourage." J. C. Predmore, Napoleon bureau agent, reported that planters snared freedmen in debt, then released them from contracts. Jacksonport's J. T. Watson believed planters extended credit to sharecropping freedpersons to control their expenses and to keep them bound to a place—their place. J. L. Thorpe of Camden agreed with Watson, insisting that merchants had sunk "their hooks" in freedpersons.[53]

"In not one case in fifty," Helena's Major J. T. Watson noted in 1867, "have the freedmen made anything this year." Sebastian

Geisreiter discovered that nearly all blacks in Pine Bluff ended the year in debt. Freedmen at South Bend complained to agent Albert Coats that they worked all year and received no money. Although escaping slavery undoubtedly elated freedmen, they must have puzzled over their new bondage under capitalism.[54]

Exorbitant merchant prices and fraud posed serious problems. V. V. Smith, bureau agent in Lewisville, decried plantation stores "where goods, cheap jewelry, and intoxicating liquors are sold at exorbitant prices." Agent Hiram Willis denounced the outrageous prices levied by Washington merchants: $8 for a straw hat, $4 for a belt, and $4 for a net. Jacksonport and Lewisville agents continually uncovered merchant fraud in the form of overcharged goods, usurious interest rates, or intentional mathematical error. As an Arkansas freedman remarked, "A man that didn't know how to count would always lose."[55]

Agents responded to this fraud by auditing freedpersons' accounts. At Lake Village Lieutenant Glasshof and freedman Columbus Paul audited Paul's 1867 bill from a Drennan Plantation merchant. Paul insisted the February charge of medicine was exorbitant when compared to the price of corn, denied that he purchased onions in May, and contested the charge of $1.58 for cash loaned at Sunnyside. Glasshoff adjusted the bill downward and encouraged the merchant to advise freedpersons weekly of their debt. Merchant markups of 30 percent to 100 percent appalled J. S. Taylor of Hamburg. After reviewing prices such as $1.00 for a dozen apples or one orange and $5.00 for three pounds of coffee or sugar, he slashed most bills by one-third. Hiram Willis cut bills even further, slicing them by 50 percent in Rocky Comfort.[56]

It is impossible to read page after page of the accounting ledgers of merchants, recording debtor after debtor, without despair. But perhaps there is more revealed by the numbers. The cold and impersonal figures of the merchants' and planters' ledgers reveal that many freedpersons made, for the first time, real choices about what to buy. Necessities for subsistence, such as sugar, flour, coffee, bacon, corn meal, and molasses, made up most purchases. But freedpersons also bought large quantities of shoes, boots, calico, "domestic" cloth, brogans, handkerchiefs, overcoats, blankets, candles, brooms, and hatchets.[57]

That this was a new beginning, a start from scratch, is revealed in

TABLE 4.8

Average Merchants' Prices: 1866–1867

Item	Price	Item	Price
Fishhooks	$.15–$2.50	Cups/saucers	$3.00
Buckets	$.60	Set of plates	$1.25
Scissors	$1.00	Bowls	$.90
Skillet	$3.60	Tin cups	$.30
Coffee pot	$1.00	Fry pan	$.75
Knives/forks	$1.50–$5.00	Water bucket	$2.00

the myriad utensils purchased by freedpersons. A list of purchases and prices indicates what freedpersons bought at this time; the price of the purchases, fairly substantial given their poverty, enhances our appreciation for the difficulties freedpersons faced (see Table 4.8). Although such items are unimpressive to a twentieth-century observer, in 1866 and 1867 they made life easier and healthier for many freedpersons.[58]

Freedpersons asserted their new identities and freedom while shopping at a country store. One pictures Joseph Scott buying "a fine hat bought in Memphis" for $5.00, or Reuben Williams purchasing a speller for Henry for $1.45. One can imagine the thrills David Moody's family felt when the tick-tock of the clock he purchased filled their cabin, or how Sam Shillings smiled as he secured whatever precious items he possessed with his padlock. Here was a man who only ten years before could himself have been padlocked, who was himself thought of as property, now locking up *his* property. Imagine Saul Franklin putting *his* money in *his* purse, or Henry Jones parading with his new umbrella, perhaps neglecting to close it long after the rain stopped.[59]

The meaning and significance of owning clocks, earrings, and new hats becomes clear when considered in the context of the antebellum world in which blacks could not own such things. Such "stuff"— skillets, blankets, knives, and forks—reified not only acceptance of Lockean notions of private property but, even more significantly, reassured blacks of their freedom. Such purchases also constantly reminded freedpersons of their new identities and status. These purchases assured blacks that slavery was no more.

The material aspects of life deeply affected freedpersons' conceptualizations of freedom and of the new identities they were forging. The material level of life equally limited Freedmen's Bureau agents' schemes to bring the economic good life to Arkansas blacks. Living in materialistic, postbellum Victorian America, freedpersons confronted wealthier and poorer whites and blacks, all with differing levels of material wealth which epitomized status, comfort, and spiraling or declining fortunes. The paucity of goods owned by blacks confirmed the overt or subtle racism of many whites, including bureau agents, by reaffirming their belief that blacks possessed little because they deserved little. The work of the bureau in Arkansas cannot be understood solely by orders issued from headquarters in Washington or Little Rock, nor even by local agents' reports. Rather, the material context in which such orders were issued has to be recalled when trying to capture the bureau's accomplishments and failures.

The economists Roger Ransom and Richard Sutch believe that "luxuries" such as hams, canned fish, cheese, candy, new clothing, and whiskey reaffirmed in freedpersons' minds that they were really free and just as human as whites. For example, merchant records indicate freedpersons bought what merchants called "Negro brogans." When freedmen wore such, they lived up to white expectations. But other entries, such as a "suit bought in Memphis" or calico, reveal that blacks fashioned their own identity through clothing. Such purchases not only hinted that freedpersons perceived a world beyond the plantation but were also confirmation ceremonies symbolizing that freedmen and Southerners embraced Northern consumption communities. Many whites grew apprehensive over black purchases, fearful perhaps that they soon might not be able to compete favorably with blacks. Lewisville's V. V. Smith spoke for many whites when he reported of local blacks, "In nearly every instance they have been very extravagant."[60]

Extravagant would not be the word chosen by many to describe the housing of most freedpersons in Arkansas. An "average" freedperson's cabin was described as "a small hut of pine logs or rough hewn boards, roofed with shingles split out with an ax." Rosa Simmons of Pine Bluff, remembering these primitive conditions, recalled, "When my folks first come to Arkansas we lived in a cabin that just had a balin' sack hangin' in the door and one night a bear come in."[61]

If former slaves' memories are reliable, the bed was the centerpiece of the freedmen's home. Marion Johnson of El Dorado recalled, "Mammy's beds was ticks stuffed with dried grass and put on bunks built on the wall, but they did sleep so good. I can most smell that clean dry grass now." Solomon Pattille of Little Rock noted, "We lived in old log cabins. We had bedsteads nailed to the wall. Then we had them old fashioned cardboard springs. They had ropes made into springs. That was a high class bed." Primarily, the oldest and youngest family members used beds, with four or five people sleeping together in cold weather. Julia Haney of Little Rock remembered not only her mother's bed but also described other contents of the house: "The furniture was a bed with high posters. It didn't have slats, it had ropes. It was a corded bed. They had boxes for everything else—for bureaus, chairs, and things." Most black homes reflected their occupants' poverty. The *Batesville North Arkansas Times* reported, "The only thing that detracts from our town is a large number of shabby huts occupied by the negroes." But perhaps such criticisms hid the real, underlying meaning of freedmen shanties; such poor housing reassured whites that blacks were "in their place."[62]

Cooking utensils were just as sparse as cabin furnishings. Lizzie Barnett, who moved to Conway in 1867 from Memphis, cooked in an iron skillet over coals. She still used the same skillet in the 1930s. Anthony Taylor, who remembered the difficulties encountered while cooking, recalled:

> We had no skillet at that time. We would rake the fireplace and push the ashes back and then you would just put the cake down on the hearth or on a piece of paper or a leaf and then pull the ashes over the cake to cook it. Just like you roast a sweet potato. Then when it got done, you would rake the ashes back and work the cake and you would eat it. Sometimes, you would strike a little grit or gravel in it and break your teeth.[63]

Freedpersons worried about both how and what to cook, often finding little food to prepare. Poor diets contributed to poor health among many freedpersons. If diet indicates socioeconomic class and

reflects poverty, then the freedpersons' diet signals blacks "in their place."
Most freedmen's diets consisted of hominy, corn bread, fat bacon, coffee, molasses, rice, pork, and vegetables. Mattie Mooreman of Hot
Springs claimed that life during Reconstruction was far harsher than it
was in the 1930s. She recalled, "We didn't get such good food. Nobody
had all the kinds of things we have today. We had mostly buttermilk and
cornbread and fat meat."[64]

Although freedpersons slowly and sadly learned that white
Arkansans could not be counted on for aid, they recognized and relied
upon the natural bounties within the state for sustenance. Grinding
parched okra, meal, or corn produced ersatz coffee, while fermented
persimmons produced beer. Snuff and tobacco served as excellent
fishing bait. An abundance of bear and wild game provided much
needed protein. Warren McKinney of Hazen experienced what many
freedmen must have felt when he noted, "There was so much wild
game [that] living was not so bad." In contrast to the urban poor of
1867 or 1967, poor Arkansas freedpersons fell back upon bountiful
nature as a safety net during harsh winters or summer droughts. But
even then, some freedmen were stalked by hunger and anxiety. Thomas
Ruffin of Little Rock poignantly recalled harsh conditions. "I got along
hard after I was freed," he noted. "We used to dig up dirt in the smoke-
house and boil it and dry it and sift it to get the salt to season our food
with. We used to go out and get old bones that had been throwed away
and crack them open and get the marrow and use them to season the
greens with." Material disparities and deprivations sorely hampered
Arkansas freedmen's freedom in the immediate postwar years.[65]

Freedmen faced more than just debt and poverty in 1866 and 1867.
Farmers live tenuous lives, eyes ever squinching heavenward, trying to
conjure either the sun or rain clouds at certain critical moments. In
Helena in 1866, scant rain in July and August retarded crop growth.
Then rain flooded river bottomlands in September and October,
drowning much of the already stunted cotton. The Ouachita,
Arkansas, and Mississippi Rivers flooded in 1867, washing planting
after planting away and causing many freedmen to abandon their
efforts in disgust. Cut worm infestation also stunted the 1867 crop.
Although freedmen replanted in corn and wheat, their replacements
offered less profit. Even when freedpersons successfully ginned their

year's cotton, competition with India and South America had forced the price of cotton from an 1864 high of $1.02 per pound to $.43 in 1866 and $.32 in 1867. "Entire Arkansas counties are bankrupt," moaned bureau state head General C. H. Smith.[66]

Although freedmen faced many staggering economic problems in 1866 and 1867, they did not succumb to despair. Instead, just as under slavery, many creatively and ingeniously continued struggling to improve their conditions. Such psychological testing strengthened some blacks' perseverance and undoubtedly began to make others wonder if all the trials were really worth it. How a black responded to these challenges greatly affected personality development.

Nearly everyone assessed the 1867 crops as a disaster. Napoleon's J. C. Predmore summarized what most agents and freedmen felt in December 1867: "The cotton crop in this county has been a decided failure this year." Although some people expected that a declining supply, coupled to England's continued demand for cotton, would accelerate prices, just the opposite occurred. Marion, Helena, Dardanelle, and Princeton agents all bemoaned the low cotton prices which devastated freedpersons who had purchased goods on credit throughout 1867 in anticipation of higher-priced cotton. C. H. Smith, Arkansas bureau head, visited the Southern agricultural centers of Washington, Camden, and Pine Bluff and found "a gloomy foreboding" caused by low cotton prices. Smith noted crop prices dropped by 75 percent from July expectations. William Morgan of Lewisburgh predicted freedmen in his area would be forced to "seek employment elsewhere." The depressed cotton market compounded freedmen's troubles by greatly increasing their debt. That which freedmen knew best—cotton production—could not be counted on to improve freedmen's living standards.[67]

Freedmen continued to move from farm to farm in 1866 and 1867 in search of more lucrative economic conditions. "A scarcity of labor has helped freedmen," noted Pine Bluff agent William Dawes. E. W. Gantt observed that in Washington "many farms will lie out of want of labor, but the laborers are not here." A comparison of Southern states in 1867 and 1868 reveals Arkansas male farm laborers received the highest wages in 1868, making Arkansas an economic magnet for blacks elsewhere who were looking for more profitable work (see Table 4.9).[68]

Blacks clearly recognized that movement could improve economic

TABLE 4.9

Wages and Value of Rations: Agricultural Labor

State	1867			1868		
	Men	Women	Youth	Men	Women	Youth
Virginia	102	43	46	102	41	45
North Carolina	104	45	47	89	41	39
South Carolina	100	55	43	93	52	42
Georgia	125	65	46	83	55	47
Florida	139	85	52	97	50	44
Alabama	117	71	52	87	50	40
Mississippi	149	93	61	90	66	40
Louisiana	150	104	65	104	75	60
Texas	139	84	67	130	72	63
Arkansas	158	94	78	115	75	67
Tennessee	136	67	65	109	51	45

standing. Many gravitated toward the higher wages along the Mississippi River, a migration which troubled many bureau agents in western Arkansas. Planters at South Bend lured blacks from other areas in Arkansas by offering to pay them extra for work performed outside the cotton fields. Arkansas freedpersons moved throughout the state, ever trying to solidify their economic freedom.[69]

Insufficient numbers of Arkansas blacks forced planters to look to other states for farm emigrants. Washington planters journeyed to St. Louis in search of workers. Pine Bluff landowners toured the Atlantic and Gulf coasts to hire additional help. Planters also utilized labor agents to supply farm hands. One such agent was John C. Calhoun, namesake and grandson of the famous antebellum senator from South Carolina. He and a Montgomery, Alabama, agent settled blacks in the Yazoo Valley in Mississippi and in Chicot County in southeastern Arkansas. Amsy O. Alexander of Little Rock recalled, "Agents came from Arkansas trying to get laborers. So about seven or eight families of us emigrated from North Carolina. That is how my folks got here." Henry Green remembered Arkansas described as a place "dat de hogs jes laying er round already baked wid de knives an de forks stickin' in 'em ready for to be et." George Johnson of Virginia heard that "money grew like apple on a tree in Arkansas." Agents told Ishe Webb that cotton grew "as high as a man in Arkansas." Webb thought that overblown but did think the situation in Arkansas better than the one in Georgia, and so the Webb family, like many others, moved westward to Arkansas.[70]

Labor agents often became, from the bureau's viewpoint, unwanted middlemen who lied to freedpersons about wages and working conditions. Fred Thibaut of Washington spoke for many of his fellow bureau agents when he disgustedly called labor agents "dealers in human flesh." Offering freedmen thirty to forty dollars a month plus whiskey to move to Arkansas, agents received twenty to thirty dollars per laborer for those secured for planters in southwestern Arkansas. As it turned out, the freedpersons, abandoned far from home, earned only fifteen to twenty dollars a month. Atlanta, Georgia, labor agents induced freedmen to leave Georgia's red hills for the promised land of Arkansas where they, upon arriving in Mississippi County, were deemed "vagrants" by local county officials and sent to a Dr. McGarock's estate. An agent named Shriver wooed over sixty Carolina blacks to follow him, supposedly to Mississippi. Forsaken by Shriver at Vicksburg, the freedpersons trekked to Lewisville upon hearing that good jobs awaited them there. Agent V. V. Smith reported that no preparations had been made for them: "No houses, no wood, no clothes. They had to lay in the rain and cold until they could build themselves houses."[71]

An agent in Cherokee County, Texas, made contracts with over sixty-five freedpersons who agreed to migrate to Pine Bluff. Traveling by wagon train from the Lone Star State to Pine Bluff for nearly the entire month of January, these freedpersons upon arrival insisted planter James Sheppard had promised them the highest wages in the area. Upon discovering other planters paid better salaries, the Texas freedmen "struck immediately for higher wages." Labor agents often helped freedpersons move to better-paying locales.[72]

Although many blacks found a better life in Arkansas, many did not. Nineteen field hands from Alexandria, Virginia, illustrate the trouble some freedmen found in Arkansas. Brought to Laconia Landing on the Mississippi River in early 1866, the nineteen workers were crowded into two small rooms and were inadequately fed. Over two-thirds of the nineteen fell ill at one time and received no medical attention from their employer, C. A. Norton. Four of these freedmen, enduring all they could, decided to go to Helena to report their mistreatment to bureau officials. County whites, privy to these plans, chased, captured, and beat these four. In the middle of the beating, armed freedmen arrived to disburse the white molesters and liberate the Virginians who now probably wished someone would "carry them back to 'ol Virginia."[73]

Those failing to find Arkansas a land of milk and honey continued their quest by exiting Arkansas in 1866 and 1867. A Pine Bluff reporter chronicled, "Our streets are flooded with people going to Texas." Pine Bluff agent Sebastian Geisreiter admitted that "many of the freedmen are leaving the valley. They are either going to the hills or to Tennessee." Helena's James Watson also recognized freedpersons' despair and desolation caused by their inability to find employment. Freedmen, he noted, "lived as best as they could, many of them wandering from place to place, being unable to find employment of any kind." Such movement, however, testified to their new condition of freedom.[74]

Many bureau agents discouraged this black exodus from Arkansas. Thomas J. Abel of Batesville advised freedmen with "all persuasive means" within his power not to leave. E. G. Barker of Fort Smith requested permission from state headquarters to prohibit freedmen from leaving for the North, but his superiors ordered him to desist and to treat freedmen "as white free men and in no other way."[75]

Many agents and freedpersons continued to see landownership as the means of escape from debt and poverty. John Goodrum of Des Arc recalled his parents' dream that the government would "divide up the land and give them a start." Five hundred in a black camp meeting held at Fort Smith in 1866 urged the local Freedmen's Bureau to help them find farms of their own. "Freedmen seem to be keenly alive," commented Hiram Willis of Sevier County, "to the importance and advantages of obtaining property."[76]

It looked for a time as if blacks' dreams for land would become reality. Congress passed the Southern Homestead Act in 1866 which opened up over nine million acres of public land in Arkansas. Union loyalists could obtain eighty-acre tracts until January 1, 1867, at which time anyone could purchase the remainder. Land offices in Little Rock, Clarksville, and Washington recorded over twenty-six thousand original entries which claimed over two million acres. Congress prohibited purchases of large tracts from 1866 to 1876 in hopes that freedpersons

and poor whites would buy the smaller sections and become economically self-sufficient. Blacks prayed Congress's vision would not
evaporate.[77]

Many local agents tried to ensure land for African Americans under
the new law. Albert Coats of South Bend repeatedly urged local freedpersons to take advantage of the Homestead Act. He also requested
maps to safeguard freedpersons from settling on land not in the public domain. Agent John Tyler successfully lobbied for the creation of
local land offices which facilitated purchases.[78]

Surveyor Dr. W. W. Granger worked more than anyone else to see
that freedpersons received land available to them under this new law.
No one advertised the land's bountifulness more than Granger. He
exhorted a Little Rock black congregation to make a pilgrimage to the
opened area. When blacks requested maps of the region to help them
decide where to move, Granger surveyed and drew up twenty-four
maps for the use of the bureau and freedpersons. As over one hundred
Helena families prepared to move, Granger discussed logistics and
helped them finalize their plans.[79]

But enormous problems crippled the homestead legislation. Ineptly
maintained antebellum land records made it difficult to ascertain what
land lay unclaimed. Disputes over landownership between the federal
government, the state of Arkansas, and railroads hampered sales. It
was not unusual for surveyor Dr. W. W. Granger to write a local official,
"I cannot find out whether it is railroad land or not." Great distances
separated land offices from the actual land, compounding the difficulties faced by blacks. Even when offices could be found nearby, corrup-
tion and fraud marred their operations. And if all these problems were
not enough to discourage blacks, the head of the Freedmen's Bureau
in Arkansas during most of this time, General C. H. Smith, displayed
no concern about freedmen and homestead possibilities. When southwestern Arkansas blacks implored him to help them get land, he
advised them to remain where they were for another year. Typically, the
Arkansas Gazette lampooned blacks for "coming to our city, bridle in
hand, fully expecting to lead the coveted mule home to the promised
forty acres."[80]

Though faced with nearly insurmountable barriers in acquiring
homestead land, a substantial number of freedpersons succeeded in
becoming landowners. The best example of freedpersons taking advan-

tage of the Homestead Act occurred in Franklin County where nearly 150 families from Green County, Georgia, began to investigate the possibilities of moving to Arkansas. A delegation, led by Abraham Colby, arrived in Fort Smith in February 1867 to reconnoiter the area. Over 72 families each took eighty-acre plots and began their lives anew in Arkansas in March 1867. Over 100 black Fort Smith families joined these Georgians in their efforts to gain their own farms. In Pulaski County as early as October 1866, 14 black families paid for land surveys, dug wells, and built "double log cabins, so common throughout the West." About 50 Washington families planned an all-black colony in southwestern Arkansas. Of the 26,395 claims made in Arkansas under the Southern Homestead Act, only 10,807 (44 percent) were completed. African Americans in Arkansas entered approximately 1,000 of these original claims, with 250 (25 percent) completing their entries. Historian Michael Lanza's assessment that "the assurance of homestead land for the freedmen proved, in the end, to be nothing more than another dream deferred" seems corroborated by contrasting the lofty expectations of freedmen for land in 1865 and 1866 with the limited number of actual homesteads farmed by blacks in 1868.[81]

By New Year's Day in 1868, freedpersons, Freedmen's Bureau agents, and Arkansas whites had witnessed many changes which transformed blacks from chattel slaves into persons not yet totally free but far freer than before emancipation. New identities and personas had been created, discarded, and modified. But despair engulfed many freedpersons and bureau agents that year. The loss of interest in the South and in African Americans was evident in Congress's decision to limit bureau appropriations in July 1868 to educational projects. Albert Coats of Arkansas County resonated the dirge which echoed throughout Arkansas, "Great dissatisfaction prevails among all classes . . . The suffering among the Freedmen is intense." Agent E. G. Barker of Marion despondently noted, "The people financially are badly shipwrecked and catching at any little thing like drowning men." In Madison, agent Thomas Williams sensed a "gloom pervading [freedmen's] minds engendered by the knowledge of the probability of the Freedmen's Bureau being discontinued."[82]

Although planters continued to face economic difficulties, they became more empowered and assertive as they forged new chains around freedpersons. Agents in Jefferson, Chicot, Arkansas, Clark,

Bradley, and Phillips Counties recorded that planters repeatedly drove blacks off their land after harvest but before settlement. Manpower shortages and the absence of troops forced bureau officials to respond nominally to recalcitrant planters. The Crittenden County agent typically noted, "Many of the colored people are being swindled out of their year's work and the cold winter which is approaching will find them destitute of even the common necessaries of life." Planters devised new methods, such as hiring only healthy males while denying contracts to less productive family members. They also won court cases which offered them new advantages in liens. "The present laws," E. G. Barker reported, allow "the merchant, landlord, planter, and others" to take "the entire crop made by the laborers and leave them without anything." Jacksonport's William Brian grew increasingly embittered that planters practiced "barbarous subterfuge" in settling accounts with freedpersons and that planters wanted, most of all, compulsory or "peonage" labor.[83]

Arkansas blacks, still supervised by remaining bureau agents, continued to weave their patchwork quilt of various labor systems in 1868. They utilized sharecropping, land tenancy, land rental, and wage labor. In Lewisburg many worked for wages of ten to fifteen dollars per month, while others rented land to make their own crop. In Napoleon, freedpersons split about evenly in contractual arrangements, half working for shares and half for wages. Freedmen who had been swindled under one system absolutely refused to try it again. For example, Marion blacks, having lost on wages the year before, balked at any semblance of wage contracts. Skyrocketing land rent denied land to many freedmen. Stock prices and land rental soared beyond the reach of Jacksonport blacks, which caused the local bureau agent to opine, "The prospect for the coming year looks gloomy."[84]

Freedpersons often protested work injustices. In a poignant, remarkable letter to the Freedmen's Bureau, freedmen Peter James, John Johnson, C. Mitchell, A. Ayers, and Thomas Gibson pleaded "for one officer" to ensure justice from the planter. "It is no infrequent thing," they documented, "to see our people come here all bruised and mangled and drove off without any pay for labor they have done for months." Others protested more vociferously and actively than with a petition. Arkansas County freedmen working for John Campbell refused to cut wood in May 1867, insisting that the woods were too wet. When

Campbell ordered the freedmen to obey and they again balked, he fired them all and told them to leave the plantation. Freedman Charles Montgomery cursed this summary dismissal. Something in Campbell then snapped; this new world where blacks refused to work and to follow a white man's orders seemed unfathomable to him. He therefore shot Montgomery in the head, killing him instantly.[85]

Not all work protests ended in a freedman's murder. More subtle protests occurred with work slowdowns, refusals to work on Saturdays and Sundays, and determination not to work. Planters meticulously documented "lost-time" when freedpersons failed to work, but from the freedpersons' viewpoint the time was not lost at all. It was time well spent in fishing, hunting, or staying inside and listening to the rain tapping on the roof.[86]

Although the horizon looked bleak for many freedpersons, some agents continued to work on their behalf. V. V. Smith of Lewisville, in one example of bureau action, confiscated thirty bales of cotton as the freedpersons' just portion. E. G. Barker of Crittenden County warned a planter, "No cotton will be moved off the place till the hands are *paid not one bale* under any circumstances or pretense what ever use all the shot guns and men necessary to hold it." Marion's E. M. Main ordered freedpersons who had been dismissed for joining the State Guard, a paramilitary organization, reinstated in their jobs. Jacksonport agent William Brian warned planter Stinger Thomas to "immediately stop moving" the cotton crop. Brian also ordered the county sheriff to confiscate all cotton and corn raised on Levi Terrel's farm by freedpersons until he could properly arbitrate. But there were too few agents and too many fraudulent planters. In so far as contracts and labor orchestration was concerned, the bureau left Arkansas in 1868 not so much with a bang as with a whimper.[87]

Pro-planter bureau agents worried that the political activism of 1868 hindered cotton production, so they often counseled political quietism. Madison agent Thomas Williams urged blacks "to abstain from attending any political meetings, to refrain from discussing any political questions, to apply themselves to the labor of their crops." E. M. Main, Marion agent, agreed and exhorted freedmen to "make no noisy demonstrations of their political opinions." Although freedpersons often ignored such advice, the agents' recommendations clearly reveal that planters had co-opted many agents by 1868.[88]

In evaluating the impact of the Freedmen's Bureau on the Arkansas economy, statistics are revealing. The bureau oversaw an economy in which blacks chose to work fewer hours, but which also demonstrated undeniable improvements. The 1866–1868 United States Department of Agriculture "Report of the Commissioner of Agriculture" reveals a recovery in the Arkansas economy during bureau supervision (see Tables 4.10 and 4.11).[89]

But statistics reveal only a partial picture. Freedpersons testified to the positive and negative aspects of bureau intrusion in the economy. Cora Gillam of Little Rock sang no praises of the bureau's economic work in Arkansas. She insisted that freedpersons remained "just about where we was in slave days." John Hunter, also of Little Rock, remembered ironically, "When the slave was freed, he was looking to get a home. They were goin' to do this and goin' to do that but they didn't do nothin'." But Joni Martin assessed the situation differently and insisted, "My greatest pleasure was independence—make my money, go spend it as I see fit." As so often is the case in history, economists and historians shuffle evidence as they wish, but the freedmen who were actually involved discerned no overriding pattern or conspiracy in what occurred. Rather, freedpersons perceived what happened to them economically in richly variant hues: some bitterly believed the

TABLE 4.10

Arkansas Farm Production: 1866–1868

Product (in bushels)	1866	1867	1868
Indian corn	11,585,332	21,243,000	32,449,000
Wheat	584,137	870,000	1,000,000
Rye	39,046	39,000	39,000
Oats	308,924	392,000	439,000
Barley	4,737	4,000	4,000
Potatoes	263,346	323,000	350,000
Tobacco*	1,425,571	1,739,000	2,521,000
Hay**	7,578	9,000	9,400

*pounds   **tons

TABLE 4.11

Arkansas Farm Annual Inventory: 1866–1868

Animal	1866	1867	1868
# of horses	89,502	104,717	109,952
Average price	$66.49	$59.40	$71.64
# of mules	42,287	48,435	52,309
Average price	$84.08	$61.56	$88.56
# of cows	100,103	108,111	120,003
Average price	$22.77	$20.76	$21.75
# of other cattle	132,694	138,001	151,801
Average price	$10.57	$9.92	$11.24
# of hogs	480,864	591,462	768,900
Average price	$4.94	$4.95	$4.20

government betrayed them, while others celebrated freedom as a most exhilarating experience indeed.[90]

Historians have judged the economic activities of the Freedmen's Bureau just as divergently as did the actual freedmen involved. W. E. B. DuBois believed that not much really changed. He argued, "The slave went free, stood a brief moment in the sun; then moved back again toward slavery." Willie Lee Rose contended, "When the excitement of the war and Reconstruction subsided, freedmen were left largely with what they had themselves made of their new freedom." Leon Litwack asserted that the job of transforming and guiding the Southern economy was too big for the Freedmen's Bureau, that limited resources and the local environment restricted major redistributions of wealth at that time. Edward Royce argued that the Freedmen's Bureau "never set forth a clear and unambiguous policy with respect to the regulation of labor relations in southern agriculture." He continued by noting that "the Bureau served the interests of both planters and freedpeople, but only as those interests conformed to the requirements of the plantation system, an economic arrangement that served their respective interests quite unequally."[91]

Bureau agents kept a debit and credit ledger sheet for each freedman, marking on one side earnings in wages or cotton shares and on the other side credit purchases at the local store. So, too, can historians devise a credit and debit analysis of the economic activities launched by the Freedmen's Bureau between 1865 and 1868.

The debit side is tragically full, for the Freedmen's Bureau was guilty of both sins of omission and commission. Bureau agents failed to see the importance of freedmen landownership and often did little to help realize the vision of the Southern Homestead Act. Planters often co-opted the Freedmen's Bureau with the result that agents moved freedmen across the South and to different parts of Arkansas, not for freedmen's benefit but to accommodate planters. Agents often accepted freedmen's indebtedness to such an extent that newly freed slaves became shackled to a life of servitude. In an age of popular mass political participation, agents often encouraged freedmen to stay in the fields hoeing or chopping instead of going to town and speaking, listening, and voting. Individual agents must be held responsible. Some never appreciated what was really happening in Arkansas and tried to change things as minutely as possible in order to minimize violence. Others clearly saw what was happening and, through their actions, vaulted the "better sort"—planters—back into hegemony. Still others tried to help freedpersons gain economic independence, but they faced too many problems and too hostile an environment to ever succeed.

On the credit side, taking into account the venomous environment following a bloody civil war, the Freedmen's Bureau achieved much, including genuine economic progress for many freedmen. The bureau acquiesced to, if it did not champion, the freedmen's work ethic which insisted on the primacy of family and on the right of freedpersons to control their own time. The bureau diligently supervised freedmen contracts, making sure freedpersons received fair wages or shares. Fraud was rampant even with the watchful bureau, but one wonders how much more fraudulent the dealings of planters and merchants with freedpersons would have been without the bureau. Agents insured a modicum of merchant fairness for freedmen by carefully supervising credit accounts. Conscientious bureau surveyors helped at least 250 freedmen gain and keep their own farms under the Southern Homestead Act. Many black indigents, remembering warm coats for frosty nights or rations which filled growling stomachs, would attest to the "good deeds" performed by the bureau. The bureau provided transportation to new jobs for freedmen who wished to move to areas of higher wages. Certainly the tale of the economic activities of the Freedmen's Bureau is not one simply of betrayal, omissions, and subservience to the planter elite. The Freedmen's Bureau made genuine contributions in the long, arduous struggle for freedmen's freedom.

By 1868 the old patterns of a landowning elite, which now utilized both white and black cheap farm labor to maintain hegemony, had reemerged in Arkansas. Some freedpersons had bargained into positions of quasi freedom—positions in which they were poor but controlled much of their work and free time. Other blacks, for all practical purposes, had been reenslaved. But regardless of the economic failures or successes that blacks individually experienced, the economic underpinnings of freedom would be jeopardized unless they secured adequate health care. Freedpersons also sensed that education could be a link which insured freedom. Care of the body, mind, and morals concerned blacks as much as did economics, for they sensed that without education and health care, freedom and their newly forged identities would be jeopardized.

## CHAPTER 5

CARE OF THE BODY, MIND, AND MORALS, 1865–1869

Freedom, for Arkansas's former slaves, necessitated a health-care system. The Freedmen's Bureau, in an effort to help blacks realize genuine freedom, served as medical facilitator. A chief medical officer, assisted by surgeons-in-chief for each Southern state, managed the medical department. In many cases the bureau co-opted the army's contraband hospitals. A medical officer, steward, commissary clerk, dispensing clerk, matrons, nurses, steward, and laundresses ostensibly made up a hospital staff, but reality seldom corresponded with the legal requirement. A dispensary, manned only by a doctor and apothecary, sometimes was all that assisted freedmen in sparsely populated areas.[1]

Many freedpersons' health remained precarious as long as medical help could not be depended upon. Camden bureau officer L. H. Carhart reported in July 1865, "The town is full of hungry, naked and destitute [freedmen]. What to do with them all is yet unsettled." "The greatest destitution and suffering," state bureau head General John Sprague told the American Missionary Association, "now prevails in western Arkansas. Very many both whites and blacks will perish next winter if timely aid is not extended." Planters often expelled elderly and sick freedpersons when their productivity waned. Steamboat operators also often added to agents' woes as they dumped sick and incapacitated blacks at the nearest Arkansas port.[2]

Bureau agents expected little aid from local officials. "The case of indigent and sick freedmen at Napoleon demands aid from the Government," agent William Dawes of Pine Bluff observed, "as the people there will not provide for them unless coerced to do so and I greatly doubt the ability of many of them if they had the inclination." Rampant epidemics among large black populations left city authorities unmoved. A Little Rock agent in 1866 reported, "The civil authorities will absolutely do nothing toward the relief of even the refugees, claiming that they live outside of their jurisdiction." Henry Sweeney of Helena chastised town fathers for "doing nothing." Jacksonport mayor T. H. Phillips offered assistance to white paupers but not to poor blacks, for there "was a Freedmen's Bureau in the place for that purpose." Pine Bluff indigents, given county scrip to use for food purchases, found merchants unwilling to accept the nearly worthless county money. Little Rock city officials refused to contribute funds for freedmen's coffins after the 1867 epidemics. Local officials, having no tradition of massive aid for the needy and seething with racism and bitterness toward Yankee agents, often refused to lend a helping hand to the "Jacobin" Freedmen's Bureau.[3]

The limits of medical knowledge in the nineteenth century always constrained the bureau's health care. Some proposed remedies were obviously ludicrous, such as a cannon fired through the streets of Fort Smith to "clear away the cholera" or "ice broken in small pieces and swallowed in moderate quantities" as an "excellent remedy for cholera and similar diseases." This was the age of home remedies and fix-all medicines; egalitarianism extended to health concerns. A reader of the *Arkansas State Gazette* recommended "two ounces of Laudanum, two ounces spirits of camphor, four ounces tincture of capsicum, two ounces of peppermint, and two ounces of Hoffman's anodyne" as a cholera cure which had proved successful for over fifteen years. Ten to twenty-five drops of the concoction were to be taken, and the reader was urged to carry a small phial in his pocket for emergencies. Dr. George Lawrence of Hot Springs, offering his assessment of cholera to *Arkansas State Gazette* readers, believed that "ozone changes" caused the epidemic and that the remedy was to secure "pure air by strictest hygiene." Some of his suggestions helped. For diarrhea, he recommended drinking pure water, eating no indigestible fruits and vegetables, and consuming "copious droughts of good hot chicken broth with plenty of African Cayenne pepper," or a mixture of "rhubarb, cloves, cinnamon, ginger, capsicum, prickly ashberry, and cognac brandy." A champagne tonic, also recommended, was probably not medically beneficial but eased the pain as well as anything.[4]

The doctors and nurses employed by the bureau often increased, rather than eased, the problems faced by freedpersons. Physicians held a low, marginal status in the South. Often inadequately trained, many Northerners found themselves ill-prepared to deal with their new Southern environment. General Ord, 1867 bureau head, encouraged L. A. Edwards, the bureau's chief medical officer, to send no more doctors to Arkansas who were "not familiar with peculiar habits and diseases of freedmen." Distinguishing between white and black susceptibility to disease was not a form of racism but was, as learned in the twentieth century, genetically based. John Wells of Edmondson, a former slave, noticed differences in the races' sicknesses. He remembered, "Me and my brother waited on white folks through that yellow fever plague. Very few colored folks had it. Now when the smallpox raged the colored folks had it seem like heap more and harder than white folks." Census reports for 1860 also reflect that blacks were far more susceptible than whites to ischemia, worms, tetanus, and rickets, but more immune than whites to diphtheria, yellow fever, typhus fever, and nephritis.[5]

Inadequate funding also limited the enthusiasm of physicians for helping blacks. Sebastian Geisreiter reported that Pine Bluff doctors received inadequate fees and refused to make visits to the sick unless guaranteed pay by the county. By 1866 most physicians balked at working for the promise of future pay. South Bend physicians declared "that they are unable to furnish medicine gratis and they can get nothing for their services among the colored people for they have nothing to pay with." Three Little Rock physicians proposed that doctors' fees be deducted from the shares of sharecroppers before the freedmen were paid, but the proposal received a bureau response of "no official action. We will encourage that they pay." Support personnel also received low pay or encountered bureaucratic bumbling. Two workers in the Little Rock bureau hospital received no pay from June 1864 to 1865, and two black nurses, Milly McGee and Lucinda Washington, never received their promised hundred dollars per month at a Batesville hospital. Poor pay and collection difficulties increased the likelihood that health care would be minimal.[6]

Other problems made finding competent medical personnel

difficult. Bureau agents dismissed surgeons who performed adequately otherwise but who could not swear to the loyalty oath prescribed by the Fourteenth Amendment. Fear of reprisals prompted some doctors to refuse medical aid to blacks who had been whipped or beaten by the Klu Klux Klan. Frequent transfer of personnel also jeopardized the health-care system. Captain Thomas Abel of Fort Smith lamented that the "surgeon in charge of refugees has gone with his regiment 62 Illinois leaving one hundred patients here—they must have attention or will suffer." Civilians left as frequently as their military counterparts. For example, every medical officer stationed in Helena, Pine Bluff, Little Rock, Fort Smith, and Camden in May 1866 had been replaced by December 1867. Arkansas doctors decreased in numbers during the Civil War and Reconstruction; the number of doctors in Arkansas declined from 1,222 in 1860 to 1,026 in 1870, furthering health-care concerns.[7]

The limited number of personnel involved in each bureau location also contributed to health-care problems. The Little Rock, Fort Smith, and Washington personnel data reveals the paucity of medical personnel involved in a "hospital" (see Table 5.1). Meager pay and small staffs hindered health care for blacks. But the most critical problems that medical personnel faced were the epidemics which swept through Arkansas after the Civil War.[8]

The health staff recruited by the Freedmen's Bureau were few and inadequately trained, and the pandemics which ravaged Arkansas blacks between 1865 and 1867 challenged bureau agents most. Disease and death struck both urban and rural Arkansas throughout 1865. In Little Rock, hundreds succumbed to typhoid and intermittent fever, while "hundreds died of dysentery and other diseases with a virulence unknown before." Statistics reveal the maladies of fifty workers on an undisclosed plantation in May 1865 (see Table 5.2).[9]

Staggering numbers of African Americans died in 1866. Osceola agent Eli Hellerin reported, "Cholera has been quite severe on the freedmen in the county this and last month, some seventy cases proving fatal." Cholera killed four freedmen per day in Little Rock in August. Smallpox "alarmed the citizens of both colors to a great extent" in Camden and "ravaged many plantations and caused much loss of life" in Pine Bluff. It continued its scourge and killed hundreds of freedpersons in Little Rock, Fort Smith, and Chicot County. Brevet Major William Dawes of

TABLE 5.1
Arkansas Hospital Staffs: 1867

Employee	Birthplace	Salary	Position	Race
Little Rock Hospital				
Christian Krull	Bremen	$420	Clerk	White
William Lewis	Indiana	$480	Asst. Steward	White
John Lewis	Indiana	$360	Steward	White
Ruby Griswold	New York	$420	Matron	White
William Doharty	Ireland	$240	Ward Master	White
George Washington	Alabama	$240	Nurse	Black
Mary Walker	Alabama	$144	Nurse	White
Sally Marroll	North Carolina	$126	Nurse	Black
James Morrison	Ireland	$360	Cook	White
Mary King	Tennessee	$120	Cook	Black
Nancy Lee	Arkansas	$144	Laundry	Black
Ellen Woods	Georgia	$120	Laundry	Black
Tennessee Rogers	Arkansas	$120	Laundry	Black
Fort Smith Hospital				
Thomas Jones	Illinois	$480	Adj. Steward	White
Thomas Sweeney	Ireland	$240	Ward Master	White
Henderson Blair	Cherokee Nation	$360	Cook	Black
Louisa Blair	Cherokee Nation	$120	Laundry	Black
Amanda Black	Missouri	$120	Nurse	Black
Washington (Arkansas) Hospital				
John Smith	Ireland	$480	Acting Steward	White
Sam London	Alabama	$240	Guard	White
Carolina Hanna	Arkansas	$120	Nurse	White
Charity Evans	Virginia	$120	Cook	White

Pine Bluff mused, "A far greater percentage of sickness and death occur on plantations than before the war." A Washington, Arkansas, witness concurred and reported, "The physical condition of the Negro population is very poor. They are dying by scores most in want of proper food and also proper medical treatment."[10]

TABLE 5.2

Workers' Illnesses: May 1865

Ailment	# Suffering from	Ailment	# Suffering from
Diarrhea	12	Rheumatism	3
Opthalmia	1	Dysentery	4
Remittent fever	6	Injury	1
Congestive fever	1	Leg ulcer	3
Intermittent fever	2	Pneumonia	1
Philias	1	Measles	2
Cholera	1	Consumption	1

The dirge continued in 1867. Cholera killed scores in Forth Smith, Helena, Pine Bluff, Little Rock, and Madison. In Pine Bluff, "the cholera existed from the early part of July to the middle of October. The mortality was great." Sixty freedpersons died in Helena, and the Madison bureau officer moved his office five miles outside town "on account of the cholera raging in that place."[11]

Arkansas blacks long remembered these death-drenched days. More than half a century later, Lizzie Bennett recalled yellow fever in Memphis: "You have never seen the like. Everything was under quarantine. The folks died in piles and de coffins was placed high as a house. They buried them in trenches, and later they dug graves and buried them." "So many soon got sick and died," Liney Chambers of Brinkley recalled. "They died of Consumption and fevers and nearly froze," she continued. Warren McKinney of Hazen observed, "Many people died in piles. I don't know till yet what was de matter. They said it was the change of living. I seen five or six wooded, painted coffins piled up on wagons pass by our house. Loads passed every day lack you see cotton pass here. Some said it was cholera and some took consumption. Lots of colored people nearly starved."[12]

Neither the Freedmen's Bureau nor any other agency could handle such enormous numbers of dead. Burial became a major concern for agents. The *Pine Bluff Dispatch* discovered "bodies left too long unattended." The Fort Smith agent worried about corpses lying "unburied for two days." Freedmen's "supplications for coffins are enormous," noted Helena agent Henry Sweeney. Later that year, in typical bureaucratic form, Sweeney lamented that he used a full size coffin for a child's burial. Grisly death proved lucrative to coffin makers such as Willard Ayers of Fort Smith who found "the demand at the present is very large." Hastily performed burial often resulted in macabre results. Arkansas County agent William Dawes observed, "The river has washed the bank on which the cemetery of soldiers killed at the place are interred to such a degree that the feet and legs of bodies in graves remaining may be seen protruding from the ground by persons passing in boats on the river."[13]

Infant and child mortality was one of the most tragic components of the health-care dilemma. Fair Dale and South Bend Plantations, located in Arkansas County, noted 137 children's deaths and 251 births from 1864 to 1867. Napoleon, Arkansas, plantations recorded child mortality from 1864 to 1870 (see Table 5.3). County records from 1864 to 1867 indicated child mortality as well (see Table 5.4). Freedpersons must have questioned the reality of their freedom in the context of so much loss of life.[14]

To combat such mortality, bureau agents established hospitals in

TABLE 5.3

Napoleon, Arkansas, Child Mortality: 1864–1870

Plantation owner	Children born in last 4 years	Children 4 & under still alive
Dr. Knox Knowlton	8	4
W. R. Anderson	4	4
Sims & Ambercrombie	10	8
Col. D. H. C. Moore	1	1
A. A. Edington	5	4
David Alexander	2	2
J. W. Meal	11	11
Col. Joseph Branch	30	18
Dr. James Rawlings	30	20
W. P. Brooks	3	4
W. G. Weatherford	25	13

Little Rock, Fort Smith, Helena, Washington, Pine Bluff, Napoleon, and Camden. Although the modern hospital had already emerged in New England, Southern institutions still seemed more akin to medieval almshouses than scientific centers for diagnosis and treatment. An inspector of Arkansas hospitals in 1867 observed that he seemed "at a loss to conjecture how the life of a patient could be saved if he were seriously ill."[15]

Problems proliferated as agents utilized hospitals for health care. The Little Rock hospital had been resurrected from the dilapidated quartermaster's mess house. The Napoleon infirmary, located too close to the river, proved more "a groggery of the lowest order." The Helena edifice, also built too near the river, frequently flooded; attendants crowded all the patients into one room on the upper floor during an 1867 flood. The Pine Bluff hospice became so drafty in November 1866 that the surgeon built fires "in the open air of logs and carried his sick out and placed them around these bonfires to derive as much benefit as they could." The exterior environment of the Pine Bluff facility was as unfit as the drafty interior. "Cattle, horses, sheep, goats, and pigs" grazed around the premises freely, making the hospital grounds

TABLE 5.4

County Infant Mortality: 1864–1867

County	Children born	Children died
Ashley	99	32
Arkansas	251	137
Calhoun	200	40
Chicot	222	146
Clark	79	24
Dallas	26	9
Desha	123	30
Fulton	25	7
Mississippi	175	71
Phillips	297	212
Pulaski	220	206
Sebastian	40	28

a petri dish for fatal microbes. Inspector D. H. Williams summed up what most visitors saw when he observed that "the refugee hospital here, Dr. Flinn in charge, is the most miserable thing of the kind I have ever seen. It is a reproach to every officer of the bureau in Little Rock." Yet the old and feeble, as well as the sick, sought asylum in these hospitals. In Pine Bluff and Helena, freedpersons who "had no other place to go" entered for food and shelter.[16]

An inventory of the Pine Bluff hospital in March 1866 indicated how limited the health care was in such places. The institution contained "one counterpane, three shuck mattresses, two cotton pillow cases, three sheets, five cotton shirts, two tin wash basins, two iron bedsteads, four brooms, one candlestick, three chairs, two-hundred feet of clothes line, three feeding cups, one glass lantern, one looking glass, six chamber pots, three bedside tables, one urinal, twelve bowls, two tin dippers, one dish, one flesh fork, one bread knife, seven mugs, one pitcher, three salt cellars, and two tumblers." The medicinal inventory for another hospital in 1867 included only alcohol, alum, blue stone, borax, Castile soap, flaxseed, olive oil, linseed oil, rosin, saltpeter, sweet spirits nostrum, laudanum, an abscess knife, probe, needle, and a lance. Sparse hospital rations included only pork, flour, rice, coffee, sugar, adamantine candy, and soap.[17]

Sexual and racial mores also hampered health care. Southern Victorian propriety forced Dr. R. R. Taylor to recommend to Arkansas medical director James Smith that women and men be segregated whenever possible. A Helena female grew hysterical when she observed black and white women in the same room in the hospital and insisted "she would not stand such degradation to the white race." Bureau agent Sweeney assured the protester that "one of the white girls she saw was worse than any black girl that ever came into our hands, being nearly dead with syphilis." But she and countless other Southerners remained unconvinced.[18]

An 1867 medical tour by Henry Lilly corroborated miserable conditions existing in bureau hospitals. He declared that the Fort Smith hospital, located in an abandoned hotel, was entirely unsuited for health care. The Helena infirmary seemed "but little else than a public nuisance. There was neither floor, ceiling, nor windows. The huge cracks between the rough board walls precluded any great necessity for windows. There were no privies." The Pine Bluff hospital also jeopardized health, though it housed not the sick, but area orphans. Tragically, hospitals provided little relief for the sick.[19]

Since hospitals and doctors could not be relied on to provide adequate health care for freedmen, individual bureau agents on occasion responded innovatively to black distress. During epidemics, Pine Bluff and Little Rock agents relocated freedpersons to less contagion-ridden places. When blacks could not be moved, agents imposed quarantines to prevent the spread of disease. General Order Number 8, issued by Assistant Adjutant General O. D. Greene to prevent disease transmission, prohibited new residents from congregating in towns. The order also mandated weekly inspections of freedmen's homes to check for filth and overcrowding. General Order Number 11, issued by Major General Thomas J. Woods, ordered the "removal of all persons having the disease [smallpox], to vaccinate such as are directly exposed to the disease, and to direct and to enforce the necessary measure for the purification of the premises, such as ventilation, white-washing, airing of bedding, clothing." W. S. McCullough of De Valls Bluff placed guards to ensure that blacks washed and boiled their clothing in salt water to deter infections. Agents in Helena and Pine Bluff used barrels of lime, the age's universal disinfectant, to check contagion.[20]

The problems faced by freedpersons overwhelmed individuals. The primary responsibility for health care fell upon the bureau, which functioned as a helpful centralizing agency for the sick and needy. Transportation to centralized hospitals and the distribution of rations from central posts often alleviated the most dire suffering. Bureau agents also approved yearly work contracts of the freedpersons in an attempt to ensure that the clause "all medical attention" was fulfilled. Bureau agents often issued rations in times of famine. Rations distributed in 1866 illustrate the care provided (see Table 5.5).[21]

Rations typically consisted of ten ounces of pork or bacon, sixteen ounces of fresh beef, sixteen ounces of flour and soft bread twice a week or twelve ounces of hard bread, sixteen ounces of cornmeal five times a week, ten pounds of beans, peas, or hominy to one hundred rations, two quarts of vinegar to one hundred rations, candles, eight ounces of adamantine or star to one hundred rations, two pounds of soap to one hundred rations, two pounds of salt to one hundred rations,

TABLE 5.5

Rations Distribution: 1866

Month	# Whites receiving rations	# Blacks receiving rations
March	4,786	544
April	2,202	392
May	3,053	536
June	6,032	561

two ounces of pepper to one hundred rations, and roasted coffee or tea. Children received half-rations. As the army left a region, its "clothing, bedding, sick room and culinary apparatus and fixtures" were distributed by the Freedmen's Bureau.[22]

The Freedmen's Bureau was not alone in its concern over the health of blacks; local institutions also worked to improve the health of their new black citizens. Larger towns created local boards of health to control disease. A Little Rock Board of Health appointed in May 1866, just at the outset of the cholera season, was composed of Doctors C. Peyton, C. M. Taylor, A. W. Webb, J. A. Dibbrell, and E. V. Duvell. City funds paid for the cleaning of the streets, gutters, and alleys, the draining of all cellars, and the whitewashing of all buildings. The board's extraordinary power, "extending even to the right to tear down all shanties which might collect filth and remove all sources of nuisance without ceremony," amazed Dr. Duvell. The board even created a map that noted where freedpersons lived in order to facilitate inspection. The Pine Bluff Board of Health in 1866 prohibited the "sale of melons, green fruits, green corn, and cucumbers" and the "congregation of negroes assembled in different houses in the city." It also decreed that no more than one family could live in a house. The Fort Smith Council urged the cleaning of the town to prevent cholera. Augusta sheriff John Thorpe used his power to foster health and cleanliness by requiring that clothes be changed once every week upon punishment of a fine. The sheriff also held freedmen "responsible for the cleanliness of their children" as an incentive for health improvement.[23]

Freedmen relied upon themselves as well as on the Freedmen's

Bureau or local government agencies, thus continuing the personal health care that was prevalent in slave days. Blacks utilized folk cures and natural medicines to mend their health. Joni Martin of Madison sold herbs for "diarrhea and piles and what ails you." Rachel Perkins of Goodwin grew mint, rosemary, tansy, sage, mullein, catnip, horseradish, artichoke, and horehound—"all good home remedies." Plantation records disclose freedpersons' medical purchases. On Leek's Plantation in east Pulaski County, five of the twenty-four employees purchased medicine over a twelve-month period, costing from $.75 to $7.95, no small amount in view of their incomes. Freedmen's Bureau merchants' records reveal nearly one-half of all black creditors purchased medicine in 1867.[24]

The *Weekly Arkansas Gazette* reported in 1867 that "visible evidence" of the "rapid disappearance" of the black race could be recognized by "even the purblind." The *Daily Arkansas Gazette* noted, "It is true that it looks lately as if human life was held cheap, but for all that every man would prolong his existence." Although untold hundreds of blacks died during the bureau's tenure in Arkansas, hundreds more recovered their health due to the aid of the bureau and fellow blacks. For those who survived and sustained healthy bodies, the care of the mind through education became the next priority for African Americans struggling to realize genuine freedom.[25]

Arkansas freedpersons not only sought to gain adequate health care at emancipation, but they also pushed for schools to nourish their intellectual development. Postbellum Arkansas was virgin territory for schools and teachers. The bureau's education superintendent William Colby lamented, "30% of white voters registered and 50% of the entire population are unable to write their names." Two-thirds of the adult population, he continued, "cannot read the Lord's prayer or write their own names." While 42,271 Arkansas whites attended school during 1860, there remained over 23,000 illiterate white adults in the state. The state allocated only $120,613 ($2.82 per student) of public funds for education, compared to $385,679 ($5.80 per student) invested in public education by neighboring Mississippi, or $469,210 ($9.35 per student) spent by Louisiana. Little infrastructure or precedent existed for an educational system in Arkansas, despite an 1840 public school law.[26]

Almost immediately after liberation, Arkansas blacks began clamoring for schools. Little Rock bureau agent Joel Grant observed in 1865,

"The desire of the free people for education is unabated, and is so strong as to be deemed by some excessive, amounting almost to a passion." Former Arkansas lawyer James Tibbetts returned home in April 1866 and observed freedpersons "anxious to learn." Monticello African-American preacher Blackwell Shelton wondered, "Steeped in ignorance as our race is, it is a question of serious concern, should not something be done to improve the condition of the rising generations."[27]

Freedpersons not only expressed a profound hunger for education, they also turned to any available educational sources in the days immediately following emancipation. At Arkadelphia, for example, Private Edward R. Chandler taught eighty-four black children how to read and write. A literate freedwoman at Lake Village taught children how to read, write, "and something of arithmetic" in her home before schools and trained teachers appeared. A Little Rock lad caught crawdads, sold them to Arkansas River fisherwomen, and saved his money for school tuition. Another Little Rock youth swore to Superintendent Colby, "I'm going to work every day, and earn $3; then when school days begins again I can go all the time!"[28]

Blacks often gathered at public forums to plot strategies for bringing teachers and schools to their community. Pine Bluff blacks unanimously adopted a resolution at a public meeting which affirmed the principles of "equality of all men before the law, an education for every child." Sebastian and Fulton County blacks also conferred to devise tactics that would fulfill their dreams for education.[29]

Black adults wanted schools not only for their children but also for themselves. When William Colby quizzed adult freedpersons why they wanted to learn to read, they replied, regardless of other reasons, that they "wanted to read the Bible and to write [to] their own children." Freedpersons spent much time and energy trying to obtain literacy skills. At Branch's Plantation near Arkadelphia, for example, adult workers spent one and one-half hours of their two-hour lunch break in school. Three generations of a family studied lessons together in a Washington school. Multigenerational class attendance revealed adults' dedication to literacy and impressed children with the importance of an education.[30]

Many Freedmen's Bureau agents shared blacks' dreams for bringing schools to Arkansas. Bureau chief General John Sprague emphasized the discipline resulting from education when he wrote to Reverend

R. W. Trimble of Pine Bluff, "As slaves it was perhaps safe to let them remain in ignorance—as freedmen it is not even *safe* for the whites." Without schools, Sprague warned, blacks would be "a fearfully disturbing element in your population"; with schools, freedpersons would become "contented and cheerful and thus promote the material interest of the employer." Agent Henry Sweeney of Helena rhapsodized in a Little Rock newspaper over "the glorious cause of education—the only hope of the colored race, the only sure foundation of the wealth and virtue of a state." "Show me a community in which there is a comfortable school house and a respectable church," he argued, "and I will show you a community that is bound to prosper and flourish." Dardanelle bureau agent William Morgan articulated what many other agents believed when he observed: "There are many children within my District who are unemployed and would be much benefited were they under school discipline and instruction. There are also many adults seemingly anxious to contribute as much as they are able for the privilege of being instructed in the act of reading, writing, and arithmetic." "If these people are free," Camden agent Lewis Carhart insisted, "they must be educated to the extent of their capacity." Agent J. H. Scroggins of Hampton believed so firmly in the benefit freedpersons gained from schools that he offered to board teachers with his family. Many bureau agents, as well as freedpersons, perceived education as a prerequisite for genuine freedom.[31]

Some local whites, notably among the elite, concurred with bureau agents and supported the creation of schools for freedpersons. They advocated schools for blacks and lower-class whites to provide order and to sustain a happy work force. William Morgan of Dardanelle realized, as did other bureau agents, "There are a few of the *leading men* of this place in my opinion who would encourage an institution of this kind." Superintendent William Colby seconded local agents' reports of planters' support. After a tour in southwestern Arkansas, he commented, "In regards to schools much more favorable [reactions] among the higher classes of planters than anticipated." Chicot County sheriff Thomas Walker encouraged his county's wealthiest whites to support schools and insisted, "Intelligent unprejudiced planters will perhaps soon see the importance of educating the freedmen, because the more intellectual the more efficient and useful a laborer is."[32]

Some planters believed schools were necessary to maintain order and social control. Southeastern Arkansas planters, for example, favored schools because they kept black youth "out of mischief." Others hoped schools for freedpersons' children would keep parents steadily and contentedly working in planters' fields, satisfied as long as minimal educational opportunities were available to their children. Several planters hoped schools would spread the gospel of hard work and persuade blacks to stay in their place. Humanitarianism also motivated some as much as economic self-interest. Others believed that schools would help freedpersons press forward and become truly free.[33] In many places there was planter support for schools for blacks (see Table 5.6). Planters sometimes collectively petitioned bureau officials for schools, as was the case in Lewisville where eighteen planters in 1867 favored the creation of a local school.[34]

Newspaper editors occasionally joined planters in support of schools by writing editorials to sway public opinion in favor of educational opportunities for blacks. Controlled by or at least sympathetic toward white planters, editors supported the educational crusade as a vehicle for social control and pacification of blacks and lower-class whites. The normally anti-black *Arkansas Gazette* supported schools for blacks by assuring Arkansans, "It is the duty of our people, as a means of self-defense, to educate our freedmen, that they may be able to deprive the Radicals of their expected aid and the chief motive for enforcing their obnoxious doctrine." The *Monticello Guardian* echoed the *Gazette*'s concern and insisted, "If ever there was a time when the freed people should know how to read, write, and cipher, it is now. In their condition they are subject to the arts and devices of wicked men, who in their garb of friends, and presuming on their ignorance are making them political slaves."[35]

Many county leaders also favored schools for blacks and improved schools for whites as forces for social control and humanitarian uplift. Sheriff Thomas Walker of Chicot County exemplified the support of governing officials for education. Responsible for bringing a school teacher from Vicksburg, Mississippi, to Lake Village to instruct freedpersons, Sheriff Walker lamented, "It is a pity that not one school for white children is in the county." N. A. Britton, a Clark County clerk, offered to board a teacher at her house, also indicating elite support for schools.[36]

Upper-class white churches often supported schools for blacks. The

TABLE 5.6

Planter Support for Schools: 1867–1868

Planter	Location	Educational support
Major Henry A. Jones	Red River	Requests school
Major J. B. Burton	Fulton	Has school ready
Benjamin Hawkins	Richmond	60 children waiting for teacher
Major P. J. Andrews	Rocky Comfort	130 children ready
Judge D. E. Coulter	Sevier County	School/teacher's board
Dr. John H. Peak	Arkadelphia	40 acres for school
Dr. E. S. Grinds	Hampton	Will board teacher
Mr. John Williams	Jacksonport	Land for school
J. M. Craig	Chicot County	Will board teacher
Haynes & Main	Marion	Opened school
Colonel Stone	Paraclifta	Provide a school
James G. Lyman	Pine Bluff	43 scholars ready
Cockrell Plantation	Pine Bluff	Wants a school
Green Adkins Place	Pine Bluff	70 scholars ready
Colonel Warren Place	Pine Bluff	20 scholars ready
Colonel M. W. Lewis	Pine Bluff	50 scholars/teacher's board
General Rayns	Pine Bluff	35 scholars ready
Fisk Place	Pine Bluff	60 scholars ready
General Clayton	Pine Bluff	40 scholars ready
Lulaman Franklin	Pine Bluff	50 scholars ready
C. Stoddard Jr.	New Gascony	School/teacher's board

bureau's assistant superintendent Enoch K. Miller expressed surprise to discover the Southern clergy very supportive of his educational endeavors. Among white denominations in Arkansas, Episcopalians led the way in favor of schools for blacks. Fort Smith Episcopalians purchased books from New York for neighboring black schools, which prompted bureau agent Colonel Pinkney Lugenbeel to vow, "The Episcopalians are the only persons here who are interesting themselves in the education of the colored children."[37]

Freedpersons did not depend solely on the aid of Southern liberal white congregations, for many Northern white denominations became deeply concerned and involved in Southern education. Northern dollars, goodwill, and prayers flowed southward as the North attempted to reconstruct the South. Motivation, as always, was complex. Missionaries hoped that the schools, by furthering literacy, would increase Bible and religious tract reading. Humanitarians believed that education improved humans. Northern cultural imperialists insisted that their economic system best promoted freedom and human dignity and could most easily be disseminated in schools. And some people simply craved adventure. Many bored bourgeois Northern men and women, weary of their assigned place in society, yearned to experience thrills denied them in Chicago or Cincinnati.

Numerous forces—freedpersons, bureau agents, planters, government officials, preachers, parishioners, and carpetbaggers—supported public schools for all Arkansas children in 1865. They favored schools for a variety of reasons, including self-help and personal empowerment, humanitarianism, social control, and placating of the work force. But regardless of their motives, these supporters joined together to boost education in Arkansas.

Agents and freedpersons had to overcome many obstacles before they realized their dreams for education. Finding money for buildings and teachers constantly plagued the interested parties. The American Missionary Association, a Congregational hybrid, and Northern Quakers provided the largest portion of Northern denominational aid in Arkansas. In 1865 the AMA funded 250 teachers and missionaries throughout the South. During Reconstruction, Arkansas schools relied extensively on AMA aid. Of the money appropriated in 1867 for education in Arkansas, 54 percent came from the AMA and Quakers. This rose in 1868 to 59 percent of the total educational expenditures. The Northwestern Freedmen's Aid Commission of Chicago, the Northern Benevolent Association, and the Western Freedmen's Aid Commission of Indianapolis also contributed to teachers' salaries, school buildings, and supplies. Groups outside the United States made contributions, such as the English Birmingham Association which donated "much aid" for Little Rock schools in 1866. The Freedmen's Bureau itself contributed substantial aid to the embryonic Arkansas schools, providing 6 percent of the Arkansas school budget in 1868.[38]

Both local politicians and Freedmen's Bureau officials recognized the necessity of outside, usually Northern, funds if Arkansas schools were to become more than blueprints, dreams, or prayers. Enoch Miller journeyed North for two months in 1867 to "secure the cooperation of the Christian public in the work of educating the freedmen." Bureau agents disguised their mendicancy in a variety of ways. Educational officials often repeated the story of an eighty-year-old rheumatic Batesville freedwoman to reveal the genuine desire of blacks for an education and to encourage Northern white Christians to pull out both purses and handkerchiefs. The elderly Arkansan told her teacher that she wanted to learn to spell the name of Jesus first, convinced that "the rest will come easier if I learn to spell dat blessed name first." Such responses may have fit nicely into the campaign for contributions, but they may also have been genuine. Agents described the adventures of two AMA women as they traveled to Little River County in southwestern Arkansas "through some of the wildest portions of the state" in hopes of luring others to the Arkansas wilderness. Agents also appealed to Northern conceit and pride as they described new Pine Bluff facilities: "the school and building in all their parts would do credit to a New England village." Rumors in April 1867 that the AMA would no longer fund teachers distressed the Arkansas educational bureaucracy, but such reports proved, at least for the moment, to be false.[39]

Blacks contributed what they could to these funds. A Little Rock black congregation in July 1865, for example, heard of a $78 deficit in school operating funds. At a special church service it raised $121, $43 more than needed. Rural blacks who had similar inclinations but little or no means of realizing their wishes could not be so generous. Washington blacks, few in numbers and short on money, found themselves "hardly able to pay one teacher." In Chicot County, freedmen contributed nothing, "for it takes all they can get to sustain life." Arkadelphia and De Valls Bluff blacks retained teachers in 1867, but a poor harvest forced them to abandon their efforts. A shortage of money kept many freedpersons' dreams of schools for themselves and their children on a wish list of things unrealized from 1865 to 1867, but those who donated, even if but a pittance, gained new self-confidence.[40]

Blacks saved as much money as they could for schools from 1865 to 1867 in the days before significant Freedmen's Bureau or state funding. Fort Smith blacks donated one-half of the money needed to buy land for a night school, and their educational zeal continued undeterred in the next year as they donated over $200.00 during a fundraising campaign led by Enoch K. Miller in the spring of 1868. Jacksonport freedpersons raised $50.00 for building a school in 1868 and displayed "a lively interest on the subject of education" according to bureau agent Simpson Mason. Pine Bluff plantation workers paid for a teacher's salary from their wages and crop shares, while planters furnished the teacher's board and a schoolhouse. Washington blacks required certificates for school attendance that could be purchased at $1.25 per month in an effort to make their schools self-sufficient (see Table 5.7). In 1868, 24 percent of educational funds came from freedpersons themselves, 6 percent was donated by the Freedmen's Bureau, and 70 percent was provided by other sources.[41]

A Phillips County freedman typified the self-reliance and philanthropic spirit of freedpersons when he purchased a $300.00 lot for building a Helena black school. "I'll do it myself," he insisted, "if I never get a cent for it; I want to see my people educated." Other blacks, less able financially to contribute land, donated as much money as they could and collectively purchased land and schools. De Valls Bluff blacks organized meetings in early 1867 and raised funds "for building a permanent school house." Washington freedpersons bought an 80 foot by 198 foot school site and made certain that black trustees controlled the deed. Camden and Batesville blacks purchased lots by subscription and

TABLE 5.7
Educational Funding: 1868

Month	Paid by freedpersons	Paid by bureau	Paid by other parties
Jan.	$168.36	$115.00	$978.00
Feb.	$253.10	$105.00	$885.00
March	$387.65	$55.00	$1,048.00
April	$387.55	$55.00	$1,245.00
May	$374.13	$65.00	$917.40
June	$400.20	$74.00	$1,092.00
July	$175.00	$35.00	$300.00
TOTAL	$2,145.99	$504.00	$6,465.40

also made sure that black trustees received the title to the land. Freedpersons' ownership of a school site and building allowed them to control their educational opportunities. As blacks had predicted, the Freedmen's Bureau and the state of Arkansas occasionally tried to confiscate black schools; but as Pine Bluff agent Sebastian Geisreiter noted to national bureau chief Oliver Howard, "I cannot take up schools as Bureau property . . . [the] building being owned by the freedmen who built the house and done all the work."[42]

Although members of the local white elite often endorsed schools for blacks, other whites found the idea repugnant. Such white antagonism vexed bureau agents and freedpersons. Many whites viewed schools as even more hideous symbols than churches, which hinted at their fear that blacks might prove themselves to be equal or superior to whites if given the chance. Bureau agents from all over the state used language such as "unsafe, indifferent, unfriendly, bitterness, and opposed" to describe the antipathy toward black schools among whites in their locales. Superintendent William Colby detected that whites harbored "a secret wish that the system may prove a failure." Pine Bluff agent Sebastian Geisreiter, observing massive disdain for black schools, reported, "Some think it terrible that the people's money should be wasted for so useless a purpose, alleging that the niggers never can be taught anything." Judge J. M. Coulter of Rocky Comfort declined to build a school for his black laborers for "fear of being mobbed or having his buildings burned" by hostile whites.[43]

Teachers or officials who defied white antagonism to black schools often encountered violence and intimidation. A Lewisville planter who built a school for blacks on his plantation received warnings to leave the county immediately. Whites warned Lewisburg instructor W. J. Evans "to stop teaching niggers and leave the place or be killed." White female instructors in black schools in Jacksonport and Monticello received "insulting and obscene" notes. Wesley Grave of North Little Rock remembered "the pateroles [patrols] made my father do everything but quit. They got him about teaching night school . . . They didn't want him teaching the Negroes right after the war . . . They just kept him in the woods then." Ku Klux Klan members disguised in blackened faces attacked Arkadelphia teacher C. H. Fowler in March 1867. Such attacks, as well as the destruction of school property, occurred repeatedly and demonstrated the deep antipathy black schools engendered among whites.[44]

Arsonists demonstrated their opposition to schools at Osceola and Jacksonport by destroying them. Many bureau agents readily admitted that only the army prevented more teacher beatings and school burnings. Marion agent E. G. Barker lamented, "Nothing but the fear of the military kept the school from being broken up." At Camden, only the presence of soldiers at the school preserved the peace. Parents feared to send their children away from them to schools in such unsettled times.[45]

Ironically, opposition to schools for blacks did not consist solely of disgusted whites. Many black preachers opposed educational efforts. Superintendent William Colby recounted, "The colored preachers seem to fear also the effect of the teacher's work will be to weaken their own influence." He grew more incensed toward black ministers later and called them "a bane both to the church and the school." Greene, Craighead, and Poinsett County black preachers "refused to encourage educational work," fearful of reprisals or loss of prestige and power.[46]

The necessity of work in the cotton fields—the only work available to most freedpersons—deterred education further. Tim Haynes of Pine Bluff recalled, "[I] went to school a little while, but my father died and my mother bound me out to a white man." The call of the cotton fields disrupted many classes when parents needed children to help them in cultivating and gathering the crop. E. G. Barker of Marion, for example, discontinued his school in May 1868 because black parents kept their children at home "to assist there [sic] parents in cultivating the crop." School enrollment statistics clearly reveal that attendance plummeted during planting and harvesting seasons.[47]

Finding a suitable building in which to conduct classes became another major concern for bureau agents and freedpersons. Little Rock agent W. G. Sargent typically observed that "suitable buildings for school purposes are needed very much." In Phillips County, "the school was kept in a shady grove; the teacher's horse would stand all day hitched to a sapling near, and pupils learned to read from a primary chart hung to a tree." Other classes met in dilapidated and uncomfortable buildings. Bitter winter winds, whipping through huge cracks in the walls at the Fayetteville school, chilled both students and teachers. A Fort Smith teacher struggled to teach in a windowless building where the only light came from the opened front door. At Helena, a floorless mule stable served as a classroom, but this was at least superior to a neighboring school in "a hole in the ground, merely an excavation under the block house."[48]

Black clergymen who were enthusiastic for schools helped alleviate some of the pressure of inadequate buildings by opening their sanctuaries to freedpersons. Agents at first feared using church buildings for schools. Although Superintendent Colby applauded agents who separated schools and churches, a practical shortage of public meeting places required that buildings with large halls be used for both school classes and church services. Bureau agents at Van Buren, Washington, Little Rock, Camden, and Pine Bluff approved using abandoned churches for schools. Pine Bluff citizens agreed to an interesting arrangement which sanctioned a building for both black and white religious services but which appropriated the structure as a school for blacks only. In time schools became increasingly owned and operated by the state, but in 1868 three of thirteen black schools, and in 1868 four of fourteen, were conducted in churches.[49]

Even when adequate school buildings existed, the acquisition and retention of competent teachers was a persistent problem. After almost four years in the field, Superintendent William Colby still fumed that Arkansas schools lacked "competent teachers, white or black." Colby found teachers everywhere "very generally quite limited," but "native teachers are still more incompetent." "Indeed," he concluded, "some of the native teachers should themselves be attending a good primary school." At his most piqued, Colby worried not only over the intellectual inferiority but also over the "moral turpitude" of teachers. For example, he immediately recalled a white Camden teacher who molested black female students in February 1868.[50]

Blacks and Freedmen's Bureau agents faced a maze of complexities as they sought to bring schools to black Arkansans. A lack of educational traditions, funding, teachers, and buildings hampered educational initiatives at every turn. Many whites and some blacks feared changes that schools might bring about. The cotton season constantly intruded upon the school calendar. But freedpersons and many bureau agents innovatively faced these challenges and diligently continued their quest to establish schools in Arkansas.

Over time, the Freedmen's Bureau developed a streamlined and efficient educational bureaucracy to counter the multitude of serious problems it faced. A chain of command headed by Superintendent William Colby and Assistant Superintendent Enoch K. Miller had emerged by March 1866. Ohio native Colby received a monthly salary of $150. He allocated funds, guided local agents and teachers, reported to superiors, and frequently toured the state to measure the progress Arkansas schools made. Assistant Superintendent Miller served as Colby's eyes and ears throughout rural Arkansas. Miller, born in 1804 in England, studied at the University of Rochester in New York, served as a Presbyterian minister, and received wounds at Gettysburg as a Union soldier. A typical educational tour for Miller in November 1867 included visits to schools in Hot Spring, Clark, Hempstead, Sevier, and Little River Counties. In Little River County, he found "little encouragement for school enterprises" and a "negligent and immoral teacher" who taught students "very little."[51]

Cognizant of the desire for schools among blacks and whites, school officials established a bureaucracy which at times aided and at other times deterred the Freedmen's Bureau and blacks in creating an educational network. In 1866 the state legislature began to deal with schools for African Americans, but it postponed implementing a separate school policy in the hope that President Johnson's "forgive and forget" policies toward the South might make such revolutions unnecessary. When Johnson's counterrevolution failed, the 1868 constitutional convention devoted an entire section (Section 9) of the new constitution to education and ordered the legislature to create a free but racially segregated public school system available to all Arkansans between the ages of five and twenty-one. The reconstructed legislature divided the state into ten educational districts and created local regulations for state schools. It also created a state board of education to regulate state funding and to recommend texts for local adoption. By 1870 state aid funded 149 schools while 55 still received Freedmen's Bureau aid.[52]

Freedpersons often demanded of bureau and state officials the control of whatever educational bureaucracy emerged. Washington and

Camden blacks chose five black trustees as soon as they began school fund-raising deliberations. These African-American trustees served as conduits between the black masses and white officials. William McCullough, De Valls Bluff agent, appointed "five of the most respected colored men in this vicinity" as trustees. A Little Rock black trustee, J. M. Alexander, urged his fellows to plot the school's future especially carefully so that their names would be honored in "the coming generations of our people." Such "respected colored men" improved their status among whites and blacks as they served on local school boards and provided a valuable buffer between black aspirations and white antipathy. The Batesville black trustees—Edward Pinkney, Charles Case, and Henry Grundy—regulated school expenditures and supervised teachers.[53]

Freedpersons also closely monitored teacher selection. Bureau agent Hiram Willis in De Valls Bluff reported that blacks wanted "northern teachers as they desired to learn northern principles." Other blacks desired black teachers more than white Yankees for they believed black role models would be most beneficial. Rocky Comfort African Americans called a public meeting in October 1868 and urged bureau agent Willis to lobby state officials on behalf of a teacher whom they wanted retained, but other freedpersons rejected their local teachers. Some blacks insisted, through annual contracts with planters, that schools be located near their homes.[54] There were more black teachers than white teachers in black schools in Arkansas in 1868 and 1869 (see Table 5.8). Whether the students' teacher was white or black was crucial and affected students' perceptions of themselves, of their own race, of others, and of race in general.[55]

Once the bureau secured teachers, the next major obstacle was to find a place for those teachers to live, a difficult task in communities staunchly opposed to black schools. Early precedents by the army and Freedmen's Bureau forbid teachers to receive rent assistance or supplements. Teachers therefore scrambled to find the best possible accommodations available. Almira Pierce, a white teacher in Pine Bluff, boarded in a cabin with a black family of seven. Another Arkansas teacher returned to her "tiny" room one February night and "found her bed and floor covered with snow."[56]

Teachers not only endured poverty and inadequate housing but also braved insults. Van Buren teacher Maggie Farrar believed Arkansas

TABLE 5.8

Arkansas Teachers' Racial Composition: 1868–1869

Month-Year	Black teachers	White teachers
7-68	47	15
8-68	19	19
9-68	41	16
10-68	34	12
11-68	12	10
12-68	10	2
1-69	14	16
2-69	19	26
3-69	5	4
4-69	34	9
5-69	27	9
6-69	45	15
TOTAL	307	153

whites "treated her with more contempt than they did blacks." "Orders" from headquarters often insulted the teachers as much as opponents' jibes. Freedmen's Bureau chief General C. H. Smith in 1868 ordered "teachers and visitors not to spit on the floor or commit any other nuisance."[57]

Community gender expectations about male and female teachers further taxed instructors. Assistant Superintendent Miller asked Washington bureau agent Fred W Thibaut, "What sex teacher do you prefer?" Communities differed in their response. Helena leaders requested a male teacher while Pine Bluff officials preferred a "lady teacher." Such wishes only compounded the difficulties faced in finding suitable teachers.[58]

The army helped local teachers financially whenever possible. In March 1867 bureau clerk John Tyler ordered local bureau agents to distribute government rations to teachers. In March 1868, army quarter-masters received orders to allow teachers to buy supplies "under the same rules as officers of the Army." The army was not alone in offering aid for Arkansas schools. In 1867 Quakers supported nine teachers, the American Missionary Association funded two teachers, and other patrons financially backed eight teachers.[59]

Although state officials, bureau personnel, and freedpersons played large roles in developing and assessing schools, local teachers were largely responsible for the success or failure of their schools. Preconceived notions of blacks profoundly influenced how and what whites taught. Some instructors found black culture mysterious and alien, with the differences either repulsive or exciting. William Colby sensed, "No people can be taught through the medium of the eye better than the freedmen." James D. Eaton, Chicot County instructor, discovered that blacks became particularly "restless" during classes and needed planned games to extinguish this energy. Little Rock's Hugh Brady detected in his school "many African scholars, especially in the practice of vocal music." Davis Lake instructor August Stickle exclaimed, "I never saw people learn so fast. It generally took me three months to teach white children what these will learn in ten or fifteen days."[60]

Other pedagogues found blacks infantile and treated them accordingly. Helena bureau agent Henry Sweeney assured the *Little Rock Morning Republican*, "I was proud, I assure you, sir, when I saw the first schools of little woolyheaded unfortunates gather within the walls I had worked so hard for." Many teachers conceptualized black adults as "helpless grown up children" who required guidance for themselves and for their children. Many teachers agreed with the *Weekly Arkansas Gazette* that over "what little mind his Maker has seen fit" to endow blacks "hangs the dark pall of unqualified ignorance."[61]

The official curriculum consisted primarily of spelling, reading, writing, arithmetic, and geography. Reading allowed blacks to decipher a part of the white world denied them under slavery. Teachers primarily used McGuffey's readers to teach reading, and the books' levels of difficulty made learning to read a progressive process rather than a haphazard accident. At Little Rock in 1864, for example, 125 black students read in book one, 26 labored in book two, and 13 reached book three. Rural areas also used these graded books which allowed students to learn at their own pace. Lewisville instructor Mrs. B. T. McClelland proudly reported that her class of fifteen rose to the Fourth Reader in twelve months. Bureau agent E. G. Barker reported similar progress at Marion schools and rejoiced, "Scholars who did not know their letters at the commencement of the term now read well in the Third Reader." Rocky Comfort's Hiram Willis similarly observed, "Children who commenced in the alphabet at the beginning of the term improved so rapidly as to read in the Third Reader." Reading material indelibly impressed blacks who lived in a land devoid of many books. In the 1930s Pasky Hawkins of Pine Bluff recalled to a WPA investigator, "I went to school down here in Arkansas in Lincoln County. I got so I could read in McGuffey's Fourth Reader. I member the story bout the white man chunkin' the boy down out of the apple tree."[62]

Teachers also dedicated themselves to inculcating Victorian norms about character and proper behavior. In what historian James McPherson called "the new Puritanism," teachers spread an ethic that extolled sobriety, hard work, self-reliance, cheerfulness, cleanliness, and a host of other virtues that synthesized Protestantism, bourgeois morality, and even patriotism.[63]

Freedmen's Bureau personnel and teachers clearly worried as much about morals as they did about the intellectual life of black Arkansans. Agent John H. Scroggins of Hampton found blacks "much given to the habits of fornication and adultery" and therefore in need of "education and moral training." R. W. Trimble visited Pine Bluff in 1866 and hoped to "inaugurate a system of moral and educational training" that would not be overturned in a few years. "Let us move," he urged, "with caution and lay down such principles as will be accepted through *all time to come.*" Trimble expressed quintessentially a Victorian sentiment in its certainty of eternal verities that must be accepted by all people for all times. Teachers also encouraged a work ethic. Monticello agent E. G. Barker wrote to J. R. Barnett, "We must try to teach the colored folks that it is by the sweat of the brow that man eats bread." Agent J. C. Predmore of Napoleon informed bureau chief General Ord that he supported a school since it induced "the Freedmen to work contentedly." Schools paid special attention to freedwomen and encouraged them to accept their assigned domestic roles. National educational superintendent John Alvord encouraged Arkansas teachers to emphasize *"home life"* to black women. Fort Smith females studied not only the usual fare of spelling, reading, and geography but also needlework to improve their homemaking skills. Domesticity proved difficult to include in the curriculum since Southern planters wanted black women picking cotton instead of sewing or washing clothes, but teachers and bureau personnel, perhaps unwittingly, helped freedwomen secure a new status by the special curriculum emphasized just for them.[64]

Books and school supplies became commercialized as publishers' and merchants' eyes gleamed with the promise of profits. A Chicago distributor of "Holbrook's Liquid Slate for Blackboards" sent advertisements to Camden Freedmen's Bureau agents which promised, "None can produce the smooth, enduring, dead-black surface of the Holbrook. It is the only surface that will not glaze." The same Chicago-based company also advertised to bureau officials "the best ever invented" ink well. They guaranteed against "the possibility of loosening it or of making a troublesome noise by the pupils twirling it round during school" and against "the temptation to make the well the receptacle of sticks, pencils, stems of flowers, etc." New York publishers Barnes and Burr sent bureau personnel a catalog which highlighted books that seemed to have "a special adaptation to the children of the colored schools." Arkansas merchants joined in marketing school supplies. Gibbs' Store of Little Rock notified *Daily Pantograph* readers, "Children at school, without the right kind of school books, are like soldiers in battle without ammunition." This encouraged parents to drop in and purchase books for their children.[65]

Graduation ceremonies were an integral part of the curriculum of the newly created black schools. Public examinations at school's end allowed scholars to display their learning and showed blacks that progress could be made. These ceremonies also reaffirmed for blacks and whites the importance of education. Henry Sweeney attended 1866 commencement ceremonies at Helena and noted, "We had quite a good time at Miss Carter's examination last Friday, a number of white persons were present and were very much surprised at the proficiency of the children." Equally important, such rites reassured educational bureaucrats that everything was going as planned. Superintendent Colby observed closing exercises in Pine Bluff and Washington in July 1868 and discovered that the "scholarship and discipline [were] very commendable." Newspapers usually covered the proceedings with positive reports which enhanced the school's status in a community.[66]

The Arkansas Freedmen's Bureau, freedpersons, and interested whites faced many difficulties as they established an educational system for blacks in Arkansas after the Civil War. Limited funding, poor infrastructure, violence, a lack of books and other school material, bitter opposition by some blacks and whites, a fledgling bureaucracy, and inadequately trained teachers all hampered educational efforts. Blacks struggled in many cases to influence and determine their own education; they demanded a share in the financial support of schools and in the selection of teachers and curriculum. For teachers, inculcation of a bourgeois Victorian morality often became as important as teaching rudimentary reading and mathematical skills. From the macrohistorical viewpoint, the Freedmen's Bureau helped freedpersons obtain for themselves the rudiments of an education. When viewed from the perspective of antebellum Arkansas where slaves were forbidden basic educational privileges, the achievements made by blacks and by the Freedmen's Bureau are impressive. But viewed within the context of goals unattained at the time the bureau exited Arkansas in 1870, much remained to be done if blacks were to be truly free. And planters, still controlling much of freedpersons' lives, influenced when and for how long schools were in session.

A black African Methodist Episcopal preacher in Little Rock articulated what many felt about schools in 1868. Addressing a large crowd gathered to dedicate the Union School at Little Rock, he noted that "he felt out of time and out of place. He was born forty-seven years ago, when school houses were not built for freedmen. Even a common education had always been beyond his reach, and now to be called upon to assist in dedicating a temple of learning, was a task too exalted for his humble abilities." The minister's address might be interpreted as but a continued dissimulation before whites, and he a sort of reconstructed Sambo; but it might well have been an expression of deepest authenticity. Many black dreams evaporated during Reconstruction. Forty acres and a mule, domestic peace between the races, and economic gain were never quite realized by many Arkansas blacks. Although schools appeared belatedly and in limited numbers, the toll of school bells across a land that had never heard such sounds was in itself revolutionary. Although the largest number of teachers for African Americans during the Freedmen's Bureau tenure was paltry at best— at most there were sixty-two teachers in July 1868 for 40,000 to 50,000 black school-aged children in a total population of over 110,000—many black students gained basic literary skills. These schools allowed blacks who were involved in them to gain new self-concepts which were impossible to formulate in the days before emancipation. Education, however limited, was one of the successes of Reconstruction.[67]

## CHAPTER 6

VIOLENCE AND THE FREEDMEN'S BUREAU

It would be naive to expect that the majority of Southern whites would accept peacefully the revolutions brought about by the Civil War and Reconstruction. The demise of slavery, the economic dislocation, the alteration of racial norms, the creation of black schools and churches, and the enfranchisement of black men radically transformed Arkansas society. Many whites bitterly opposed the changes. The Freedmen's Bureau protected black rights and freedom in this new environment. Random acts of individual violence revealed white anger about equality, civil rights, and freedom; but little could be done collectively by whites as long as the bureau used the threat of federal troops to stem violence toward blacks.

"We are sleeping on a volcano," declared Freedmen's Bureau agent James Predmore in 1868. Freedpersons, carpetbaggers, national and state officials, and native white Arkansans agreed. Historian George C. Rable captured the *angst* of the era when he described the South as a land where "sacrifice, suffering, and defeat had rubbed emotions raw." Planters' dreams of maintaining hegemony collided with freedpersons' yearnings to become independent. Freedmen's Bureau agents aspired to deter racism and confronted whites who needed someone to hate—blacks. Carpetbagger's hopes of metamorphosing Southerners into Northerners foundered upon centuries of white distrust of blacks. The past collided with dreams of the future. Former slaves remembered whippings and families torn apart. Planters recalled the warm, secure feeling of knowing, with certainty, that they had everything—blacks, money, family—under control. White farmers, large and small, remembered their sons who had once run in the ebony-earthed cotton fields or swam in the Ouachita River and now lay buried at Gettysburg or Vicksburg.[1]

"Society is very unsettled and life very unsafe in many parts of the country," lamented a Napoleon bureau agent. An Ashley County agent reported, "A great deal of lawlessness of every kind is practiced, and I do not consider that either life or property [is] any safer now than it was during the war." Washington bureau official Fred Thibaut insisted that "you can not imagine how terrified the people are."[2]

Violence psychologically regenerated both blacks and whites and altered identities. By fighting whites, either covertly or overtly, freedpersons gained a better understanding of their freedom and their new selves; but by outmaneuvering blacks either through litigation, intimidation, or physical coercion, whites assured themselves of their superiority and their eventual restoration to power. Violence provided both blacks and whites with others to hate and causes to join, filling the vacuum of uncertainty created by a civil war. Reconstruction's reign of terror was but a power struggle for control of the South.[3]

Whites attempted to reestablish slavery and restore white hegemony through litigation. Arkansas Freedmen's Bureau chief General Charles H. Smith recognized this in 1867 as he reported to General Howard, "Freedmen in many places are still freedmen, not freemen. The white man still arrogates ther [sic] rights and power of mastery while the freedman half acknowledges them." Agent Sebastian Geisreiter paraphrased the Dred Scott decision: "The black man has no rights that they [whites] are bound to respect." Arkadelphia agent William Stuart lamented, "The law is of no effect in these sections."[4]

Rumors of impending violence inevitably arose as a result of whites' opposition to actions taken by the Freedmen's Bureau on behalf of blacks, as well as their resentment of blacks' assertion of freedom. Planters had always feared the Christmas season, thinking that holiday celebrations would unleash violent blacks seeking revenge for past injustices. Pine Bluff planters worried during the 1867 yuletide when they heard rumblings that freedmen threatened to "settle their way this time." Whites in Madison at the same time trembled as a rumor spread that blacks had formed groups "to kill all whites." A citizen from Union, Arkansas, captured the anguish that most white Arkansans felt when he wrote to General Charles Smith: "The condition of Fulton County is really worse than actual war. Few persons are left on Bennett's Bayou and a feeling of dread pervades the community. All kinds of rumors are in circulation. Messages of threats and assassinations are frequent, and confidence is lost in a great measure."[5]

Freedpersons lived with violence daily. Camden blacks complained to Freedmen's Bureau agent J. L. Thorpe that their lives were "in constant danger." Lewisburg agent William Morgan observed, "Attacks upon and murders of freedmen are of frequent occurrence and the peaceably disposed citizens both white and colored are in a constant state of alarm for their lives and property." Many freedpersons feared to leave their cabins to work in unprotected fields. Whites often warned blacks to keep their fears to themselves and threatened them with death if they attempted to report the intimidation they faced.[6]

Whites tortured blacks to force them into submission and to humiliate them into abandonment of all notions of equality. Albert Coons of Lewisville tied America Anderson "to the limb of a tree by the thumbs and otherwise treated her cruelly." A Mississippi County planter reportedly also tied freedpersons up by their thumbs as a means of punishment. Such action reminded blacks of antebellum days when similar treatment occurred routinely and instilled in their minds the thought that whites still controlled much of their lives. Some whites in Lafayette County tied down an elderly Lewisville black man and, after drenching his feet and legs with turpentine, set him afire. Such torture presumably would be necessary only a few times to force blacks into submission as news of the incidents would spread far and wide through the freedpersons' communication network.[7]

Whites often used firearms as instruments of social control. A black itinerant preacher near Camden sustained a gunshot wound in the arm and jaw for preaching unacceptable doctrine. Violating sexual mores also drew white ire. Two whites shot freedman Granville McMillen of Marion for "keeping a black girl." Whites also sought to resurrect racial deference and reacted violently when blacks hinted at their new equality. In Arkansas County a white man shot a black man who rode by him "quickly in a hard rain—possibly splattering mud and water on him." Although few depositions remain from assault victims, Thomas Childs swore to Freedmen's Bureau agent R. W. Barnard that whites stripped him and began taking ropes from their mules to tie him up. While they were doing that, he testified, "I jumped up and run as hard as I could. One of them shot at me and I heard the bullet as it whistled past."[8]

The viciousness that characterized murders suggests that culprits used victims as object lessons for others. Jacksonport freedman James Hanover's body was discovered in December 1866, riddled with seventeen bullet holes. At about the same time in Paraclifta in southwestern Arkansas, a freedwoman and her three children were found in the woods near their home with their heads split open. In Van Buren, a black man married to a white woman was murdered in February 1868, a symbol of the sentiment many whites held toward interracial marriage.[9]

Planters resorted, as they had before the Civil War, to the use of whips to force blacks into submission. Freedmen's Bureau agents from 1865 to 1869 continually reported cases of planters who flogged freedpersons. Captain J. M. Cain toured the Camden area in 1865 and observed, "Many are whipped as formerly." Pine Bluff agent Geisreiter lamented in the summer of 1868 that planters still clamored "for old times and the lash is fast becoming up." Thomas Abel, Chicot County bureau agent, complained to his superiors that it was "tough to convince planters that flogging [was] not best." Arkadelphia agent William Stuart agreed and noted, "Every day's observation shows that the great panacea of the South would be to place a whip in the white man's hand, with the privilege of using it on the 'trifling niggers.'"[10]

Planters found a world without whips unimaginable. Whips not only reminded freedpersons of slavery and served as visible objects that reified planters' attempts to regain power over blacks, but they also suggested that planters still equated blacks with animals or children. In the summer of 1865, an Arkadelphia planter confided to the Freedmen's Bureau agent, "I will keep my niggers if I can whip them, and make them mind." With time the bureau tried to stop such barbarisms, but many planters agreed with Helena planter Bob Wallace— he did not mind paying a fine of fifteen dollars "to whip a negro now and then." An older planter swore he would "leave the country if he couldn't thrash insulting Negroes." In a new world that appeared so frightfully uncontrollable, the whip offered planters one of the few means of control. Planters also gagged at their recent military defeat and at Northern intrusion during Reconstruction which constantly forced them to yield and submit. Unaccustomed to yielding to anyone, planters viewed whips as symbols of their power in at least one area and as practical instruments to force blacks, once again, to submit to their rule.[11]

Whippings were often bestial. Freedwoman Nancy Wiley of Lewisville was held down and beaten with a horsewhip in the summer of 1867. Freedman Smart McCoy accidentally tripped a white man while in a Hamburg store. McCoy's punishment consisted of an hour-long beating, his attackers using a bailing rope and a belt; the snow outside where he was beaten reddened with his blood. Pregnant women at Hamburg and Camden received such severe beatings that they miscarried their unborn children. Planter James Cobb of Madison described his whip "as loaded, and good to keep off dogs and knock down men with." Whippings with such brutal implements often resulted in the death of those punished.[12]

Freedpersons were not the only recipients of the brunt of Reconstruction violence. Whites who interfered with those whites who were desperately trying to turn the clock back and reenslave blacks were threatened with punishment for their violation of racial norms. Regulators, a terrorist organization, threatened to kill any De Valls Bluff planter who rented land to freedmen. White supremacists beat an El Dorado white citizen who voted for a pro-black congressional candidate, while political intimidation in Poinsett County included conspiracies "to incite a mob to attack and assassinate the Registrars for the County." Civil authorities who obeyed the Fourteenth Amendment and offered blacks justice and "equal protection under the law" often faced attacks. Helena justice of the peace Samuel Delaney was beaten in court after he fined a white man twenty-five dollars for aggravated assault against a freedman. As mentioned previously, white teachers often jeopardized their lives while teaching in the South. W. J. Evans, a Lewisburg instructor, was ordered to "quit teaching niggers and leave the place or be killed." Whites who attempted to transform racial relations, whether in their support of black landownership, voting rights, civil rights, or education, were threatened by whites who sought to reassert white hegemony. Seen as traitors to their race by white supremacists, these pro-black whites often faced death as they sought to accomplish their goals in the South.[13]

Bureau agents became targets just as other whites in the region who tried to ensure freedom and justice for freedpersons. Agent Captain John Williams was assaulted on the streets of Pine Bluff while performing his duties. Rebel sympathizers beat Arkadelphia agent Anthony Habricht in March 1868. The Klan threatened Chicot County agent A. G. Cunningham with "tar and feathering" if he did not leave. Other bureau officials faced threats more ominous than tar and feathers. Drew County bureau agent E. G. Barker was "shot and dangerously wounded" while he ate supper in a hotel at Harrisburgh in Ashley County. Doctors removed buckshot from his face, hand, and wrist and eventually had to amputate his arm. Two bureau agents were assassinated in the line of duty—Simpson Mason in Fulton County and Hiram Willis in Little River County. "I am to be the next man killed," chillingly penned agent Mason to Governor Isaac Murphy in January 1868, a prediction realized within the year. Such fear of violence, as well as actual violence toward agents, explains the conservatism of many agents. Whites often invoked force and violence in an attempt to compel bureau agents to accept their plans for the postwar South.[14]

Freedpersons, bureau agents, and carpetbaggers not only faced violence from individuals, they also confronted terrorist groups that sought to return blacks to their "proper place" and to expel from the state whites who sympathized with blacks. These outlaws "had no respect for God, man, or the devil," agent Hiram Willis had observed from his southwestern Arkansas post, an area filled with marauders from both eastern Texas and Indian Territory. Gangs found the heavily wooded terrain perfect for quick hiding. "[They] escape to the woods and [are] impossible to find," lamented Willis. Although some gangs roamed throughout the region leaderless and nameless, ex-Rebel soldiers formerly led by Joseph O. Shelby and Cullen Baker's gang became the most infamous desperadoes of the day.[15]

"Shelby men" named themselves after their beloved cavalry leader. Most men in this group had no land and therefore preyed upon freedpersons at least partially to steal money. But racial intimidation and coercion played as large a part in their motivation as robbery. Horses and guns were frequently stolen to deprive blacks of both the means of mobility and self-defense. Disguised with blackened faces, Shelbyites often forced freedpersons from their cabins at night for whippings, another way of keeping blacks "in their place."[16]

No less fearsome to bureau agents and freedpersons was the Cullen Baker gang. Baker, born in Tennessee in 1835, moved to an area near the Sulphur River on the Arkansas-Texas border in 1854. The typical frontiersman, Baker knew little of reading and writing but excelled at brawling, fighting, and drinking. Drafted by the Confederates in 1862 but unable to endure army discipline, Baker escaped into the swamps of east Texas for a time and eventually found refuge in Union-occupied Little Rock under the facade of Union loyalty. Rebel sympathizers in and around Perry County joined Baker in 1864 and engaged Union guerrillas in savage combat. Eventually expelled from the Perry County region, Baker returned to his old home along the Sulphur River in 1865 and began guerrilla operations from there which continued until his death in 1868. Enlisting fifteen Rebel true-believers to join him, he robbed, whipped, and killed scores of blacks in both Arkansas and Texas. At Bright Star in Miller County, for example, he told black residents that he would kill any black who voted, a threat which kept many freedpersons away from the polls. By 1866 Baker had become a cult hero to many area whites who believed he was a Robin Hood standing up courageously against carpetbaggers and Union troops.[17]

Guerrillas waged war against freedpersons and their sympathizers in Fulton County along the Arkansas-Missouri border. Agent J. P. Martin observed that the situation was "really worse than actual war." Part of this excitement was but a carry over from the guerrilla fighting that shook the region during the Civil War. William Monks of Missouri led pro-Union bands of armed men against Arkansas Klansmen who refused to accept Confederate defeat.[18]

Northeastern blacks and white sympathizers faced similar depredations. Woodruff County agent Simpson Mason reported to bureau officials, "In my judgment assistance is as much needed here as anywhere owing to the devastation of the homes of refugees by bushwhackers." "Desperadoes" held "civil authorities in fear" in the county and hindered black opportunities. Similar terror occurred in adjoining

Jackson County. Outlaws with blackened faces drove freedpersons from their homes and crops and randomly murdered them as a means to reassert white supremacy.[19]

Northwestern Arkansas freedpersons and Unionists faced their share of violence, too. In Fort Smith, a band of seventy men supposedly disciplined horse thieves but actually murdered blacks and Unionists and warned white Unionists to leave. In Scott County, to the south of Fort Smith, William Gibson and Isaac Backwell led a guerrilla force that warned loyalists to leave and whipped those who ignored their advice.[20]

Violence and guerrilla terrorism plagued southeastern Arkansans, especially those who lived in the Arkansas River basin. A "Vigilance Committee" hounded impudent and assertive blacks and their supporters. Bureau agent Captain E. T. Wallace observed, "Civil authorities are powerless, sheriff timid, and military not authorized to act without being called on . . . Loyal men are preparing to leave unless their safety is guaranteed."[21]

Guerrilla bands existed not only to control freedpersons and to restore white domination, but often to rob blacks and white Unionists. But the Ku Klux Klan emerged in Arkansas in late 1867 as a direct response to that year's elections and served as a terrorist organization to prevent blacks from voting. Although the Klan had emerged in many Southern states much earlier and had become a planters' paramilitary organization to regain economic control, in Arkansas it appeared in 1867 and 1868 to oppose black voter registration and voting. The Klan also became a Southern response to military Reconstruction and the reinvasion by the Union Army and served white supremacists as a means to keep blacks on the plantation.[22]

Jacksonport agent William Brain clearly recognized that the Klan wanted to reenslave "the colored people in both mind and body as in former years." A Klan warning issued at Searcy revealed the class goals of the Klan; it advised A. B. Gwin that "you are breeding dissension among the negroes of our community—you are arraying them against the old [white] citizens of this community." The Klan visited Poinsett County sheriff W. S. Wade in April 1868 and declared that "They were determined not to let any but White Men rule and that they would die before they would let the niggers rule." Many anti-black Southerners perceived Klan members as "harbingers of the millennium" and hoped that freedpersons could be driven back to their former subservience.[23]

Marion agent E. G. Barker observed, "I have been through the bloody rebellion from first to last but with all its horrors I have never seen anything to equal the state of affairs in this county [Mississippi]." "I was as scared of the Ku Klux Klan as rattlesnakes," freedperson Henry Walker of Hazen recalled. The Klan created such fear in many blacks and whites by applying its various methods of intimidation.[24]

Many citizens awoke to find warnings had been left at their homes during the night. The Klan reminded Jackson County sheriff-elect Riley Kinman: "We have come! We are here! Beware! Take heed! Speak in whispers and we hear you. Dream as you sleep in the inmost recesses of your house, and, hovering over your beds, we gather your sleeping thoughts, while our daggers are at your throat. Ravishers of liberties of the people for whom we died and yet live, begone ere it is too late. Unholy blacks, cursed of God, take warning and fly." Other officials also received threats, such as the *Clarksville Standard* editor whom the Klan warned "to become right or leave forthwith." A cavalry trumpet, gun shots, and shouts awakened the Poinsett County registrar in March 1868 as the Klan tried to persuade him to deny blacks' voter-registration rights for the forthcoming election. On eight consecutive nights the Klan visited freedman John Wilburn in an effort to force him to stop distributing election tickets. Camden Klan members harassed black farmers in the Ouachita River valley throughout the spring of 1868 and instilled "fear and dread" among them.[25]

The Klan also used tricks or illusions to frighten superstitious blacks and whites. Freedman John Johnson of Clarendon believed that the Klan "wanted colored folks [to] think they was haints and monsters from the bad place." The elaborate uniforms of Klan members heightened their image as apparitions, especially while riding horseback at night. Moses Jeffries of Little Rock remembered a Klan trick in which the white-robed "spirits would ask for a drink of water and they had some way of drinking a whole bucketful to impress the Negroes that they were supernatural."[26]

Klan members sought control over public places for blacks in order to increase their power over freedpersons and to prevent them from plotting strategies in self-defense. Vergil Jones of Brinkley recalled,

"The Ku Kluxes didn't want much big gatherings among the black folk. They break up big gatherings." Rachel Harris of Pine Bluff recollected, "I remember once we had a big ball. We was cuttin' a dash that night. The Ku Klux came and made out they was dead. Some of the folks run they was so scared." The Klan also frequently disrupted religious services. Napoleon blacks, for example, had gathered for a prayer meeting in November 1868 when the Klan interrupted their service and told them "not to meet again."[27]

Many learned that a man's home was not his castle in the South, especially if the man was black. A Klan detail rode out nightly from Marion and "robbed men and ran them out of the country." Children grew especially frightened as these white-sheeted figures appeared in the night at their homes. Laura Hart of Pine Bluff explained, "They came and surrounded the house, hundreds of 'em. We had a loose plank floor and we'd hide under the floor with the dogs and stay there, too, till they'd gone." John Jones, also of Pine Bluff, recalled a similar experience, "I remember one night the Ku Klux came to our house. I was so scared I run under the house and stayed till ma called me out. I was so scared I didn't know what they had on." Since black parents dedicated themselves to protecting their children and to sustaining a safe, secure environment for their offspring, white terrorists could find no more effective method of psychological torture than to terrorize black children, exposing their parents' impotence.[28]

The Klan also attempted to disarm freedpersons so they could not defend themselves. In August 1868 Pine Bluff Klansmen "carried off every gun and pistol to be found in possession of the colored men." De Witt and El Dorado blacks faced similar confiscations of firearms in 1868.[29]

The Klan orchestrated a crescendo of violence against freedpersons and white Unionists during the 1868 elections. In Ashley County the sheriff was assaulted and abused and two freedmen were hanged. Five blacks were murdered in a ten-day "reign of terror" in Columbia County. Union men slept "in the woods or [were] driven out of the country" in Sevier County. In Little River County the sheriff was wounded, the Freedmen's Bureau agent murdered, and a black farmer killed. A legislator was killed and another political leader "badly wounded" in Monroe County. A bureau agent was assassinated and a judge's office destroyed in Craighead County. A mob demolished a courtroom, and innumerable blacks were murdered in Conway County. A deputy sheriff and freedman were killed and then tied together as a public warning and a black preacher was taken from his cabin and "not heard from again" in Drew County. "A reign of terror was being inaugurated in our state," declared newly elected Republican governor Powell Clayton. Fear of the Klan soared. Green Williams, Pulaski County freedman, shot at what he thought was a Klansman in a field near his cabin; but it turned out to be freedwoman Aggie Thomas who prayed nightly in the field. No Arkansan in 1867 or 1868 would have believed the Civil War was really over.[30]

Pro-Confederate newspaper editors heightened racial animosities and often sparked violence. The *Pine Bluff Vindicator* called for the assassination of bureau agents, leading freedmen, and black sympathizers in 1867. Philip Gatewood, *Chicot Press* editor and unrepentant Southern sympathizer, swore "he was a *North American white man* and would not allow the town in which he lived to be overrun with Negro worshippers." He eventually backed up his anti-black editorials with a murder attempt on several freedmen who stayed at bureau agent Benson's house. Army officers arrested and sent him to Vicksburg, Mississippi, for trial. The *Arkansas Gazette* constantly printed anti-black editorials and stories which excited white prejudice. In May 1867 the paper warned, "The enfranchisement of the negro has stirred the slimy sediments of society, and bad men have applied themselves to the work of engendering hatred and bad feeling among the negroes, toward the white masses of the community."[31]

Editors sometimes tried to drum up antimilitary sentiment, but they had to take care not to antagonize military officers. *Camden Constitutional Eagle* editors Dr. Anson W. Hobson and Rufus Lycurgus Linscott publicly protested the presence of drunken soldiers who made "such obscene exhibitions of themselves as they would make the most obdurate negro blush, if such a thing was possible, to say nothing of respectable ladies and children." Radical Republican government officials in 1868 charged editor John George Ryan of the *Southern Vindicator* with "obstructing reconstruction and inciting disturbances of the peace by incendiary publications." They also jailed and fined editors Colonel J. W. Gaulding and Adam Clark of the *Arkadelphia Southern*

Standard for criticizing a circuit judge. In an era when newspapers forged public opinion and molded public attitudes and behavior, many editors fanned anti-black or anti-bureau sentiment which contributed to outbreaks of violence.[32]

Although violence was a real part of daily Southern life during Reconstruction, freedpersons and their compatriots did not passively endure it. Many bureau agents, white government officials, the army, and blacks themselves stood up against white terror and demanded protection for black life, liberty, and the pursuit of happiness.

Freedmen's Bureau agents, whether racist or sympathetic toward blacks, wanted normalized, peaceful relations to be established quickly in Arkansas and in the South so that the remainder of the bureau's agenda could be realized. E. W. Gantt, Washington bureau agent, saw the need for bureau protection of freedpersons. He feared blacks would be "starved, murdered, or forced into a condition more horrible than the worst stage of slavery!" And he understood the reason for that rage: "I say this sorrowfully of our people, but I know it is but too true. Their wrath over defeat would be poured upon the hands of the helpless ones once their slaves."[33]

Sometimes bureau agents used threats to force whites into complying with their orders. Bureau chief General E. O. C. Ord notified Arkansas planters, "I will send a force of colored cavalry to sweep the country and remove every free person from it as a measure of safety to that class of people." On yet another occasion, Ord repeated, "Notify the wealthy land owners and planters a colored cavalry [is] coming if they don't get [the] desperadoes to cool it." Hiram Willis threatened southwestern Arkansas planters with taxes to compensate "if depredations" continued. Apparently Willis's ploy worked; the planters immediately called a meeting to halt the violence.[34]

When threats failed, agents resorted to orders backed by threats of military intervention to coerce whites into accepting the bureau's dictates. Whipping of blacks required much bureau attention and activity. Washington agent E. W. Gantt reported, "I am still asked the question of what kind of punishment persons will be allowed to inflict upon disobedient negroes, meaning that they whip with the lash, or tie up by the thumbs, etc. My response is 'neither.'" Arkadelphia agent William Stuart typified many agents' responses to whipping when he fined a culprit ten dollars and confined him to hard labor for ten days. Agents also often dealt with black ownership of guns, so necessary for freedpersons' self-defense. Agent E. G. Barker of Marion advised a planter, "You are not authorized to refuse to pay them [freedmen] because some of them have revolvers." Many agents cautiously guarded freedpersons' crops and economic livelihood. Agents blocked planters who tried to force blacks to leave their crops and often ordered planters to allow them to supervise crop harvests.[35]

Bureau officials also worried about the newly gained legal rights granted to blacks by civil-rights legislation and by the Fourteenth and Fifteenth Amendments. South Bend agent Albert Coats requested a copy of the Civil Rights Act of 1866 so that he would know, with certainty, what it guaranteed freedpersons. Agent E. W. Gantt of Union lobbied state officials for black jurors as he queried government leaders whether freedpersons could receive fair trials when blacks were not permitted to serve on juries. Little Rock agent John Tyler in 1867 issued a circular which clearly announced to planters and all other interested parties that former slaves or free persons of color now had legal rights such as the right of contract, the right to sue or be sued, property rights, right of testacy, and the right to testify in and serve on juries in state courts.[36]

Agents often adjudicated conflicts between blacks and whites in the days before state courts allowed blacks to participate in the judicial process. An Arkadelphia bureau agent's docket processed in August 1865 included cases involving a variety of disputes (see Table 6.1). The Lewisville bureau agent in the summer of 1867 wrestled with dilemmas that included domestic quarrels, the whipping of freedpersons, contract annulments, and rape. Before state courts permitted black testimony and allowed blacks on juries, the Freedmen's Bureau tried to settle disputes between blacks and whites equitably.[37]

But many agents did not want to risk their own safety and position in the community by standing up against planters who abused freedpersons. In Lewisville in the summer of 1867, for example, agent Volney Voltaire Smith fined freedman Tobey Warren ten dollars for his "insolent and disobedient manner," an action which must have pleased local planters. Inexplicably, agent Hiram Willis voiced support of a state law in June 1867 which prohibited blacks from possessing

TABLE 6.1

Arkadelphia Litigation: August 1865

Dispute	# of cases
Contract dispute	15
Theft	7
Assault	5
Whipping	5
Disorderly conduct	2
Firearms possession	1
Murder	1
Threat of murder	1
Kidnapping	1

guns—at a time when blacks were confronting a veritable civil war in southwestern Arkansas. Such a law would clearly have made blacks as defenseless as in antebellum days. The *Arkansas Gazette* praised bureau agent Lewis Carhart of Camden after he refused to release black corn thieves whom a state judge had freed due to insufficient evidence. In each of these cases, agents forgot their task was to become a buffer between planters and freedpersons and became, instead, surrogates for planters who tried to reenslave blacks.[38]

State and county authorities, especially before passage of the Fourteenth Amendment, prohibited blacks from holding office and felt no need to help freedpersons receive justice. Indeed, they seemed to fear retribution from whites if they did so. State bureau head General Ord observed, "The pistol worn by almost every white man in Arkansas settles the dispute." "The people here are very much worked up about the Civil Rights Bill," witnessed Monticello agent E. G. Barker, "and are so *bitter* and irritable in their feelings that it appears nothing but *fear* controls them." But who controlled whom presented a major problem to many civil authorities, such as those in Ashley County who were "afraid to arrest any of the rowdies and bullies who infest the country." By 1868 many people feared to accept civil appointments and refused to get involved, an abdication which allowed violence to go unchecked against freedpersons.[39]

Most bureau officials reported from 1865 to 1867 that no help could be expected from civil authorities. Napoleon agent J. C. Predmore believed, "The civil law gives no protection here for life and the whole criminal practices in this county is [sic] a farce, and it has been so for years and it will take a long time to make a change for the better." Agent Hiram Willis agreed: "The civil courts are of no account here . . . The sheriff dare not to undertake to enforce his duties from fear of the mob law." Agents offered to bureau leaders specific proof of the do-nothing attitude of government officials. In Lewisville, when white David Semay murdered freedwoman Mandy Landers, local officials "did nothing." In Madison the white justice of the peace acquitted a white man of beating a black man to death. In Augusta a man raped a freedperson's daughter while his friend held her parents at gun point. The sheriff insisted that no jury would convict the rapists, and after holding them in prison for the night, he released them at dawn.[40]

Civil authorities not only offered no resistance as whites took the law into their own hands, but some also used the law to intimidate and coerce freedpersons. Justices of the peace in Washington issued frivolous arrest warrants against blacks who favored the new 1868 constitution and would not allow them to call witnesses in their own behalf. Officials also levied exorbitant bail to keep blacks in prison. In Dardanelle, for example, a judge set a three thousand dollar bail for a freedman, which proved, of course, impossible for him to pay. In Monticello freedpersons received heavy sentences of from one to two years for "very light offenses (such as stealing an axe, a bushel of corn)." At De Valls Bluff, leaders charged blacks with larceny after whites had loaned them the supposedly stolen objects.[41]

Blacks saw through these legal ruses and thought "bringing civil cases folly." V. V. Smith of Lewisville summed it up best when he reported, "In Columbia County I should judge that the whites done [sic] about as they please with the blacks."[42]

Although many civil authorities "uttered not a word" when whites abused, discriminated against, or harmed blacks, some officials proved to be exceptions and tried to bring justice to freedpersons. Helena justice of the peace Samuel Delaney fined a white man twenty-five dollars for assault of a freedman. The guilty party then assaulted Delaney and called him a "nigger's man." Although it was rare, county officials occasionally requested that federal troops be sent to their area. Monroe County sheriff R. C. Carlton asked for military aid to maintain order in November 1867 when a white man killed an elderly, highly respected black man. Little Rock agent Frank Gross believed that civil magistrates increasingly dealt "justly between whites and colored." Although his estimates may have been too generous, most state and local officials elected in 1868 tried to follow the Fourteenth and Fifteenth Amendments and to provide "equal protection under the law" for freedpersons—as long as the army policed Arkansas justice.[43]

Local, county, and state judges often blocked blacks in their efforts to obtain justice, as did their executive counterparts. Agent Hiram Willis echoed what many of his fellow agents observed in 1865 and 1867, "The civil courts are of no account here even on civil matters." As late as July 1867, Lewisville whites found it unfathomable that they were actually expected to appear at court with blacks.[44]

Whites found many ways to tamper with the judicial process. Sebastian Geisreiter of Augusta reported, "Whites swear to shoot the first damned nigger who sues a white man." Obtaining evidence necessary for convictions often proved difficult. At Fort Smith in 1866, blacks obtained judgments against whites only if there were white witnesses. Lake Village judges continually dismissed cases brought by blacks in 1867 by claiming that "insufficient evidence" warranted no prosecution. The Yell County prosecuting attorney shielded a potential white witness whose testimony would have acquitted a freedman charged with murder.[45]

Determined to make a mockery of the Fourteenth Amendment and civil-rights legislation, white zealots in Arkansas pressured jurors to stay within the bounds of white domination. Community pressure forced an integrated jury in Lewisburg to sentence only the black litigant in a dispute over a fight between a white and black man. Marion jurors, facing reprisals, acquitted all Klan members for any crimes committed. The bureau agent in Lafayette County in early 1867 insisted, "I am certain no jury could be empounded who would decide a case against a white in favor of a black."[46]

But over time, new laws enforced by the army offered blacks at least the semblance of fair trials for as long as the military regulated Southern life. Integrated juries became the norm by late 1867 and afforded freedpersons at least a modicum of judicial fairness.[47]

The Arkansas General Assembly wrestled with the problem of how to legislate order out of the chaos which prevailed after the Civil War. The 1866 unreconstructed legislature, which contained many former Confederates, rejected the Fourteenth Amendment, deferred an educational clause that would have established state-funded schools for blacks and whites, and refused to give black men the right to vote. The 1866 legislature did, however, guarantee freedpersons the "rights of contract, right to sue and be sued, give evidence, inherit and hold property, and to purchase, lease, sell or assign property."[48]

Radical Republicans won the constitutional convention and legislative elections in early 1868 and began reconstructing Arkansas according to a more revolutionary blueprint. The 1868 constitutional convention recognized federal supremacy, insured "equality of all persons before the law," enfranchised black men over the age of twenty-one, and provided for a common-school system. The new constitution was ratified by a margin of 54,501 votes in April 1868 and guided the new state legislature in its deliberations. The 1868 radical legislature ratified the Fourteenth Amendment, guaranteed no discrimination against persons regarding public carriers and public accommodations, established a system of free but racially segregated common schools, granted laborers a lien upon what they produced, and set up punishments of not less than five hundred dollars and a prison sentence of from one to ten years for instigating civil disturbances.[49]

The presence of United States troops throughout Arkansas served as the largest restraint on violence against freedpersons and deterred civil-rights violations. Freedmen's Bureau agents could order, county officials could enforce, courts could adjudicate, and the legislature could legislate; but it was the army that best commanded the attention of anti-black forces and stemmed their violence. The army best bridged the glaring gap between the legal promises guaranteed blacks by the new constitution and legislation and the de facto discrimination that often controlled Arkansas.

Most bureau agents agreed with John Scroggins' assessment: "The people [are] hostile to every official act and [are] only acquiescing through fear of the military." Agents from Arkadelphia, Dardanelle, Lewisburg, Washington, Columbus, De Valls Bluff, and Helena constantly clamored for armed reenforcements from 1865 to 1868. Sometimes the threat of troops was enough to stabilize a region, as when state bureau chief General Ord warned local planters that black troops would be sent if violence against freedpersons continued.[50]

Often warnings proved inadequate, and actual detachments of troops had to be sent throughout Arkansas. Camden agent Joseph Thorp believed that only troops offered freedpersons security and safety. Monticello agent E. G. Barker agreed and observed that it was "unsafe to travel or stay in the country without soldiers." Soldiers not only protected freedpersons but also provided refuge for bureau agents. "I am not satisfied," Napoleon agent J. C. Predmore asserted, "that my only safety here is their [whites] fear of swift justice by the military authorities." Paraclifta agent A. W. Ballard agreed and observed that the agent's "office will amount to very little without military participation." With the passage by Congress of the Reconstruction Act of 1867, Arkansas was placed in the Fourth Military District. Although Arkansas head General Ord opposed the legislation "in toto" and dispatched troops sparingly throughout the Fourth District of Arkansas and Mississippi, the renewed threat of military intervention proved a limited deterrent to escalating violence.[51]

Troops occasionally proved more of a curse than a blessing for bureau agents who tried to promote domestic tranquillity. In Fort Smith agent Thomas Abel condemned nearby troops as a bane to both blacks and whites. Jacksonport agent J. M. Bowler gave strict orders to Lieutenant Phil Skilman to keep his men "in complete control," to allow "no wandering around the countryside," and to have "little to do officially as possible with the civil authorities and the people." Agents who tried to control the army may have been trying to prevent bloodshed and a further escalation of violence, or they may have not wanted soldiers, and especially their officers, to interfere in their pro-planter agenda.[52]

The most serious army-community confrontation erupted in August 1867 in Camden. The episode was spawned by an anti-army editorial in the local newspaper, the *Constitutional Eagle*, which condemned soldiers for public drunkenness and reprehensible conduct. The soldiers' commander, Brevet Major George S. Pierce, led a group of thirty men to the newspaper office where they demolished the press, destroyed the half-finished edition of the next week's newspaper, and dumped the case and types into the Ouachita River. Pierce's superior, Colonel Charles C. Gilbert, supported his subordinate and brashly retorted that the military were "not the servants of the people of Arkansas, but their masters." Furthermore, insisted Colonel Gilbert, "It is felt to be a great piece of impertinence for a newspaper in this state to comment upon the military under any circumstances whatever." Bureau head General Ord countered Gilbert's "impudence" and insisted that "the military forces are the servants of the laws, and the laws are for the benefit of the people." Although the army usually maintained peace, law, and order in Arkansas, it was altogether capable of exacerbating the difficulties inherent in Reconstruction.[53]

Although soldiers at times worried bureau agents more than they helped them, most officials despaired at the thought of the army leaving Arkansas. Civil authorities who opposed bureau work grew emboldened at the thought of the army's evacuation. When troops actually left, threats of retaliation against freedpersons became reality. In Osceola, for example, five freedmen were killed within a month of the army's departure.[54]

Governor Powell Clayton, elected in 1868 in the first elections in which freedmen voted, decided within six months of his inauguration that martial law was needed to quell violence in Arkansas. "A reign of terror was being inaugurated in our state," insisted the governor, "which threatened to obliterate all the old landmarks of justice and freedom, and to bear us onward to anarchy and destruction." Allen Trelease, historian of the Ku Klux Klan and of the violence of this era, accepts Clayton's assessment and estimates that more than two hundred murders occurred in Arkansas on the eve of the November 3, 1868, presidential election. To counter these murders and the unrest and agitation stirred by the Klan, Governor Clayton began planning clandestinely to create a militia to thwart anti-black forces. Failing to receive aid in buying arms from the Illinois governor, Clayton turned to a private distributor in Detroit who sold him in July 1868 "4000 rifles, 400,000 cartridges, 1,500,000 percussion caps, and a large quantity of gun powder." The materiel arrived by train at Memphis, but no steamboat would transport the explosives across the Mississippi River for fear of reprisals by the Klan. The *Hesper* finally agreed to transport the goods and set sail from Memphis on October 15. The Klan vessel *Netty Jones* intercepted the *Hesper*, grounded the boat, and threw the materiel overboard.[55]

Clayton proclaimed martial law on November 4, 1868, and divided the state into four military districts. Militia men "constituted a motley force." Disheveled in dress, they foraged from the land they protected. Major clashes between the militia and Rebel sympathizers occurred at Center Point in southwestern Arkansas, near Monticello in southeastern Arkansas, and in Woodruff, Conway, Greene, Mississippi, and Craighead Counties. By early 1869 martial law ended in most counties with the rout of the Klan. According to historian Trelease, Governor Clayton "accomplished more than any other Southern governor in suppressing the Ku Klux conspiracy."[56]

Freedpersons also formed militias and played an integral role in defending themselves. Although most black militiamen were adjuncts of Clayton's forces, blacks had formed a paramilitary organization in the autumn of 1867 and commenced drilling almost six months before Clayton's inauguration. Black militias formed in Florida, Tennessee, Texas, Louisiana, Mississippi, North Carolina, South Carolina, Georgia, and Arkansas as a response to the Ku Klux Klan and as a black military arm of radical Reconstruction. Texarkana freedman Doc Quinn recalled, "We would ride up to a negro settlement, and tell de niggers we wuz organizing a colored militia to catch Cullen Baker and his gang. Most ob de negroes would join."[57]

Blacks drilled nightly in Little Rock in August 1868. Freedmen outside of the state capital similarly bonded together and formed defensive militias in Marion, Rocky Comfort, Pine Bluff, and Washington.[58]

Planters and many other Arkansas whites trembled as they conjured up images of armed black militias. Marion bureau agent E. M. Main reported, "A very bitter feeling exists among the planters toward the colored people in consequence of the latter joining the State Guard." Rocky Comfort agent Hiram Willis uncovered similar white antipathy and noted that there was "considerable excitement and a great many harsh words said by the whites against organizing the colored militia in this county." Whites breathed easier in Washington in 1867 when "military authorities interfered promptly" with armed black militiamen who "disturbed the peace." But to the dismay of many whites, the army intervened less willingly between whites and the black militia during the 1868 elections. At Marion, planters dismissed freedmen who joined black militias, but Freedmen's Bureau agent E. M. Main declared this illegal and forced planters to reinstate the laid-off freedmen. Even after the Klan's defeat and the end of martial law, black militiamen in southwestern Arkansas continued scouting forays to insure no resurrection of the Klan. Providing self-defense and fostering self-worth and a sense of power, black militias enabled freedpersons to express their determination to care for themselves.[59]

Blacks struggled fiercely between 1865 and 1868 to obtain the right to possess guns, and they used such arms to protect themselves from white violence. Planters tried to disarm freedpersons in 1865, and they were still trying to take their guns away in 1868. Occasionally, even Freedmen's Bureau agents wanted to disarm freedpersons, as when Pine Bluff agent Captain Edward Wallace was reminded by state bureau chief General John Sprague that "Negroes have the same right to carry arms that white men have and will be protected in it." Blacks clearly recognized that gun ownership insured protection and survival. Napoleon agent J. C. Predmore observed that the "practice of carrying pistols is almost universal." Freedmen carried guns to the fields when they went to work. And when they attended political meetings which they feared might be disrupted, they went heavily armed. Little Rock blacks had a communication network that allowed large numbers of them to coalesce quickly and be armed when necessary.[60]

Life in Arkansas after the Civil War combined both a Southern and a frontier heritage of violence which made existence for most blacks and whites extremely tentative and anxious. Rumors of intended horrors, torture, shootings, murders, and whippings accompanied blacks' struggles for freedom. Both individual whites and white guerrilla groups tried to force freedpersons to submit to white supremacy. To counter the violence, the Freedmen's Bureau often served as a buffer between blacks and their opponents by issuing orders to planters and by adjudicating disputes between blacks and whites. Although the legislative and judicial branches of the state opposed blacks until 1868, at the beginning of radical rule in that year, both branches began to offer blacks a closer approximation of justice and equal protection under the law. Both the army and Governor Powell Clayton, inaugurated in 1868, protected freedpersons and their rights. Freedpersons defended themselves as well as relying on the army, Freedmen's Bureau agents, and sympathetic whites. As long as the bureau and a radical governor were in Arkansas, freedpersons could expect aid in the defense of their new liberties.

When the bureau left Arkansas in early 1869, violence escalated in some areas as planters sought to regain economic, political, and social dominance. Large-scale riots occurred at places such as Dardanelle and in Pope County in late 1869 and Chicot County in late 1871. The violence culminated in the Brooks-Baxter War of 1874, which ended radical rule in Arkansas. It is likely that if there had never been a Freedmen's Bureau, such class and racial violence would have erupted immediately at war's end in 1865 and would have seriously jeopardized black freedom. Also, freedpersons' successful resistance to the Klan's attempts to disenfranchise them and reinstitute slavery powerfully reminded blacks of their new identity as United States citizens.[61]

CHAPTER 7

FAREWELL TO THE FREEDMEN'S BUREAU

The Freedmen's Bureau Act of July 1866 provided for a two-year extension of the agency. In 1868 Congress overrode President Andrew Johnson's veto and funded the bureau for another year, but with severe reductions in agent salaries. Most local agents received word of their dismissal, effective January 1, 1869, but had sensed their approaching dismissal throughout 1868. A skeletal bureaucracy at the national level and minimal personnel to supervise schools and hospitals at the state level lingered in Southern states until 1870.[1]

Bureau agents often became targets for disgruntled whites, as did other whites in the region who tried to ensure freedom and justice for blacks. Ruffians assaulted agent Captain John Williams on the streets of Pine Bluff in Jefferson County while he performed his duties. Rebel sympathizers beat Arkadelphia agent Anthony Habricht in March 1868. Bureau opponents assassinated two agents, Simpson Mason in Fulton County and Hiram Willis in Little River County.[2]

In 1868 many blacks and some whites feared for a future without the bureau. Thomas Williams of Madison detected the despair and reported, "There seems to be a gloom however pervading their [blacks'] minds engendered by the knowledge of the probability of the Freedmen's Bureau being discontinued."[3]

In contrast to freedpersons, many whites rejoiced at the prospect of the bureau's demise. Planters resented bureau interference in contract disputes and longed for a return to antebellum days with no outside intermediary for blacks. South Bend planter Robert G. Hunt ordered his laborers in November 1867 to ignore any directives coming from the bureau. In the *Arkansas Gazette,* planters A. H. Garland, W. Byers, and A. B. Williams lambasted the Freedmen's Bureau by arguing, "If the negro be equal to the white man, and so very capable of taking care of himself, why establish and keep in operation, as his special guardian, a bureau at an annual cost of $50 million."[4]

White yeomen despised the bureau's intrusion into Southern life as much as planters. A small-scale, white farmer from Camden swore to bureau agent Fred Thibaut that he would not "report to any Bureau for charges proffered against him by a Negro." Individuals sometimes protested the bureau's presence with ridicule, as when William Callaway of Clark County tied ginger cake on the doorknobs of all businesses which adjoined the "rad hole" ("as the negro bureau and carpetbaggers' offices were called") for "bait for the rads." Over one hundred Hamburg citizens, representing all classes, declared in a petition to state bureau officials that their problems stemmed not from black and white confrontations but rather from bureau interference. Antipathy toward the bureau united all classes of Southern whites against Northern "trespassers." Napoleon agent J. C. Predmore recognized that all elements of white society demonstrated a "bitter feeling against the bureau which is intensified by its officers being northern men."[5]

Arkansas newspaper editors raised anti-bureau animus whenever possible. The *Weekly Arkansas Gazette* reminded white Arkansans, "The sooner we supersede, by the enactment of proper laws, the necessity of the Freedmen's Bureau, the less excuse there will be for forcing upon us that obnoxious and expensive excrescence." The *Daily Arkansas Gazette* agreed, calling the bureau an institution "fraught with peril" and its agents "a scandalous sort of knaves."[6]

Opposition occasionally came from unexpected quarters. The army often resented the additional duties forced upon it by the bureau. Soldiers at Paraclifta openly spoke "against the Bureau" and declared themselves "not there for its support." Black politicians sometimes feared that the bureau served as but "a political machine from which the black race had never reaped the benefit for which it was intended."[7]

The constitutional convention, meeting in Little Rock in early 1868, debated whether to request Congress "to continue the Freedmen's Bureau until reconstruction is accomplished." Opponents believed the Freedmen's Bureau too meddlesome and restrictive of both whites and blacks. Many of the elite offered self-serving criticisms of the bureau. Bradley County representative John Bradley insisted, "The negroes in my country became very sick of the Freedmen's Bureau." The bureau's absence from his county for parts of 1866 and 1867, he elaborated, had allowed blacks and whites "to get along more peacefully and quietly than before." Ashley County lawyer and convention delegate W. D. Moore agreed, calling the Freedmen's Bureau "a curse to the colored man, the greatest curse ever inflicted upon the black man." On the other hand, a former bureau agent and delegate, John R. Montgomery of Sevier County, supported continuance of the bureau. "In southwestern Arkansas," he explained, "not only the colored man, but the Union men, are, on account of their principles, denied justice in the courts." Freedman William Grey of Phillips County eloquently defended the bureau. He insisted that it alone guaranteed civil rights for African Americans. "Take away the Freedmen's Bureau," he insisted, "and it is beyond the power of mortal man to predict what would be the consequence." Chicot County's Oberlin-educated black postmaster and delegate James W. Mason, incensed at the incompetence of local bureau agent Thomas Hunicutt, proposed an amendment to the proposal which encouraged "more honest and efficient" bureau officials, but delegates viewed the amendment as a negative reflection on the bureau and defeated it by a vote of thirty-seven to twenty-four. The resolution which encouraged continuation of the Freedmen's Bureau passed by a vote of forty-three to seventeen on February 1, 1868.[8]

Although the Arkansas Constitutional Convention urged Congress to maintain the bureau, Congress ignored its pleas and began the restriction of bureau operations in early 1869. Less money and fewer agents (confined to the state capital to supervise funds for schools and hospitals) restricted the influence of the bureau. By the summer of 1869 the role of the Freedmen's Bureau in Arkansas and in the South had, to use Langston Hughes's metaphor, "dried up like a raisin in the sun."

Historians have rightly criticized the Freedmen's Bureau for its conservatism and lethargy in protecting freedom, civil rights, and economic opportunities for freedpersons. Eric Foner argues that the bureau "never quite comprehended the depths of racial antagonism and class conflict in the postwar South." Eric McKitrick insists that the bureau stayed too conservative and labored to restore planter hegemony. "The political, constitutional, legal, and administrative changes effected in the United States through the Civil War and Reconstruction," he believes, "were almost invisible compared with those that remained in France after the French Revolution." William McFeely agrees with McKitrick and argues that the bureau "betrayed" freedpersons by "substituting supervision for man to man respect."[9]

Regardless of the Reconstruction goals of Freedmen's Bureau agents, Southern white planters, carpetbaggers, or scalawags, African Americans themselves often rejected suggestions from these surrogates and chose for themselves how to live. Paternalistic paradigms which fail to appreciate the freedom freedpersons demanded, struggled for, and often gained during Reconstruction distort the realities of Reconstruction. It is true that many bureau agents viewed blacks as children, but it is erroneous to assert that blacks accepted these views of themselves. African Americans demanded ballots, schools, churches, teachers, preachers, fair contracts, family protection, and civil and legal rights to a degree that makes paternalistic paradigms too simplistic. William McFeely calls bureau head General O. O. Howard the blacks' "Yankee Stepfather," but the metaphor fails when looking at the bureau from the freedpersons' perspective. Many blacks insisted that they wanted neither Howard nor anyone else as a father or stepfather. Other blacks dissembled as in antebellum years, letting white caretakers appear to control their existence. Still other blacks succumbed completely to the wishes of whites in power, whether bureau agents or planters.

In a more recent work, McFeely applies the metaphor of a carpet, woven by bureau agents and black sympathizers, which protected freedpersons. "With emancipation and Reconstruction," he observes, "official, public promises were made—and broken. Expectations rose and were dashed; psychological damage was done. The rug was pulled out from under them; during slavery there had been no rug." What some blacks in Arkansas clearly recognized was that they had to weave their own rug, that they could not depend upon others to preserve their freedom. Their varying responses to the bureau only accentuated the real possibility of choices and the genuine alternatives available to freedpersons.[10]

Paternalistic paradigms are also too present minded. They decontextualize Reconstruction and judge 1865 and 1866 from the perspective of the New Deal or the Great Society. Forgetting that Andrew Johnson was not Lyndon Johnson, that telegraph lines (often down in Arkansas after Civil War) were not television screens to help mobilize public opinion, and that the Holocaust had not yet seared human consciousness with the imprint of racism, these historians make history a morality play. They are inclined to find angels and demons too readily when, in reality, mixtures of good and evil warred in almost every human during Reconstruction. The struggles to make sense of the horrible destructive forces of the Civil War must be viewed as a dialectic in which each individual—black and white, Northerner and Southerner, male and female—had different views of the future. The complex dialectic of change and continuity must also be remembered. The situation was not at all dichotomous. Neither blacks nor whites neatly discarded some values and institutions while keeping others; rather, they groped for new understandings of freedom while often subconsciously clinging to old values and patterns of behavior and thought. Even after revolutions, such as the Civil War and Reconstruction in the United States, much remains unchanged. The struggle over what institutions and values from the past are worth saving is always complicated and angst riddled, and to reduce such dilemmas to simplistic tales of good and evil is to betray all who lived in the 1860s.

Freedpersons, often with the help of sympathetic bureau agents, moved toward economic freedom. By moving to areas of better economic opportunities, by demanding control of the time spent in farm labor, and by refusing to work in gangs, African Americans mastered much of their own household economies. Freedpersons approved or rejected contracts negotiated by bureau agents between themselves and planters, thereby establishing a precedent for mastery over wages or shares which endured into the twentieth century. Although cliometricians rightly reveal that indebtedness quickly tied many freedpersons to a particular farm, it must not be assumed that African Americans upheld bourgeois values about debt. Although many freedpersons soon became "mired deep in the trials of Job," indebtedness from the freed-persons' viewpoint was a long way from chattel slavery.

Adapting self-help ideology promulgated by the Freedmen's Bureau, blacks took their lives and their freedom into their own hands and shaped much of their own destiny. Freedpersons developed their own identities by moving to areas far from painful plantation memories, by finding and supporting lost family members, by creating historical myths to help explain their existence, by perceiving gender and race from their own unique and individualistic perspectives, and by joining communities (churches, clubs, and political parties) which offered them greater choices and alternatives. Freedpersons made economic choices which often influenced the quality of their lives by demanding for freedwomen more time for work in the home, by purchasing desired goods at local stores, by insisting on bureau regulation of contracts with conniving planters, and by striking against unfair working conditions. Freedpersons often protested overtly and loudly. They reported grievances against bureau agents or teachers to their supervisors, committed petty crimes such as small-scale theft, and joined a self-defense (and at times, perhaps, offensive) militia. As they did under slavery and even more so in the postbellum world, blacks created worlds that *they* more openly mastered and controlled. Although no monolithic "freedperson" personality developed, many blacks did, with these options, become new and freer people.

Blacks nourished communal institutions which fostered individual and group identities. Churches, schools, and all-black fraternal organizations offered freedpersons opportunities for leadership, growth, and fulfillment. By refusing to allow whites to dictate theology, school curriculum, or political agendas, African Americans constructed new identities and created new ideological milieus in which to live.

By actively participating in the elections of 1867 and 1868, blacks guaranteed that they would be political forces to be reckoned with in the future. Political activism offered them new venues for freedom and opportunities for new roles which strengthened their commitment to freedom.

The bureau, freedpersons, and Southern whites constantly confronted the Southern lodestars of race and class. For freedpersons, the bureau often encouraged positive understandings of "blackness" that could be developed only covertly under slavery. Although little was done or probably could have been done to ameliorate white racism, many whites looked at black churches, schools, voters, and farm owners and perhaps, to a degree, reevaluated their thoughts about blacks. Although white planters ultimately regained their power after the departure of the Freedmen's Bureau, they had to deal with blacks more equitably while the bureau supervised Reconstruction. A black elite openly brokered with white elites, a circumstance unheard of in antebellum days. Subtle yet important changes in understandings of race and class occurred while the Freedmen's Bureau labored in Arkansas.

Even though the class structure stayed much the same, power was an extraordinarily complex reality. Planters controlled the outward symbols of power, including government positions, land, and money. But a closer look reveals how tenuously planters held that power and shows that the "powerless" tenant farmers and sharecroppers often controlled cotton production. In a dramatic sense, freedpersons did gain tremendous power when their role is looked at from the bottom up, instead of the usual top-to-bottom perspective. Blacks worked where and how they wished, received enough credit to purchase necessities and a few luxuries, fished and hunted the bounties of natural Arkansas, feared whippings less than in slavery, loved their families with a constancy denied them under slavery, prayed to their God in their own way in their churches, learned to read and write, and watched with pleasure as their children read and wrote. It was not everything dreamed of in 1865 at emancipation, but neither was it chattel slavery.

"The world struggles to be happy," sighed the *Little Rock Daily Pantograph* editor in 1865. Blacks as well as whites continued to struggle after the Civil War, caught in the webs of poverty, defeat, and guilt. The world ushered in by many Freedmen's Bureau agents, carpetbaggers, and freedpersons from 1865 through 1868—a new world full of black voters, churches, schools, and renewed families—allowed African Americans for the first time real glimpses of Jefferson's dream of "life, liberty, and the pursuit of happiness." War's wake brought no utopia to Arkansas freedpersons, but it did bring new dimensions of freedom and new opportunities of self and group fulfillment, due in large part to the work of the Freedmen's Bureau. [11]

Although the work of the Freedmen's Bureau is much more complex than historians have previously suggested, the mere presence of such a federal agency effectively checked much white animosity against blacks. What if there had been no Freedmen's Bureau in the South after the Civil War? It is easy to imagine that planters would have reenslaved blacks and denied them economic freedom, opportunities, the hope for change, and new work roles; that black churches would have been controlled, as in antebellum days, by white planters; that schools for blacks would have remained dreams; that black families would not have been protected, and blacks would most likely have been continually treated as sexual objects; that black men would have neither registered nor voted; that more blacks would have died than did due to lack of medical care, clothing, or food. When viewed in their complexity, the achievements made by freedpersons were remarkable. At times they were aided by the Freedmen's Bureau, at other times they co-opted it, and sometimes they were manipulated by planters, the white majority, or the bureau. Although it was not, as blacks had dreamed, the Day of Jubilee, it was a beginning of freedom and an end of slavery. Freedpersons made what freedom they possessed a reality.

NOTES

CHAPTER 1

1. George P. Rawick, ed., *Arkansas Narratives*, The American Slave, 1st ser. (1941; reprint, Westport, Conn.: The Greenwood Publishing Company, 1972), 9:164, 8:8, 327, 47, 10:124

2. Joe H. Mays, *Black Americans and Their Contributions toward Union Victory in the American Civil War, 1861–1865* (New York: University Press of America, 1984), 128. For the struggles black soldiers faced in the Civil War, see also Joseph T. Glatthar's *The Civil War Alliance of Black Soldiers and White Officers* (New York: Free Press, 1990), or Dudley T. Cornish's classic *The Sable Arm: Black Troops in the Union Army, 1861–1865* (1956; reprint, Lawrence, Kans.: University Press, 1987). John F. Walter, *Capsule History of Arkansas: Military Units in the Civil War* (Middle Village, N.Y.: n.p., 1971), 412–43; James M. McPherson, *The Negro's Civil War: How American Negroes Felt and Acted during the War for the Union* (New York: Random House, 1965), 146; James McPherson, "Who Freed the Slaves?" *Reconstruction* 2, no. 3 (1994). 35–44.

3. Ira Don Richards, "The Battle of Poison Springs," *Arkansas Historical Quarterly* 18 (winter 1959): 349; Cornish, *The Sable Arm*, 177.

4. Carl H. Moneyhon, "From Slave to Free Labor: The Federal Plantation Experiment in Arkansas," *Arkansas Historical Quarterly* 53 (summer 1994): 137–60; John Eaton, *Grant, Lincoln, and the Freedmen* (1907; reprint, New York: Negro Universities Press, 1969), 2. For a biographical sketch of Eaton see *The National Cyclopedia of American Biography*, vol. 8 (New York: James T. White & Co., 1924), 390–91. Grant's description of Eaton's work can be found in *Personal Memoirs of U. S. Grant*, ed. E. B. Long (New York: World Pub. Co., 1952), 221.

5. Eaton, *Grant, Lincoln, and the Freedmen*, 124, 58, 158; John Eaton, *Report of the General Superintendent of Freedmen, Department of the Tennessee and the State of Arkansas, For 1864* (Memphis, Tenn.: n.p., 1865), 36.

6. Martha Mitchell Bigelow, "Freedmen of the Mississippi Valley, 1862–1865," *Civil War History* 8 (March 1962): 44–45; Gibson to Sargent, January 17, 1864, Field Office Records, Arkansas, Bureau of Refugees, Freedmen, and Abandoned Lands, Record Group 105 (hereafter cited as FOR-A), National Archives; Benjamin Quarles, *The Negro in the Civil War* (New York: Russell and Russell, 1953), 284.

7. Louis S. Gerteis, *From Contraband to Freedmen: Federal Policy toward Southern Blacks, 1861–1865* (Westport, Conn.: Greenwood Press, 1973), 121; Harlan to Sargent, February 5, 1864, FOR-A, National Archives; Todd to Whipple, July 4 and June 2, 1864, Arkansas, American Missionary Association Manuscripts (hereafter cited as AMA Manuscripts), National Archives; Joe M. Richardson, *Christian Reconstruction: The American Missionary Association and Southern Blacks, 1861–1890* (Athens: University of Georgia Press, 1986), 60; Palmer to Sargent, September 30, 1865, Records of the Assistant Commissioner for Arkansas, Bureau of Refugees, Freedmen, and Abandoned Lands, Record Group 105 (hereafter cited as AC-A), National Archives.

8. Todd to Whipple, July 4, 1864, Arkansas, AMA Manuscripts; Register of Sickness and Death, June 1864, FOR-A, National Archives.

9. Eaton, *Grant, Lincoln, and the Freedmen*, 127–33. For an overview of the health care problem, see Gaines M. Foster, "The Limitations of Federal Health Care for Freedmen, 1862–1868," *Journal of Southern History* 48 (August 1982): 355. *Fort Smith New Era*, March 19, 1864; *Little Rock Weekly Arkansas State Gazette*, May 13, 1865; Sweeney to McCook, April 21, 1865, AC-A, National Archives; Wheelock to Sargent, July 16, 1864, FOR-A, National Archives; Sprague to Howard, July 23, 1865, AC-A, National Archives; July 31, 1865 Report, AC-A, National Archives.

10. Thomas Kennedy, "Southland College: The Society of Friends and Black Education in Arkansas," *Arkansas Historical Quarterly* 42 (autumn 1983): 209; Larry Wesley Pearce, "The AMA and the Freedmen in Arkansas, 1863–78," *Arkansas Historical Quarterly* 30 (summer 1971): 124; Sprague to Howard, June 2, 1865, AC-A, National Archives; James McPherson, *The Civil War and Reconstruction* (New York: Alfred A. Knopf, 1982), 386; G. K. Eggleston, "The Work of Relief Societies during the Civil War," *Journal of Negro History* 14 (July 1929): 273.

11. Young to Fowler, February 4, 1864, AMA Manuscripts; May School Report, May 28, 1865, FOR-A, National Archives; Joel Grant Report, March 21, 1865, FOR-A, National Archives; Young to Whipple, May 30, 1864, AMA Manuscripts.

12. Special Order #11, October 31, 1864, FOR-A, National Archives; Joel Grant Report, February 28, 1865, FOR-A, National Archives; Hugh Brady Report, December 30, 1864, FOR-A, National Archives; Young to Fowler, February 4, 1864, AMA Manuscripts; Heilman to Whipple, March 4, 1864, AMA Manuscripts.

13. John G. Sproat, "Blueprint for Reconstruction," *Journal of Southern History* 23 (February 1957): 34; David Donald, *Charles Sumner and the Rights of Man* (New York: Alfred A. Knopf, 1970), 587. For a brief sketch of Sumner's life, see *The National Cyclopedia of American Biography*, vol. 3 (New York: James T. White & Co., 1924), 300–301. The best scholarly biography of Sumner remains David Donald's two-volume work, *Charles Sumner and the Coming of the Civil War* (New York: Alfred A. Knopf, 1960), and *Charles Sumner and the Rights of Man. Congressional Globe*, 38th Cong.,

1st sess., 2800; Charles Sumner, *The Works of Charles Sumner,* vol. 8 (Boston: Lee & Shepard, 1874), 476. Other Sumner speeches on slavery and the Freedmen's Bureau can be found in *The Works of Charles Sumner* on pp. 476–524.

14. Sproat, "Blueprint for Reconstruction," 34–35; Benjamin P. Thomas and Harold M. Hyman, *The Life and Times of Lincoln's Secretary of War* (New York: Alfred A. Knopf, 1962), 263–64; *The National Cyclopedia of American Biography,* vol. 8 (New York: James T. White & Co., 1924), 372–73; Harold Schwartz, *Samuel Gridley Howe: Social Reformer, 1801–1876* (Cambridge: Harvard University Press, 1956), 261; *The National Cyclopedia of American Biography,* vol. 9 (New York: James T. White & Co., 1924), 222; *Official Records of the War of the Rebellion,* 3rd ser. (Washington, D.C.: Government Printing Office, 1899), 3:73–74, 4:380–82.

15. *Congressional Globe,* 38th Cong., 1st sess., 567, 2799.

16. Ibid., 2802, 709, 761, 3300, 2933.

17. George R. Bentley, *A History of the Freedmen's Bureau* (New York: Octagon Books, 1970), 49; *Statutes at Large,* vol. 13 (Boston: Little, Brown, and Co., 1866), 507–8; Richard F. Bensel, *Yankee Leviathan: The Origins of Central State Authority in America, 1859–1877* (Cambridge: Cambridge University Press, 1990), 123.

18. William S. McFeely, *Yankee Stepfather: General O. O. Howard and the Freedmen* (New Haven: Yale University Press, 1968), 29–31; John Carpenter, *Sword and Olive Branch: Oliver Otis Howard* (Pittsburgh, Pa.: University of Pittsburgh Press, 1964), 44–72, 83; Bentley, *Freedmen's Bureau,* 54–55; Oliver Otis Howard, *Autobiography of Oliver Otis Howard,* vol. 2 (New York: Baker & Taylor Co., 1907), 164; Edward M. Coffman, *The Old Army: A Portrait of the American Army during Peacetime, 1784–1898* (New York: Oxford University Press, 1986), 235.

CHAPTER 2

1. James E. Sefton, *The U.S. Army and Reconstruction, 1865–1877* (Baton Rouge: Louisiana State University Press, 1967), 8; Coffman, *The Old Army,* 219; Bentley, *Freedmen's Bureau,* 58; Howard, *Autobiography,* 218.

2. *The National Cyclopedia of American Biography,* vol. 5 (New York: James T. White & Co., 1924), 5.

3. " E. O. C. Ord File," Adjutant General Report: Appointment, Commission, and Personnel Branch Document File (hereafter cited as AGR: AC & PBD File), National Archives; Dean S. Thomas, *Civil War Commanders* (Arendtsville, Pa.: Thomas Publications, 1986), 38. See also Bernarr Cresap, *Appomattox Commander: The Story of General E. O. C. Ord* (San Diego: A. S. Barnes & Co., 1981).

4. "Charles H. Smith File," AGR: AC & PBD File, National Archives; Torlief S. Holmes, *Horse Soldiers in Blue* (Gaithersburg, Md.: Butternut Press, 1985), vi–vii, 227–29.

5. "Station Books, 1865–1869," AC-A, National Archives.

6. "Edward T. Wallace File," "Fred W. Thibaut File," "Frank Gross File," and "Francis Springer File," AGR: AC & PBD File, National Archives.

7. "Henry Sweeney File," AGR: AC & PBD File, National Archives; Sweeney

to Sprague, April 3, 1865, AC-A, National Archives; Sweeney to Sprague, June 6, 1866, AC-A, National Archives; Sweeney to Ord, February 14, 1867, AC-A, National Archives.

8. Fay Hempstead, *Historical Review of Arkansas*, vol. 3 (Chicago: Lewis Pub. Co., 1911), 1242–44; Dallas Tabor Herndon, ed., *Centennial History of Arkansas*, vol. 2 (Chicago: S. J. Clarke Pub. Co., 1922), 92–95.

9. 1860 Manuscript Census, Arkansas.

10. Register of Marriages, 1865, FOR-A, National Archives; Marriage Certificates, 1865, FOR-A, National Archives; Registrar of Marriages, 1864–1866, FOR-A, National Archives.

11. Sprague to Howard, May 22, 1866, AC-A, National Archives; Sprague to Cullen, April 19, 1866, AC-A, National Archives; Tisdale Report, 1865, AC-A, National Archives; Wallace to Sprague, April 9, 1866, AC-A, National Archives.

12. Dawes & Abel to Williams, July 27, 1866, AC-A, National Archives; Lt. J. W. Shaw Report, June 8, 1867, AC-A, National Archives; De Wolf to Bennett, February 4, 1868, AC-A, National Archives.

13. Barker to Elliott, January 12, 1868, FOR-A, National Archives; Sprague Circular #17, AC-A, National Archives.

14. Cole to Tyler, December 31, 1866, FOR-A, National Archives; Geisreiter to Watson, February 4, 1867, FOR-A, National Archives; Habricht to Williams, November 22, 1866, FOR-A, National Archives.

15. Chicot County Report, undated, FOR-A, National Archives.

16. Benson to Colby, October 26, 1867, FOR-A, National Archives; Ord to Taylor, January 24, 1867, FOR-A, National Archives; Sprague to Howard, March 2, 1866, AC-A, National Archives.

17. Gross to Bennett, May 31, 1867, AC-A, National Archives; Geisreiter to Mills, September 30, 1868, AC-A, National Archives; John P. Walker Report, July 23, 1867, FOR-A, National Archives.

18. Eric Foner, *Politics and Ideology in the Age of the Civil War* (New York: Oxford University Press, 1980), 98–105; Howard Circular, May 15, 1865, *Acts of Congress Relative to Refugees, Freedmen, and Confiscated and Abandoned Lands* (Washington, D.C.: Government Printing Office, 1865).

19. Barker to Bennett, June 15, 1866, FOR-A, National Archives; Gantt to Sprague, December 23, 1865, FOR-A, National Archives.

20. Sprague to Howard, June 22, 1865, AC-A, National Archives.

21. Rawick, *Arkansas Narratives*, 1st ser., 9:353, 243; *Little Rock Morning Republican*, October 13, 1868.

22. Rawick, *Arkansas Narratives*, 1st ser., 9:24, 8:20, 143.

23. Thorp to Tyler, January 6, 1867, AC-A, National Archives; *Little Rock Weekly Arkansas State Gazette*, January 15, 1867.

24. Nate Coulter, "The Impact of the Civil War upon Pulaski County, Arkansas," *Arkansas Historical Quarterly* 41 (spring 1982): 69; *Ninth Census of the United States, 1870* (Washington, D.C.: Government Printing Office, 1872), 83–89.

25. Rawick, *Arkansas Narratives*, 1st ser., 9:56; Richardson, *Christian Reconstruction*, 248.

26. Rawick, *Arkansas Narratives*, 1st ser., 9 (pt. 3):347; Carroll to Hines, July 6, 1867, FOR-A, National Archives.

27. Leon F. Litwack, "The Ordeal of Black Freedom" in *The Southern Enigma: Essays on Race, Class, and Folk Culture*, ed. Walter J. Fraser Jr. and Winfred B. Moore Jr. (Greenwood, Conn.: Greenwood Press, 1983), 13; *Little Rock Weekly Arkansas State Gazette*, May 2, 1867; *Little Rock Evening Republican*, June 4, 1867.

28. Tisdale Report, October 31, 1865, AC-A, National Archives; Stuart to Sargent, October 31, 1865, AC-A, National Archives; Dawes to Tyler, November 30, 1866, AC-A, National Archives; Record and Account Book of Bayner Plantation, February–December 1867, FOR-A, National Archives.

29. Montgomery to Sargent, September 27, 1865, AC-A, National Archives; Tisdale to Sargent, September 27, 1865, AC-A, National Archives; *Little Rock Daily Arkansas Gazette*, September 13, 1866.

30. Reed to Sprague, January 10, 1866, AC-A, National Archives; V. V. Smith Report, July 17, 1867, AC-A, National Archives; Predmore to Dawes, October 14, 1866, AC-A, National Archives.

31. Smith to Bennett, July 17, 1867, FOR-A, National Archives; Mason to Smith, April 30, 1867, AC-A, National Archives; Stuart to Sargent, September 8, 1865, AC-A, National Archives.

32. J. P. Walker Report, July 23, 1867, FOR-A, National Archives; Ord to Howard, February 22, 1867, AC-A, National Archives.

33. Smith to Bennett, July 8, 1867, FOR-A, National Archives; Cole to Tyler, November 30, 1866, FOR-A, National Archives; Sprague to Howard, June 28, 1865, AC-A, National Archives; Sprague to Barker & Ballard, September 5, 1865, AC-A, National Archives.

34. Barker to Sprague, November 25, 1865, AC-A, National Archives.

35. Sprague to Thibaut, August 28, 1866, AC-A, National Archives; Dawes & Abel to Williams, July 27, 1866, AC-A, National Archives; Sprague to Reed, October 10, 1866, FOR-A, National Archives; Howard Letter, March 28, 1866, FOR-A, National Archives; Lafayette County Letters Received Register, July 1867 to January 1868, FOR-A, National Archives; Ord to Howard, June 11, 1868, AC-A, National Archives.

36. De Wolf to Bennett, May 31, 1868, AC-A, National Archives; Barnard to Mills, September 30, 1868, AC-A, National Archives; Cresap, *Appomattox Commander*, 238; Adair to Sprague, April 30, 1866, AC-A, National Archives; De Wolf to Bennett, May 31, 1868, AC-A, National Archives; D. H. Williams Report, September 18, 1865, AC-A, National Archives; Smith to Bennett, July 6, 1867, FOR-A, National Archives; Barker to Sargent, July 11, 1865, AC-A, National Archives.

CHAPTER 3

1. Eugene Genovese, *Roll, Jordan, Roll: The World the Slaves Made* (New York: Random House, 1872); George Rawick, *From Sundown to Sunup: The Making of the Black Community* (Westport, Conn.: Greenwood Pub. Co., 1972); John Boles, *Black Southerners, 1618–1869* (Lexington: University of Kentucky Press, 1983); Charles Joyner, *Down by the Riverside: A South Carolina Slave Community* (Urbana: University of Illinois Press, 1984); John Blassingame, *The Slave Community: Plantation Life in the Antebellum South* (New York: Oxford University Press, 1973); Lawrence W. Levine, *Black Culture and Black Consciousness* (New York: Oxford University Press, 1977); Deborah Gray White, *Ar'n't I a Woman? Female Slaves in the Plantation South* (New York: W. W. Norton & Co., 1985). For a provocative look at the romanticism in much of African-American historiography, see Clarence Walker, *Deromanticizing Black History: Critical Essays and Reappraisals* (Knoxville: University of Tennessee Press, 1991). See also Elizabeth Fox-Genovese, *Within the Plantation Household: Black and White Women of the Old South* (Chapel Hill: University of North Carolina Press, 1988).

2. Quoted in Leon F. Litwack, *Been in the Storm So Long: The Aftermath of Slavery* (New York: Alfred A. Knopf, 1979), 247; Sterling Stuckey, *Slave Culture: Nationalist Theory and the Foundations of Black America* (New York: Oxford University Press, 1987), 195–99.

3. Litwack, *Been in the Storm So Long*, 248–51; Genovese, *Roll, Jordan, Roll*, 446–49; Rawick, *Arkansas Narratives*, 1st ser., 9:207; Herbert Gutman, *The Black Family in Slavery and Freedom* (New York: Pantheon Books, 1976), 186.

4. Rawick, *Arkansas Narratives*, 1st ser., 9:244, 255, 2:134.

5. Joel Williamson, *The Crucible of Race: Black-White Relations in the American South since Emancipation* (New York: Oxford University Press, 1984), 45; Gutman, *The Black Family*, 142–290, 365–400; Genovese, *Roll, Jordan, Roll*, 450–519; Litwack, *Been in the Storm So Long*, 229–46. See also Steven Mintz, *A Prison of Expectations: The Family in Victorian Culture* (New York: New York University Press, 1983).

6. Jacqueline Jones, *Labor of Love, Labor of Sorrow: Black Women, Work, and the Family from Slavery to the Present* (New York: Vintage Books, 1985), 46; O'Brien to Sprague, July 7, 1865, AC-A, National Archives; Carhart Letters, November 23 and 29, 1865, FOR-A, National Archives.

7. Little Rock Report, September 24, 1866, AC-A, National Archives; Litwack, *Been in the Storm So Long*, 229–38.

8. Dianna Brown letter, September 6, 1866, FOR-A, National Archives; Polly Goodloe Petition, April 26, 1867, FOR-A, National Archives; Letter to George Waller, June 4, 1867, FOR-A, National Archives; Ellen Hands Letter, March 13, 1868, FOR-A, National Archives; Stuart to Sargent, October 11, 1865, FOR-A, National Archives; Johnson to Abel, April 27, 1866, FOR-A, National Archives; Dawes to Smith, May 16, 1867, AC-A, National Archives.

9. Murphy to Sprague, March 22, 1866, AC-A, National Archives; Deposition, *Smith v. Owen*, October 29, 1866, FOR-A, National Archives; Deposition, *Taylor v. Nickelson*, March 3, 1868, FOR-A, National Archives.

10. Rawick, *Arkansas Narratives*, 1st ser., 10:266; Froth to Bell, April 18, 1867, FOR-A, National Archives.

11. John Scroggins Letter, July 25, 1867, FOR-A, National Archives; Dawes to Tyler, November 30, 1866, FOR-A, National Archives; Predmore to Smith, July 31, 1867, FOR-A, National Archives; Predmore to Dawes, October 14, 1866, FOR-A, National Archives.

12. Genovese, *Roll, Jordan, Roll*, 458–81; Blassingame, *The Slave Community*, 149–91.

13. Winthrop Jordan, *White over Black: Attitudes toward the Negro, 1550–1812* (Chapel Hill: University of North Carolina Press, 1968), 3–43.

14. *Little Rock Daily Pantograph*, February 24, 1866; *U.S. v. John Roger*, September 6, 1865, AC-A, National Archives; Sprague Circular, March 31, 1866, AC-A, National Archives; *Little Rock Arkansas Daily Gazette*, December 10, 1868.

15. Thorp to Tyler, January 6, 1867, AC-A, National Archives; Jennings Report, July 26, 1867, AC-A, National Archives.

16. Dyer to Pofoe, September 21, 1867, FOR-A, National Archives; Mary Reed Deposition, July 22, 1867, FOR-A, National Archives; *Green v. Skearrer*, Entry 329, FOR-A, National Archives; *Harris v. Robinson*, September 25, 1867, FOR-A, National Archives; Andrew Bateman Deposition, undated, FOR-A, National Archives; Sprague to Sweeney, July 3, 1867, AC-A, National Archives.

17. Predmore to Ord, November 30, 1866, FOR-A, National Archives; Predmore to Stevenson, October 19, 1866, FOR-A, National Archives.

18. DeWolf to Bennett, February 4, 1868, AC-A, National Archives; Shaw Report, June 8, 1867, AC-A, National Archives.

19. Bayner Plantation Record, April 13, 1867, FOR-A, National Archives.

20. Rawick, *Arkansas Narratives*, 1st ser., 9:320.

21. Hempstead County Marriage Records, Entry 495, FOR-A, National Archives; Arkadelphia Marriage Records, Entry 285, FOR-A, National Archives; Jacksonport Marriage Records, Entry 349, FOR-A, National Archives; Pine Bluff Marriage Records, Entry 419, FOR-A, National Archives; Madison Marriage Records, Entry 383, FOR-A, National Archives.

22. Ibid.

23. Pine Bluff Marriage Records, Entry 419, FOR-A, National Archives.

24. Rawick, *Arkansas Narratives*, 1st ser., 8 (pt. 2):47

25. Sprague to Sweeney, March 22, 1866, AC-A, National Archives; Pine Bluff Marriage Records, Entry 419, FOR-A, National Archives; Arkadelphia Marriage Records, Entry 285, FOR-A, National Archives; Barker to Sprague, July 10, 1866, FOR-A, National Archives.

26. Miller to Colby, November 1, 1867, AC-A, National Archives; William Brian Report, August 31, 1867, FOR-A, National Archives; E. G. Barker Report, December 9, 1867, FOR-A, National Archives.

27. Predmore to Mills, October 1, 1868, FOR-A, National Archives; Geisreiter to Bennett, August 7, 1868, FOR-A, National Archives; E. G. Barker Report, December 9, 1867, FOR-A, National Archives.

28. *Harry Smith v. Dr. L. G. Williams*, October 7, 1867, FOR-A, National Archives; Brian to Scott, December 16, 1867, FOR-A, National Archives; William Brian Report, April 30, 1868, AC-A, National Archives; Eliza Ebberson Affidavit, May 10, 1866, FOR-A, National Archives.

29. Sweeney Report, April 28, 1867, AC-A, National Archives; *Fort Smith Weekly Herald*, October 12, 1867; Stuckey, *Slave Culture*, 200.

30. Plymouth Hale Deposition, March 10, 1867, FOR-A, National Archives; Richardson, *Christian Reconstruction*, 157; Clarence Walker, *A Rock in a Weary Land: The African Methodist Episcopal Church during the Civil War and Reconstruction* (Baton Rouge: Louisiana State University Press, 1982), 82.

31. Pine Bluff Marriage Records, Entry 419, FOR-A, National Archives; Rawick, *Arkansas Narratives*, 1st ser., 10:328; Joel Williamson, *New People: Miscegenation and Mulattoes in the United States* (New York: Free Press, 1980), 65.

32. Sprague Report, May 14, 1867, AC-A, National Archives.

33. *Little Rock Weekly Arkansas State Gazette*, February 18, 1868; Paul C. Palmer, "Miscegenation as an Issue in the Arkansas Constitutional Convention of 1868," *Arkansas Historical Quarterly* 24 (summer 1965): 100, 104; Cal Ledbetter Jr., "The Constitutional Convention of 1868: Conqueror's Constitution or Constitutional Continuity?" *Arkansas Historical Quarterly* 49 (spring 1985): 28–30; Palmer, "Miscegenation," 111; *Little Rock Arkansas Daily Gazette*, February 11, 1868.

34. *Little Rock Arkansas Daily Gazette*, August 9, 1867; *Batesville North Arkansas Times*, August 3, 1867.

35. Columbia County Church Records, #47, Little Rock, Arkansas History Commission; Springer to Sprague, December 31, 1865, AC-A, National Archives; Walker, *A Rock in a Weary Land*, 53.

36. Hamburg Petition, February 13, 1867, AC-A, National Archives; *Little Rock Morning Republican*, September 7, 1867; Rawick, *Arkansas Narratives*, 1st ser., 8:170, 9:77, 195; Harriet Bailey Bullock Daniel, *A Remembrance of Eden: Harriet Bailey Bullock Daniel's Memories of a Frontier Plantation in Arkansas, 1849–1872* (Fayetteville: University of Arkansas Press, 1993), 102.

37. *Little Rock Weekly Arkansas State Gazette*, December 9, 1865.

38. Sprague to Howard, October 4, 1865, AC-A, National Archives; Pine Bluff Report, Entry 417, June 10, 1867, FOR-A, National Archives; Bennett to Miller, September 9, 1867, AC-A, National Archives; E. T. Wallace Report, July 12, 1866, AC-A, National Archives.

39. Colby to Tyler, December 30, 1866, AC-A, National Archives; Arnold H. Taylor, *Travail and Triumph: Black Life and Culture in the South since the Civil War* (Westport, Conn.: Greenwood Press, 1976), 146; Richardson, *Christian Reconstruction*, 157; Walker, *A Rock in a Weary Land*, 82.

40. Carter G. Woodson, *The History of the Negro Church* (Washington, D.C.: Associated Publishers, 1921), 164–241; Adair to Sprague, March 31, 1866, AC-A, National Archives; Sargent to Perry, March 31, 1865, FOR-A, National Archives.

41. Genovese, *Roll, Jordan, Roll*, 255–79.

42. Inman to Williams, July 31, 1866, AC-A, National Archives; *Little Rock*

Evening Republican, July 1, 1867; Sprague to Howard, May 29, 1866, AC-A, National Archives; Millard to Sprague, April 26, 1866, AC-A, National Archives.

43. Colby to Tyler, November 26, 1866, AC-A, National Archives; Colby to Smith, August 15, 1867, and March 1, 1868, AC-A, National Archives; Inman to Williams, July 31, 1866, AC-A, National Archives.

44. Walker, *A Rock in a Weary Land*, 44; Vetter to Kership, February 6, 1866, FOR-A, National Archives; Entry 319, March 24, 1866, FOR-A, National Archives; Williams to Sargent, August 22, 1865, FOR-A, National Archives; Springer to Sprague, December 31, 1865, AC-A, National Archives; *Little Rock Morning Republican*, May 28, 1868.

45. W. E. B. DuBois, *Black Reconstruction in America: An Essay toward a History of the Past in Which Black Folk Played in the Attempt to Reconstruct Democracy in America, 1860–1880* (New York: Russell and Russell, 1935), 122; Sweeney to Sprague, May 31, 1866, AC-A, National Archives.

46. *Little Rock Daily Arkansas Gazette*, December 13, 1867; Geisreiter to Bennett, September 30, 1867, FOR-A, National Archives; *Little Rock Daily Arkansas Gazette*, March 26, 1868; *Little Rock Weekly Arkansas State Gazette*, September 24, 1867; *Little Rock Daily Arkansas Gazette*, March 26, 1868.

47. Dawes to Tyler, November 23, 1866, FOR-A, National Archives; Barker Report, July 31, 1866, AC-A, National Archives.

48. Predmore to Mills, August 1, 1868, FOR-A, National Archives; E. G. Barker Report, June 29, 1867, FOR-A, National Archives; Sweeney Report, June 30, 1865, FOR-A, National Archives.

49. Predmore to Mills, August 1, 1868, AC-A, National Archives; Willis to Williams, October 31, 1866, AC-A, National Archives; Thorpe Report, April 9, 1868, AC-A, National Archives; Mix to Smith, June 30, 1868, AC-A, National Archives; Sweeney to Tyler, January 22, 1867, AC-A, National Archives.

50. Kay Lehman Schlozman, ed., *Elections in America* (Boston: Allen & Unwin, 1987), 404–1. For a good analysis of the cultural context of politics, see Paul Kleppner, *The Cross of Culture* (New York: Free Press, 1970).

51. John H. Scroggins Report, July 25, 1867, FOR-A, National Archives; Hale to Tyler, May 1, 1867, FOR-A, National Archives; V. V. Smith Report, March 4, 1868, AC-A, National Archives; Geisreiter to Mills, September 30, 1868, AC-A, National Archives; Carhart to Bennett, February 29, 1868, AC-A, National Archives; Carhart to Bennett, May 30, 1868, AC-A, National Archives; Geisreiter to Mills, August 31, 1868, AC-A, National Archives; Mallett to Smith, September 1, 1868, AC-A, National Archives; Inman to Mills, August 31, 1868, AC-A, National Archives; Inman to Mills, October 31, 1868, AC-A, National Archives; Predmore to Smith, November 3, 1868, AC-A, National Archives; Williams to Mills, August 3, 1868, AC-A, National Archives.

52. Rawick, *Arkansas Narratives*, 1st ser., 10:56; *Batesville North Arkansas Times*, August 17, 1867; Diane Neale, "Seduction, Accommodation, or Realism? Tabbs Gross and the *Arkansas Freeman*," *Arkansas Historical Quarterly* 48 (spring 1989): 57–64.

53. William Morgan Report, September 1, 1867, FOR-A, National Archives; Roots to Williams, February 15, 1868, FOR-A, National Archives.

54. Thibaut to Bennett, November 1, 1867, AC-A, National Archives; Gross to Bennett, August 1, 1867, FOR-A, National Archives; Geisreiter to Bennett, September 30, 1867, FOR-A, National Archives.

55. *Little Rock Evening Republican*, June 11, 1867; Carhart to Bennett, August 31, 1867, AC-A, National Archives; Minutes of the Little Rock Republican Club, 1867–1868, Minutes, August 17, 1867, SMC, Box 65:4, Arkansas History Commission, Little Rock.

56. Edward Magdol, *A Right to the Land: Essays on the Freedmen's Community* (Westport, Conn.: Greenwood Press, 1977), 123; Bentley, *Freedmen's Bureau*, 199; Geisreiter to Mills, November 2, 1868, AC-A, National Archives; *Little Rock Evening Republican*, November 1, 1867.

57. *Little Rock Weekly Arkansas State Gazette*, May 14 and October 22, 1867; Taylor, *Travail and Triumph*, 13; Union League of America: State Council of Arkansas, 1871, October 7, 1871 Report, SMC, Box 21, No. 6, Arkansas History Commission, Little Rock.

58. *Little Rock Weekly Arkansas State Gazette*, September 24, 1867; *Little Rock Daily Arkansas Gazette*, March 26, 1868; *Little Rock Weekly Arkansas State Gazette*, April 9, 1867; Dawes Letter, April 3, 1867, FOR-A, National Archives.

59. Minutes of the Little Rock Republican Club, 1867–68, Minutes, December 14, 1867, Box 64, No. 4, Arkansas History Commission, Little Rock.

60. *Little Rock Daily Arkansas Gazette*, July 12, 28, 1867, August 11, 1868.

61. *Little Rock Evening Republican*, June 4, 11, 1867.

62. *Little Rock Daily Arkansas Gazette*, August 28, 1868; Colby to Smith, August 15, 1867, AC-A, National Archives; Larry W. Pearce, "The AMA and the Freedmen's Bureau in Arkansas, 1868–78," *Arkansas Historical Quarterly* 31 (autumn 1972): 251; *Little Rock Weekly Arkansas State Gazette*, October 15, 1867; *Little Rock Daily Arkansas Gazette*, November 13, 1867.

63. Geisreiter to Bennett, September 1, 1867, AC-A, National Archives; *Little Rock Daily Arkansas Gazette*, September 27 and October 21, 1868.

64. Geisreiter to Mills, August 31, 1868, AC-A, National Archives; Main to Mills, August 31, 1868, AC-A, National Archives; Inman to Mills, August 31, 1868, AC-A, National Archives; *Little Rock Weekly Arkansas State Gazette*, September 15, 1868; *Little Rock Daily Arkansas Gazette*, January 19, 1869.

65. *Little Rock Weekly Arkansas State Gazette*, August 18, 1868; *Little Rock Daily Arkansas Gazette*, August 19, 22, 23, 1868, January 19, 1869; *Fort Smith Weekly Herald*, September 19, 1868; *Pine Bluff Daily Dispatch*, September 21, 1867.

66. *Pine Bluff Daily Dispatch*, April 27, 1867; *Little Rock Weekly Arkansas State Gazette*, April 16, 1867; Williams to Mills, August 31, 1868, FOR-A, National Archives; Inman to Mills, July 31, 1868, AC-A, National Archives; William Brian Report, October 31, 1868, AC-A, National Archives.

67. Predmore to Smith, September 7, 1867, FOR-A, National Archives; Benson to Smith, August 23, 1867, AC-A, National Archives; McCullough to Bennett, August 31, 1867, AC-A, National Archives; Benson to Smith, July 31, 1867, AC-A, National Archives; Smith to Howard, April 23, 1868, AC-A, National

Archives; Watson to Mills, August 31, 1868, AC-A, National Archives; *Little Rock Morning Republican*, October 26, 1868.

68. Rawick, *Arkansas Narratives*, 1st ser., 11 (pt, 7):4; *Little Rock Morning Republican*, March 25 and September 15, 1868; Inman to Bennett, March 31, 1868, AC-A, National Archives; Barker to Mills, September 30, 1868, AC-A, National Archives; Predmore to Smith, November 3, 1868, AC-A, National Archives.

69. *Little Rock Morning Republican*, March 25, 1868.

70. William Morgan Report, September 1, 1867, FOR-A, National Archives; *Little Rock Evening Republican*, July 8, 1867; Roots to Williams, February 15, 1868, FOR-A, National Archives; *Little Rock Evening Republican*, August 6, 1867.

71. *Pine Bluff Daily Dispatch*, April 27, 1867; *Little Rock Weekly Arkansas State Gazette*, April 19, 1867; *Pine Bluff Daily Dispatch*, November 16, 1867; *Little Rock Weekly Arkansas State Gazette*, November 12, 1867; Geisreiter to Mills, November 2, 1868, AC-A, National Archives.

72. *Little Rock Weekly Arkansas State Gazette*, September 24, 1867. Counties with a black majority of voters were Chicot, Crittenden, Desha, Jefferson, Lafayette, Monroe, Phillips, and Pulaski. Blacks and whites were nearly equally divided in Ashley, Hempstead, Little River, Mississippi, Ouachita, St. Francis, and Union Counties. Taylor, *Travail and Triumph*, 14.

73. E. G. Barker Report, March 18, 1868, FOR-A, National Archives; *Little Rock Morning Republican*, May 2, 1868; Carhart to Bennett, November 30, 1867, AC-A, National Archives.

74. Predmore to Mills, December 21, 1868, AC-A, National Archives; Inman to Bennett, March 31, 1868, AC-A, National Archives; Willis to Bennett, February 21, 1868, AC-A, National Archives; Mix to Smith, March 31, 1868, AC-A, National Archives; Ledbetter, "The Constitutional Convention of 1868," 23; Rawick, *Arkansas Narratives*, 1st ser., 8:48, 172, 9:94.

75. *Little Rock Weekly Arkansas State Gazette*, March 31, 1868; *Little Rock Daily Arkansas Gazette*, March 26, 1868.

76. Thibaut Report, November 12, 1867, FOR-A, National Archives.

77. Eric Foner, "Reconstruction and the Black Political Tradition," in *Political Parties and the Modern State*, ed. Richard L. McCormick (New Brunswick, N. J.: Rutgers University Press, 1984), 60–64.

78. Benson to Colby, October 26, 1867, FOR-A, National Archives; Ord to Taylor, January 24, 1867, FOR-A, National Archives; Predmore to Smith, September 7, 1867, FOR-A, National Archives; Joseph M. St. Hilaire, "The Negro Delegates in the Arkansas Constitutional Convention of 1868: A Group Profile," *Arkansas Historical Quarterly* 33 (spring 1974): 42–46.

79. Willard B. Gatewood, "The Arkansas Delta: The Deepest of the Deep South," in *Shadows over Sunnyside: An Arkansas Delta Plantation in Transition, 1830–1945*, ed. Jeannie Whayne (Fayetteville: University of Arkansas Press, 1993), 3–28.

80. Dyer to Bennett, September 21, 1867, FOR-A, National Archives; Rawick, *Arkansas Narratives*, 1st ser., 10:3; E. M. Main Report, August 31, 1868, Entry 387, FOR-A, National Archives; Willis to Mills, August 31, 1868, FOR-A, National

Archives; Brusard to Mills, August 31, 1868, AC-A, National Archives; *Little Rock Daily Arkansas Gazette,* December 1, 1868, and January 14, 1869.

81. Sprague to Wallace, May 4, 1866, AC-A, National Archives; Predmore to Smith, January 31, 1868, AC-A, National Archives; Geisreiter to Cabel, August 2, 1866, FOR-A, National Archives; Sumner Report, November 14, 1867, AC-A, National Archives; *Little Rock Weekly Arkansas State Gazette,* December 17, 1867; *Little Rock Daily Arkansas Gazette,* December 13, 1867; Gross Report, June 3, 1867, AC-A, National Archives.

82. Eric Foner, *Reconstruction: America's Unfinished Revolution, 1863–77* (New York: Harper & Row, 1988), 95.

83. O. O. Howard Circular, May 15, 1867, FOR-A, National Archives; George Murrell Hunt, "A History of the Prohibition Movement in Arkansas," (M. A. thesis, University of Arkansas, 1933), 34–52; V. V. Smith to Bennett, October 1, 1867, AC-A, National Archives; Thibaut to Bennett, October 1, 1868, AC-A, National Archives; Colby to Smith, October 23, 1867, AC-A, National Archives; Colby to Smith, March 1, 1869, AC-A, National Archives; Smith to Howard, June 29, 1867, AC-A, National Archives; Sweeney to Bennett, July 31, 1867, AC-A, National Archives; Sweeney to Bennett, May 31, 1867, AC-A, National Archives; Thorp to Bennett, August 31, 1867, AC-A, National Archives.

84. Miller to Smith, September 23, 1867, AC-A, National Archives; Colby to Smith, January 1, 1868, AC-A, National Archives.

85. Sweeney to Bennett, May 31, 1867, AC-A, National Archives; Thorp to Bennett, August 31, 1867, AC-A, National Archives.

86. *Pine Bluff Daily Dispatch,* January 5, 1867; Dawes to Ord, January 1, 1867, AC-A, National Archives.

87. Thibaut to Mills, September 1, 1866, FOR-A, National Archives; Rawick, *Arkansas Narratives,* 1st ser., 9:180, 320.

CHAPTER 4

1. Pete Daniel, "The Metamorphosis of Slavery, 1865–1900," *Journal of American History* 66 (June 1979): 88; J. T. Trowbridge, *A Picture of the Desolated States; and the Work of Restoration, 1865–1868* (Hartford, Conn.: L. Stebbins, 1868), 391.

2. Montgomery to Sargent, July 23, 1865, FOR-A, National Archives; Stewart to Sargent, September 30, 1865, AC-A, National Archives; Carhart to Sargent, July 28, 1865, FOR-A, National Archives; William Tisdale Report, September 1865, AC-A, National Archives; Sprague to Howard, August 21, 1865, AC-A, National Archives; Sprague Circular Letter, December 11, 1865, FOR-A, National Archives; Sheriff John Thorp Rules, December 5, 1865, AC-A, National Archives.

3. Report of A. W. Ballard, July 31, 1865, AC-A, National Archives; Roger L. Ransom and Richard Sutch, *One Kind of Freedom: The Economic Consequences of Emancipation* (Cambridge: Cambridge University Press, 1977), 60; James Sellers, "The Economic Incidence of the Civil War in the South," *Mississippi Valley Historical Review* 14 (September 1927): 184–89; Charles E. Seagrave, *The Southern Negro*

Agricultural Worker, 1850–1870 (New York: Arno Press, 1975), 27; *Little Rock Weekly Arkansas State Gazette,* June 30, 1865.

4. Howard Circular #1, July 25, 1865, FOR-A, National Archives; Sprague to Thorp, December 19, 1865, AC-A, National Archives; *Little Rock Daily Pantograph,* July 6, 1865.

5. William Cohen, *At Freedom's Edge: Black Mobility and the Southern Quest for Racial Control, 1861–1915* (Baton Rouge: Louisiana State University Press, 1991), 56, 65; River Passes, February to March 1865, Entry 316, FOR-A, National Archives; Williams to Carhart, September 5, 1865, AC-A, National Archives.

6. Montgomery to Sprague, July 25, 1865, FOR-A, National Archives; Ballard to Sargent, August 5, 1865, FOR-A, National Archives; O'Brien to Sprague, July 7, 1865, AC-A, National Archives. For background on "apprenticeships," see Eric Foner's *Reconstruction: America's Unfinished Revolution, 1863–1877* (New York: Harper and Row, 1988), 201.

7. Apprenticeship Agreement by C. W. Draper, 1865, FOR-A, National Archives; Herbert Gutman, *The Black Family in Slavery and Freedom, 1750–1925* (New York: Pantheon Books, 1976), 410.

8. Saunders to Sprague, October 30, 1865, AC-A, National Archives.

9. Labor Contracts, 1865, Entry 284, FOR-A, National Archives.

10. Labor Contracts, February–March 1865, FOR-A, National Archives.

11. George P. Rawick, ed., *Arkansas Narratives,* The American Slave, 2nd ser. (1941; reprint, Westport, Conn.: Greenwood Press, 1972), 1:91.

12. Joseph D. Reid, "Sharecropping as an Understandable Market Response—The Postbellum South," *Journal of Economic History* 33 (March 1973): 120–25; Harold Woodman, "Post Civil War Agriculture and the Law," *Agriculture History* 53 (January 1979): 322–24; Stuart to Gantt, December 18, 1865, FOR-A, National Archives.

13. Claude F. Oubre, *Forty Acres and a Mule: The Freedmen's Bureau and Black Land Ownership* (Baton Rouge: Louisiana State University Press, 1978), 38; William Tisdale Report, October 31, 1865, AC-A, National Archives.

14. Montgomery to Sargent, July 23, 1865, FOR-A, National Archives; Register of Complaints, August 8, 1865, Entry 283, FOR-A, National Archives; Barker to Williams, December 31, 1865, AC-A, National Archives, Complaints, February 1865, Entry 316, FOR-A, National Archives.

15. Camden Reports, October 30, 1865, FOR-A, National Archives; Rawick, *Arkansas Narratives,* 1st ser., 10:204.

16. Springer to Sargent, August 30, 1865, FOR-A, National Archives; Montgomery to Sargent, August 19, 1865, FOR-A, National Archives; Tisdale Report, September 1865, AC-A, National Archives.

17. Peter Kulchin, *American Slavery, 1619–1877* (New York: Hill & Wang, 1993), 103–4; Ralph Shlomowitz, "The Squad System on Postbellum Cotton Plantations," in *Toward a New South? Studies in Post–Civil War Southern Communities,* ed. Orville V. Burton and Robert C. McMath Jr. (Westport, Conn.: Greenwood Press, 1982), 266–72. This is clearly evidenced in De Valls Bluff's work register where the average planter employed three to four men and an equally small number of women. This

system not only reflected freedperson's demands but also could be the only economically viable numbers that planters could fund. Ransom and Sutch, *One Kind of Freedom*, 9, 44; Edward Royce, *The Origins of Southern Sharecropping* (Philadelphia: Temple University Press, 1993), 84–85.

18. Rawick, *Arkansas Narratives*, 1st ser., 10:340, 90, 246–47, 340, 2nd ser., 2 (pt. 6):267.

19. Foner, *Reconstruction*, 70–71. Foner thinks the phrase "forty acres and a mule" most likely derived from General William T. Sherman's Special Field Order #15 which allocated forty acres of South Carolina Sea Island land and a mule to freedmen. Joyce Appleby, *Capitalism and a New Social Order* (New York: New York University Press, 1984).

20. United States Congress, *Report of the Joint Committee on Reconstruction*, 39th Cong., 1st sess., pt. 3 (1866; reprint, Westport, Conn.: Negro Universities Press, 1969), 77.

21. Kenneth M. Stampp, *The Era of Reconstruction, 1865–1877* (New York: Alfred A. Knopf, 1965), 123; Howard, *Autobiography*, 229; Sweeney Report, June 30, 1865, FOR-A, National Archives; Rains to Williams, August 16, 1865, AC-A, National Archives; U.S. Congress, *Joint Committee on Reconstruction*, 71.

22. Oubre, *Forty Acres and a Mule*, 1, 8–9, 17. See also Edward Magdol's *A Right to the Land: Essays on the Freedmen's Community* (Westport, Conn.: Greenwood Press, 1977), 152–56, for a good overview on the history of confiscatory legislation. Foner, *Reconstruction*, 70–71, 58–59; Paul Skeels Peirce, *The Freedmen's Bureau: A Chapter in the History of Reconstruction* (Iowa City, Iowa: University Press, 1904), 22; Eaton, *Grant, Lincoln, and the Freedmen*, 124, 132–33.

23. Richard N. Current, *Old Thad Stevens: The Story of Ambition* (Madison: University of Wisconsin Press, 1942), iii, 214–15.

24. LaWanda Cox, "The Promise of Land for the Freedmen," *Mississippi Valley Historical Review* 45 (December 1958): 431; Patrick W. Riddleberger, *George Washington Julian: Radical Republican* (Bloomington: Indiana Historical Bureau, n.d.), 238; "George Washington Julian," *National Cyclopedia of American Biography*, vol. 5, (New York: James T. White & Co., 1924), 502.

25. Cox, "The Promise of Land for the Freedmen," 413–19; Howard Circular #15, July 28, 1865, FOR-A, National Archives; Sweeney to Williams, August 17, 1865, AC-A, National Archives.

26. Sprague to Howard, August 7, 1865, AC-A, National Archives; County List of Abandoned Plantations, December 1865, AC-A, National Archives; Crawford County Confiscated Property, 1865, FOR-A, National Archives; Abandoned Property, 1864 to 1867, Entry 421, FOR-A, National Archives.

27. Kenneth Stampp, *Andrew Johnson and the Failure of the Agrarian Dream* (Oxford: Clarendon Press, 1962), 15; *Papers of Andrew Johnson*, ed. Paul Bergeron (Knoxville: University of Tennessee Press, 1989), 8:129; Oubre, *Forty Acres and a Mule*, 38; Special Orders Received, December 1865, Entry 418, FOR-A, National Archives.

28. Mason to Ord, March 31, 1867, AC-A, National Archives; A. S. Dyer Report, August 31, 1866, AC-A, National Archives; Mason to Smith, November 30, 1867, AC-A, National Archives; Smith to Bennett, July 17, 1867, FOR-A, National

Archives; Captain J. M. Cain Report, September 29, 1865, FOR-A, National Archives.

29. Smith to Bennett, July 31, 1867, AC-A, National Archives; Smith to Bennett, July 17, 1867, FOR-A, National Archives; *Batesville North Arkansas Times*, December 21, 1867; J. A. Thorp Report, undated, FOR-A, National Archives; Cole to Thibaut, February 1, 1867, AC-A, National Archives.

30. Complaints, June 22, 1866, Entry 303, FOR-A, National Archives; Thomas Abel Circular Letter, August 10, 1866, FOR-A, National Archives; Campbell to Bennett, December 7, 1867, FOR-A, National Archives; *Acts of Arkansas,* 1866–1867, 298–300; *Acts of Arkansas,* 1868, 225–27.

31. Witenberg to Churchill, September 16, 1867, FOR-A, National Archives; Letters Received, October 1867, Entry 389, FOR-A, National Archives.

32. Geisreiter to Watson, February 4, 1867, FOR-A, National Archives; Lewisville Complaints: *Rhodes v. Lee,* July 4, 1867, *Burston v. Johnston,* July 22, 1867, *Merriman v. Merriman,* July 24, 1867, *Chapman v. Cole,* July 23, 1867, *Wiley v. Williams,* July 23, 1867, Entry 362, FOR-A, National Archives; Predmore to Smith, June 19, 1867, FOR-A, National Archives.

33. Banzhoff to Saunders, October 4, 1867, FOR-A, National Archives; Benson to Bennett, November 28, 1867, FOR-A, National Archives; Cole to Tyler, December 1866, FOR-A, National Archives; Circular Letter, May 4, 1866, Entry 390, FOR-A, National Archives; Circular Letters, July 22, 1866, Entry 390, FOR-A, National Archives.

34. Dyer to Perry, February 2, 1867, FOR-A, National Archives; E. G. Barker Directive, November 30, 1867, FOR-A, National Archives.

35. Orders to South Bend Citizens, October 24, 1867, Entry 428, FOR-A, National Archives; Barker to Sprague, November 10, 1866, AC-A, National Archives; Sweeney Circular, November 12, 1866, AC-A, National Archives.

36. Willis to Bennett, October 31, 1867, AC-A, National Archives; Willis to Tyler, February 1, 1867, FOR-A, National Archives.

37. Lewisburg Labor Contracts, 1866, Entry 312, FOR-A, National Archives; W. C. Cotley Contract, January 1, 1867, AC-A, National Archives; H. W. Ratcliff Contract, February 3, 1868, AC-A, National Archives; Samuel McKaye Contract, December 30, 1865, AC-A, National Archives.

38. Madison Contracts, Sytle & Dumas, November 1866, FOR-A, National Archives.

39. W. C. Cotley Contract, January 1, 1867, AC-A, National Archives; Conway County Contracts, December 3, 1866, AC-A, National Archives.

40. Dunn & Nupell Contracts, December 9, 1865, FOR-A, National Archives; Samuel McKaye Contract, December 30, 1865, AC-A, National Archives.

41. Jones/Hicks Contract, January 4, 1868, AC-A, National Archives; Dunn & Nupell Contracts, December 29, 1865, FOR-A, National Archives; White, *Ar'n't I a Woman?* 161–67.

42. Hamburg Contracts, 1867, Entry 330, FOR-A, National Archives; F. S. Hobbs Contract, Big Rock, Pulaski County, 1866, SMC, Box 9, No. 2, Arkansas History Commission, Little Rock.

43. M. L. Hawkins Report, January 27, 1868, AC-A, National Archives; Shlomowitz, "The Squad System," 266; Lewisburg Work Contracts, 1866, Entry 312, FOR-A, National Archives; Chicot County Contracts, 1867, Entry 354, FOR-A, National Archives.

44. Demographics, 1864–1867, AC-A, National Archives.

45. Hamburg Contracts, 1867, Entry 330, FOR-A, National Archives; F. S. Hobbs Contract, Big Rock, Pulaski County, 1866, SMC, Box 9, No. 2, Arkansas History Commission, Little Rock.

46. Time-Keeping Records, 1866–67, AC-A, National Archives.

47. Dallas County Contracts, Entry 424, FOR-A, National Archives.

48. "Record and Account Book of Mrs. Bayner's Plantation," February–December 1867, Entry 422, FOR-A, National Archives.

49. Ibid.

50. Ibid.

51. Ibid.

52. Ransom and Sutch, *One Kind of Freedom*, 149–70; Lawrence N. Powell, *New Masters: Northern Planters during the Civil War and Reconstruction* (New Haven: Yale University Press, 1980), 88; Henry L. Swint, "Northern Interest in the Shoeless Southerner," *Journal of Southern History* 16 (November 1950): 462; Thomas D. Clark, *Pills, Petticoats, and Plows: The Southern Country Store* (New York: Bobbs-Merrill Co., 1944), 26.

53. Predmore to Sprague, August 4, 1866, AC-A, National Archives; Watson to Tyler, December 31, 1866, AC-A, National Archives; Thorp to Tyler, December 31, 1866, AC-A, National Archives.

54. Watson to Bennett, December 31, 1867, AC-A, National Archives; Geisreiter to Bennett, December 31, 1867, AC-A, National Archives; Coats to Bennett, December 31, 1867, FOR-A, National Archives.

55. V. V. Smith Report, July 9, 1867, AC-A, National Archives; Willis to Bennett, October 31, 1867, AC-A, National Archives; Brian to Bennett, July 31, 1867, AC-A, National Archives; Smith Report, July 9, 1867, AC-A, National Archives; Foner, *Reconstruction*, 408.

56. Glasshoff Report, November 15, 1867, FOR-A, National Archives; Taylor to Tyler, December 31, 1866, AC-A, National Archives; Willis to Bennett, October 31, 1867, AC-A, National Archives.

57. Merchant-Planter Account Ledgers, 1866–1867, AC-A, National Archives.

58. Ibid.

59. Ibid.

60. Ransom and Sutch, *One Kind of Freedom*, 5–11; Clark, *Pills, Petticoats, and Plows*, 26, 124–41; Smith to Bennett, January 9, 1868, FOR-A, National Archives.

61. Henderson H. Donald, *The Negro Freedman: Life Conditions of the American Negro in the Early Years after Emancipation* (New York: Henry Schuman, Inc., 1952), 53; Rawick, *Arkansas Narratives*, 1st ser., 10:157.

62. Rawick, *Arkansas Narratives*, 1st ser., 9:117, 112, 10:293; Donald, *The Negro Freedman*, 71; *Batesville North Arkansas Times*, April 27, 1867.

63. Rawick, *Arkansas Narratives*, 1st ser., 8:114, 10:262.

64. Donald, *The Negro Freedman*, 47; Rawick, *Arkansas Narratives*, 1st ser., 10:130.

65. Rawick, *Arkansas Narratives*, 1st ser., 9:136, 157, 187, 10:28, 99.

66. Sweeney to Tyler, December 31, 1866, AC-A, National Archives; *Little Rock Daily Arkansas Gazette*, June 16, 1867; Habricht to Bennett, May 31, 1867, AC-A, National Archives; Predmore to Smith, June 30, 1867, FOR-A, National Archives; Hale to Bennett, June 30, 1867, FOR-A, National Archives; Gross to Bennett, July 1, 1867, FOR-A, National Archives; Conway County Letters, September 1, 1867, Entry 306, FOR-A, National Archives; *Little Rock Daily Arkansas Gazette*, August 28, 1867; Predmore to Smith, June 1, 1867, FOR-A, National Archives; Fort Smith Letters Received, June 30, 1868, Entry 318, FOR-A, National Archives; Ransom and Sutch, *One Kind of Freedom*, 64; Smith to Howard, December 28, 1867, AC-A, National Archives.

67. Predmore to Smith, July 12, 1867, FOR-A, National Archives; Ransom and Sutch, *One Kind of Freedom*, 64; E. G. Barker Report, November 30, 1867, FOR-A, National Archives; Watson to Bennett, January 12, 1867, AC-A, National Archives; Morgan to Bennett, December 1, 1867, AC-A, National Archives; George Mallett Report, December 2, 1867, AC-A, National Archives; Smith to Howard, December 28, 1867, AC-A, National Archives; William Morgan Report, December 1, 1867, FOR-A, National Archives.

68. Dawes to Tyler, November 30, 1866, AC-A, National Archives; Gantt to Sprague, January 13, 1866, FOR-A, National Archives; Robert Higgs, *Competition and Coercion: Blacks in the American Economy, 1865–1914* (Chicago: University of Chicago Press, 1980), 44.

69. Habricht Report, January 2, 1867, FOR-A, National Archives; Hale to Page, February 28, 1867, FOR-A, National Archives.

70. *Little Rock Daily Arkansas Gazette*, March 7, 1866; Dawes to Tyler, January 23, 1867, FOR-A, National Archives; Willard Gatewood, "The Arkansas Delta," 9; Rawick, *Arkansas Narratives*, 1st ser., 8:25, 11:78–79.

71. Thibaut to Tyler, January 31, 1867, FOR-A, National Archives; Howard to Sprague, January 24, 1866, AC-A, National Archives; Smith to Bennett, March 24, 1868, AC-A, National Archives.

72. Sheppard to Sprague, February 17, 1866, AC-A, National Archives.

73. Edward Smith Deposition, July 29, 1866, AC-A, National Archives.

74. *Little Rock Weekly Arkansas State Gazette*, November 5, 1867; Geisreiter to Bennett, December 31, 1867, AC-A, National Archives.

75. Thomas J. Abel Report, September 30, 1866, AC-A, National Archives; Oubre, *Forty Acres and a Mule*, 91.

76. Rawick, *Arkansas Narratives*, 1st ser., 9:56; Banzhoff Report, September 10, 1866, AC-A, National Archives; Willis to Tyler, May 7, 1867, FOR-A, National Archives.

77. Michael Lanza, *Agrarianism and Reconstruction: The Southern Homestead Act* (Baton Rouge: Louisiana State University Press, 1990), 13–22; Martin Abbott, "Free Land, Free Labor, and the Freedmen's Bureau," *Agricultural History* 30 (October 1956): 150–56; Paul W. Gates, "Federal Land Policy in the South, 1866–1888," *Journal of Southern History* 6 (August 1940): 303–4.

78. Coats to Bennett, November 7, 1867, FOR-A, National Archives; Coats to Bennett, July 7, 1867, AC-A, National Archives.

79. Granger to Tyler, November 30, 1866, AC-A, National Archives; Granger to Mills, August 31, 1868, AC-A, National Archives; Granger to Bennett, July 1, 1867, and October 31, 1868, AC-A, National Archives.

80. Ord to Howard, October 12, 1866, AC-A, National Archives; Granger Report, April 24, 1868, FOR-A, National Archives; Oubre, *Forty Acres and a Mule*, 103; Lanza, *Agrarianism and Reconstruction*, 85; Mark W. Summers, *Railroads, Reconstruction, and the Gospel of Prosperity: Aid under the Radical Republicans, 1865–1877* (Princeton, N.J.: Princeton University Press, 1984), 85–97; Granger Report, May 27, 1868, FOR-A, National Archives; Thibaut to Bennett, October 1, 1868, AC-A, National Archives; Lanza, *Agrarianism and Reconstruction*, 57–59, 42–46; Oubre, *Forty Acres and a Mule*, 109.

81. Ord to Howard, March 15, 1867, AC-A, National Archives; Sebastian County Letters, Entry 318, FOR-A, National Archives; Banzhoff to Ord, March 4, 1867, AC-A, National Archives; Granger to Sprague, October 18, 1866, AC-A, National Archives; Granger Report, February 1, 1868, AC-A, National Archives; Thibaut to Bennett, November 1, 1868, AC-A, National Archives; Oubre, *Forty Acres and a Mule*, 109; Lanza, *Agrarianism and Reconstruction*, 72.

82. Peirce, *The Freedmen's Bureau*, 69–73; Coats to Bennett, January 31, 1868, FOR-A, National Archives; Barker Report, January 31, 1868, FOR-A, National Archives; Williams to Bennett, FOR-A, National Archives.

83. Barnard Report, August 14, 1868, FOR-A, National Archives; Smith to Howard, January 29, 1868, AC-A, National Archives; Arkadelphia Reports, April 15, 1868, FOR-A, National Archives; Watson to Mills, August 31, 1868, AC-A, National Archives; R. H. Barnard Report, August 14, 1868, FOR-A, National Archives; Main to Mills, November 30, 1868, FOR-A, National Archives; Jefferson County Letters, September 31, 1868, Entry 415, FOR-A, National Archives; A. G. Cunningham Report, February 10, 1868, FOR-A, National Archives; Morgan to Bennett, February 1, 1868, AC-A, National Archives; Barker Report, January 30, 1868, FOR-A, National Archives; Brian Report, April 30, 1868, AC-A, National Archives.

84. Lewisburg Reports, February 1, 1868, Entry 306, FOR-A, National Archives; Predmore to Bennett, February 29, 1868, FOR-A, National Archives; Barker to Bennett, January 31, 1868, AC-A, National Archives; Brian to Bennett, March 31, 1868, and January 31, 1868, AC-A, National Archives.

85. Peter James, John Johnson, et al., to Little Rock Freedmen's Bureau, June 24, 1866, FOR-A, National Archives; Hale to Bennett, May 29, 1867, FOR-A, National Archives.

86. Planter Records, AC-A, National Archives.

87. Barker to Bennett, January 6, 1868, FOR-A, National Archives; Brian to Thomas, March 10, 1868, FOR-A, National Archives; Brian to County Sheriff, February 1, 1868, FOR-A, National Archives.

88. Williams to Mills, August 3, 1868, FOR-A, National Archives; Main to Mills, September 30, 1868, FOR-A, National Archives.

89. Charles E. Seagrave, *The Southern Negro Agricultural Worker, 1850–1870* (New York: Arno Press, 1975), 72; Ransom and Sutch, *One Kind of Freedom*, 46; U.S. Department of Agriculture, *Report of the Commissioner of Agriculture, 1866–68* (Washington, D.C.: Government Printing Office, 1867–1869), 58 (1866), 84 (1867), 28 (1868).

90. Rawick, *Arkansas Narratives*, 1st ser., 9:30, 362, 10:51.

91. DuBois, *Black Reconstruction*, 30; Willie Lee Rose, "Jubilee and Beyond: What Was Freedom?", in *What Was Freedom's Price?*, ed. David G. Sansing (Jackson: University of Mississippi Press, 1978), 16; Litwack, *Been in the Storm So Long*, 383; Royce, *The Origins of Southern Sharecropping*, 79–83.

CHAPTER 5

1. McFeely, *Yankee Stepfather*, 20; Peirce, *The Freedmen's Bureau*, 36–44; Bentley, *Freedmen's Bureau*, 48–49; Foster, "The Limitations of Health Care," 363–64.

2. Carhart to Sprague, July 19, 1865, AC-A, National Archives; Sprague to Cobb, August 3, 1865, AC-A, National Archives; Ouachita and Union County Reports, November 30, 1866, AC-A, National Archives; Predmore to Sprague, August 4, 1866, AC-A, National Archives; James Watson Letter, April 30, 1868, AC-A, National Archives.

3. Dawes to Sprague, September 8, 1866, AC-A, National Archives; Sweeney to Tyler, April 26, 1867, AC-A, National Archives; Brian to Phillips, August 17, 1867, FOR-A, National Archives; Geisreiter to Lewis, April 6, 1868, FOR-A, National Archives; Letters Received, December 1, 1866, and September 4, 1867, Entry 318, FOR-A, National Archives.

4. *Little Rock Weekly Arkansas State Gazette*, October 23, 1867, July 25, 1867, and May 12, 1866.

5. Ronald L. Numbers and Todd Savitt, eds., *Science and Medicine in the Old South* (Baton Rouge: Louisiana State University Press, 1989), 199, 152–65; Foster, "The Limitations of Health Care," 365; Ord to Edwards, February 18, 1867, AC-A, National Archives; Rawick, *Arkansas Narratives*, 1st ser., 11 (pt. 7):87; *Eighth Census of The United States*, vol. 1 (Washington, D.C.: Government Printing Office, 1866), 283.

6. Geisreiter to Bennett, June 1, 1868, AC-A, National Archives; Coats to Bennett, February 7, 1868, FOR-A, National Archives; Sprague to Gold, December 4, 1865, AC-A, National Archives; Drs. Covington, Terry, and Carroll Letter, August 26, 1867, FOR-A, National Archives.

7. Hamburg Report, January 29, 1867, Entry 327, FOR-A, National Archives; Abel Letter, February 27, 1866, AC-A, National Archives; Report of May 1866 and December 1867, AC-A, National Archives; John S. Haller, *American Medicine in Transition, 1840–1910* (Chicago: University of Chicago Press, 1981), 327.

8. Little Rock, Fort Smith, and Washington Hospital Reports, September 1867, AC-A, National Archives.

9. *Little Rock Weekly Arkansas State Gazette*, October 28, November 4, March 24, and November 18, 1865; May 1865 Medical Report, FOR-A, National Archives.

10. Hellerin to Sweeney, October 31, 1865, AC-A, National Archives; Cole to Sprague, August 31, 1866, AC-A, National Archives; Thibaut to Sprague, September 5, 1866, FOR-A, National Archives; *Little Rock Daily Pantograph,* April 17, 1866; Abel to Sprague, May 4, 1866, AC-A, National Archives; Chicot County Report, September 30, 1866, FOR-A, National Archives; Dawes to Tyler, November 30, 1866, FOR-A, National Archives; Thibaut to Williams, August 9, 1866, FOR-A, National Archives. For more information on cholera see Charles E. Rosenberg's *The Cholera Years: The U.S. in 1832, 1849, and 1866* (Chicago: University of Chicago Press, 1962).

11. Dr. J. H. Collins Report, July 27, 1867, FOR-A, National Archives; Geisreiter to Bennett, December 31, 1867, FOR-A, National Archives; Sweeney Report, April 9, 1867, AC-A, National Archives; Dyer Report, August 7, 1867, AC-A, National Archives.

12. Rawick, *Arkansas Narratives,* 1st ser., 8:113, 8 (pt. 2):46, 10:27.

13. *Pine Bluff Daily Dispatch,* September 14, 1867; Fort Smith Report, December 1, 1866, FOR-A, National Archives; Fort Smith Report, June 11, 1867, FOR-A, National Archives; Sweeney to Tyler, April 9, 1867, AC-A, National Archives; Sweeney Report, April 9, 1867, AC-A, National Archives; Sweeney Report, July 17, 1867, AC-A, National Archives; Fort Smith Report, September 25, 1866; FOR-A, National Archives; Dawes to Greene, November 10, 1866, FOR-A, National Archives.

14. Hales to Bennett, June 1, 1867, FOR-A, National Archives; Mortality Records, March 1867, Entry 400, FOR-A, National Archives; Habricht to Tyler, March 20, 1867, AC-A, National Archives.

15. Thomas Staples, *Reconstruction in Arkansas, 1862–74* (Gloucester, Mass.: Peter Smith, 1923), 146; Charles E. Rosenberg, *The Care of Strangers: The Rise of America's Hospital System* (New York: Basic Books, 1987), 47–48; Clark to Sewall, June 5, 1867, AC-A, National Archives.

16. *Little Rock Evening Republican,* July 30, 1867; Letter from Napoleon, May 10, 1867, FOR-A, National Archives; Predmore to Howard, October 9, 1866, AC-A, National Archives; Geisreiter to Bennett, May 14, 1867, AC-A, National Archives; Dawes to Sprague, November 12, 1866, AC-A, National Archives; Duvell to Bennett, August 10, 1867, AC-A, National Archives; D. H. Williams Report, September 18, 1865, AC-A, National Archives; Dawes Report, October 30, 1866, FOR-A, National Archives; D. W. Carroll Letter, August 28, 1867, FOR-A, National Archives; Watson to Bennett, May 31, 1867, AC-A, National Archives.

17. Dunn Inventory, March 22, 1866, AC-A, National Archives; Hempstead Inventory, February–March 1867, Entry 306, FOR-A, National Archives; Hospital Rations, June–July 1867, Entry 423, FOR-A, National Archives.

18. Taylor to Smith, December 12, 1865, AC-A, National Archives; Sweeney Report, October 13, 1865, AC-A, National Archives.

19. Lilly to Ord, February 4, 1867, AC-A, National Archives.

20. Geisreiter to Bennett, May 14, 1867, AC-A, National Archives; Miller to Williams, August 31, 1866, AC-A, National Archives; Thibaut to Sprague, September 5, 1866, AC-A, National Archives; *Little Rock Weekly Arkansas State Gazette,*

February 17, 1866; *Fort Smith Weekly Herald,* July 13, 1867; O. O. Greene General Order #8, AC-A, National Archives; McCullough to Sprague, November 30, 1865, AC-A, National Archives; Geisreiter Letter, August 16, 1867, AC-A, National Archives; Sweeney Letter, April 9, 1867, AC-A, National Archives; *Little Rock Arkansas Daily Gazette,* May 14, 1867; Geisreiter to Bennett, August 7, 1867, AC-A, National Archives; *Little Rock Daily Pantograph,* October 30, 1865.

21. Stuart to Sargent, October 11, 1865, FOR-A, National Archives; Cole Letter, June 23, 1866, FOR-A, National Archives; Labor Contracts, 1867–1868, FOR-A, and AC-A, National Archives; Sprague to Howard, May 8 and July 11, 1866, AC-A, National Archives;

22. Staples, *Reconstruction in Arkansas,* 205; Springer to Sargent, August 9, 1865, FOR-A, National Archives.

23. *Little Rock Weekly Arkansas State Gazette,* May 26, 1866, May 7, 1867, September 8, 1866, and October 2, 1866; Duvell Letter, May 27, 1867, AC-A, National Archives; John Thorp Rules, December 5, 1865, AC-A, National Archives.

24. Newbell N. Puckett, *Folk Beliefs of the Southern Negro* (Chapel Hill: University of North Carolina Press, 1926), 358–92; Genovese, *Roll, Jordan, Roll,* 225–29; Rawick, *Arkansas Narratives,* 1st ser., 10:51, 317; Leek Plantation Ledger, 1867, Arkansas History Commission, Little Rock; Merchant Records, 1867, AC-A, National Archives.

25. *Little Rock Weekly Arkansas State Gazette,* January 22, 1867; *Little Rock Daily Arkansas Gazette,* June 18, 1866.

26. Colby to Smith, July 10, 1868, Educational Records, Records of the Bureau of Refugees, Freedmen, and Abandoned Lands, District of Arkansas, Record Group 105 (hereafter cited as ER-A), National Archives; Clara B. Kennan, "Dr. Thomas Smith, Forgotten Man of Arkansas Education," *Arkansas Historical Quarterly* 20 (winter 1964): 312; *Eighth Census of the United States* (Washington, D.C.: Government Printing Office, 1866), 1:508, 506.

27. Joel Grant Report, May 31, 1865, FOR-A, National Archives; *Little Rock Daily Pantograph,* April 27, 1866; *Little Rock Daily Arkansas Gazette,* April 27, 1866; *Little Rock Weekly Arkansas State Gazette,* April 2, 1867.

28. Stuart to Sprague, August 31, 1865, AC-A, National Archives; Cunningham to Bennett, March 5, 1868, AC-A, National Archives; Colby to Alvord, July 16, 1869, ER-A, National Archives.

29. Springer to Sprague, December 31, 1865, AC-A, National Archives; Simpson to Smith, July 31, 1868, AC-A, National Archives; Colby to Alvord, July 16, 1869, ER-A, National Archives.

30. Colby Report, June 30, 1866, ER-A, National Archives; Stickle to Miller, May 2, 1867, Enoch K. Miller Papers, Arkansas History Commission, Little Rock; Colby to Alvord, July 16, 1869, ER-A, National Archives.

31. Sprague to Trimble, March 26, 1866, AC-A, National Archives; *Little Rock Morning Republican,* July 17, 1868; Scroggins Report, May 1867, FOR-A, National Archives; William Morgan Report, December 29, 1866, FOR-A, National Archives; Carhart to J. M. Kelson, February 1, 1866, FOR-A, National Archives.

32. William Morgan Report, December 29, 1866, FOR-A, National Archives;

Colby Report, March 1, 1867, AC-A, National Archives; Cunningham to Bennett, February 3, 1868, AC-A, National Archives.

33. Hall to Bennett, November 7, 1867, AC-A, National Archives.

34. Alvord to Howard, July 1, 1867, ER-A, National Archives; Habricht Report, June 16, 1868, FOR-A, National Archives; J. H. Scroggins Report, May 1867, FOR-A, National Archives; Brian to Colby, June 18, 1867, FOR-A, National Archives; Hersey to Smith, April 30, 1867, FOR-A, National Archives; Barker Report, July 1, 1868, FOR-A, National Archives; Miller to Dawes, March 27, 1867, FOR-A, National Archives; Miller to Colby, March 14, 1867, AC-A, National Archives; Petition to C. H. Smith, July 5, 1867, FOR-A, National Archives.

35. *Little Rock Weekly Arkansas State Gazette,* September 18, 1866; quotes in *Batesville North Arkansas Times,* May 23, 1867.

36. Cunningham to Bennett, February 3, 1868, AC-A, National Archives; Stuart to Sargent, October 11, 1865, FOR-A, National Archives.

37. Miller to Colby, May 10, 1867, ER-A, National Archives; Lugenbeel to Bennett, February 5, 1868, AC-A, National Archives; Lugenbeel Report, May 5, 1868, FOR-A, National Archives.

38. Richardson, *Christian Reconstruction,* 37; Foner, *Reconstruction,* 477; Colby to Smith, August 15, 1867, ER-A, National Archives; Colby to Smith, July 10, 1868, ER-A, National Archives; Shiphert to Sprague, July 12, 1865, AC-A, National Archives; Sewall to Smith, October 6, 1868, AC-A, National Archives; G. K. Eggleston, "The Work Relief Societies during the Civil War," *Journal of Negro History* 14 (July 1929): 280; *Little Rock Daily Arkansas Gazette,* January 18, 1866; Colby to Smith, July 10, 1868, ER-A, National Archives.

39. Enoch K. Miller Report, May 7, 1867, AC-A, National Archives; Pamelia Hand Letter, December 1868, Arkansas, AMA Manuscripts; Colby to Smith, February 1 and May 1, 1868, AC-A, National Archives; April 15, 1868, ER-A, National Archives.

40. Sprague to Howard, July 17, 1865, AC-A, National Archives; Thibaut to Bennett, October 1, 1868, AC-A, National Archives; Colby to Smith, February 1, 1868, AC-A, National Archives; McCullough Report, July 31, 1867, FOR-A, National Archives; Habricht Report, December 20, 1866, FOR-A, National Archives.

41. Barker Report, June 6, 1867, FOR-A, National Archives; Lugenbeel Report, April 3, 1868, FOR-A, National Archives; Mason to Colby, May 31, 1868, FOR-A, National Archives; Miller to Colby, March 14 and November 1, 1867, AC-A, National Archives; Educational Statistics, ER-A, National Archives.

42. Colby to Alvord, July 16, 1869, ER-A, National Archives; Tyler to Greene, January 7, 1867, AC-A, National Archives; Alvord to Howard, July 1, 1867, ER-A, National Archives; Scovill to Shipherd, Arkansas, AMA Manuscripts; *Batesville North Arkansas Times,* May 23, 1867; Geisreiter to Howard, August 27, 1867, FOR-A, National Archives.

43. Alvord to Howard, July 1, 1867, ER-A, National Archives; Clark to Howard, January 30, 1870, ER-A, National Archives; Miller to Colby, February 28, 1867, ER-A, National Archives; Colby to Smith, March 1, 1868, ER-A, National

Archives; Colby to Alvord, July 1, 1869, ER-A, National Archives; William Morgan Report, February 3, 1868, FOR-A, National Archives; E. G. Barker Report, April 28, 1866, AC-A, National Archives; Geisreiter to Tyler, March 26, 1867, AC-A, National Archives; Colby to Smith, March 1, 1868, AC-A, National Archives; Geisreiter to Bennett, July 1, 1868, FOR-A, National Archives; Willis to Tyler, December 31, 1866, FOR-A, National Archives.

44. Smith to Mills, August 23, 1868, AC-A, National Archives; Colby Report, July 1, 1870, ER-A, National Archives; Brian to Scott, September 20, 1867, FOR-A, National Archives; *U.S. v. John A. Barker*, May 1, 1866, AC-A, National Archives; Rawick, *Arkansas Narratives*, 1st ser., 9:74; Anthony Habricht Report, March 23, 1867, FOR-A, National Archives.

45. Colby to Smith, June 1, 1868, ER-A, National Archives; Brian Report, August 8, 1867, AC-A, National Archives; Barker to Rust, June 1, 1866, FOR-A, National Archives; Carhart to Sprague, March 13, 1866, AC-A, National Archives; Colby to Smith, December 1, 1868, ER-A, National Archives.

46. Colby Report, June 26, 1867, ER-A, National Archives; Colby to Tyler, November 26, 1866, AC-A, National Archives; Colby to Smith, March 1, 1868, AC-A, National Archives.

47. Rawick, *Arkansas Narratives*, 1st ser., 9:228; E. G. Barker Report, May 31, 1868, FOR-A, National Archives; Colby to Alvord, ER-A, National Archives; Educational Statistics, 1866–1870, ER-A, National Archives.

48. Sargent Report, August 30, 1865, FOR-A, National Archives; Colby to Alvord, January 1, 1870, ER-A, National Archives; Dora Ford Report, November 18, 1868, Arkansas, AMA Manuscripts; Colby to Smith, April 15, 1867, AC-A, National Archives; Alvord to Howard, June 1, 1866, ER-A, National Archives.

49. Williams to Bennett, March 31, 1866, AC-A, National Archives; Carhart Report, November 10, 1865, AC-A, National Archives; Colby to Thibaut, October 14, 1867, FOR-A, National Archives; *Little Rock Daily Arkansas Gazette*, May 21, 1867; E. W. Gantt Report, April 23, 1866, AC-A, National Archives; Carhart Report, November 10, 1865, AC-A, National Archives; Millerd Report, January 22, 1866, AC-A, National Archives; Special Order #11, October 31, 1864, Entry 377, FOR-A, National Archives; Grant Report, November 30, 1864, FOR-A, National Archives; E. T. Wallace Report, July 12, 1866, AC-A, National Archives; Colby Education Report, October 6, 1868, ER-A, National Archives.

50. Alvord to Howard, January 1, 1867, ER-A, National Archives; Colby to Alvord, July 16 and August 1, 1869, ER-A, National Archives; Colby to Ord, December 21, 1866, ER-A, National Archives; Colby Report, July 1, 1870, and February 1, 1868, ER-A, National Archives.

51. Station Book, 1866–1869, AC-A, National Archives; Ord to Howard, January 9, 1867, AC-A, National Archives; Station Book Reports, 1866–1868, AC-A, National Archives; Larry W. Pearce, "Enoch K. Miller and the Freedmen's Schools," *Arkansas Historical Quarterly* 31 (winter 1972): 306; Miller to Colby, November 1, 1867, AC-A, National Archives.

52. Paige E. Mulhollen, "The Arkansas General Assembly and Its Effect on

Reconstruction," *Arkansas Historical Quarterly* 20 (winter 1961): 340; Arkansas Constitution, 1874, 31–33; Ledbetter, "The Constitutional Convention of 1868," 16–41; Kennan, "Dr. Thomas Smith," 303–4; Pearce, "The AMA and the Freedmen's Bureau," 247–48; *Acts of Arkansas* (Little Rock: John G. Price, 1868), 2:168–97; Colby to Alvord, November 6, 1868, January 17, 1870, ER-A, National Archives.

53. Alvord to Howard, July 1, 1867, ER-A, National Archives; Colby to Ord, March 1, 1867, ER-A, National Archives; Clark to Howard, January 30, 1870, ER-A, National Archives; William McCullough Report, July 18, 1868, FOR-A, National Archives; *Batesville North Arkansas Times*, May 23, 1867; Little Rock Public School Meeting Report, June 11, 1866, AC-A, National Archives.

54. Willis to Bennett, January 1, 1868, FOR-A, National Archives; Arnold H. Taylor, *Travail and Triumph: Black Life and Culture in the South since the Civil War* (Westport, Conn.: Greenwood Press, 1976), 122; Walker, *A Rock in a Weary Land*, 52; Willis to Mills, October 2, 1868, AC-A, National Archives; Sprague to Howard, January 10, 1866, AC-A, National Archives.

55. Colby Report, December 31, 1868, ER-A, National Archives.

56. Grant Report, March 20, 1865, FOR-A, National Archives; Williams to Tisdale, November 25, 1865, AC-A, National Archives; Pearce, "The AMA and the Freedmen's Bureau," 246; Richardson, *Christian Reconstruction*, 173.

57. Richardson, *Christian Reconstruction*, 173; Smith Order, November 2, 1868, AC-A, National Archives.

58. Mills to Thibaut, September 12, 1867, FOR-A, National Archives; Sargent to Fowler, January 27, 1867, FOR-A, National Archives; Miller to Colby, March 14, 1867, AC-A, National Archives.

59. Tyler to Crane, March 18, 1867, AC-A, National Archives; Colby to Alvord, March 11, 1868, and February 5, 1867, ER-A, National Archives.

60. Henry Lee Swint, *The Northern Teacher in the South, 1862–1870* (Nashville, Tenn.: Vanderbilt University Press, 1941), 23–76; Sandra E. Small, "The Yankee Schoolmarm in Freedmen's Schools: An Analysis of Attitude," *Journal of Southern History* 45 (August 1979): 390; Alvord to Howard, July 1, 1867, ER-A, National Archives; Colby Report, July 1, 1870, ER-A, National Archives; Hugh Brady Report, December 30, 1864, FOR-A, National Archives; Stickle to Shepherd, July 9, 1867, Arkansas, AMA Manuscripts.

61. *Little Rock Morning Republican*, July 17, 1868; Litwack, *Been in the Storm So Long*, 478; *Little Rock Weekly Arkansas State Gazette*, September 18, 1866.

62. Grant to Yearick, November 30, 1864, FOR-A, National Archives; Colby Reports, July 1, 1870, ER-A, National Archives; Barker to Rust, June 1, 1866, FOR-A, National Archives; Willis to Bennett, June 30, 1868, FOR-A, National Archives; Rawick, *Arkansas Narratives*, 1st ser., 9:209, 8:178.

63. Educational Statistics, 1865–1870, ER-A, National Archives; James M. McPherson, "The New Puritanism: Values and Goals of Freedmen's Education in America," in *The University in Society: Europe, Scotland, and the U.S. from the Sixteenth Century to the Twentieth Century*, ed. Lawrence Stone (Princeton, N.J.: Princeton University Press, 1974), 2:626.

64. Scroggins Report, July 25, 1867, FOR-A, National Archives; Trimble to Sprague, March 14, 1866, AC-A, National Archives; Barker to Bennett, June 15, 1866, FOR-A, National Archives; Predmore to Ord, March 5, 1867, FOR-A, National Archives; Alvord to Howard, January 1, 1867, ER-A, National Archives; Fort Smith Report, May 1867, Entry 325, FOR-A, National Archives.

65. Camden Reports, Entry 298, FOR-A, National Archives; Barnes & Buss to Sprague, July 10, 1865, AC-A, National Archives; *Little Rock Daily Pantograph*, November 1, 1866.

66. Sweeney to Smith, July 10, 1868, ER-A, National Archives; Colby to Smith, July 10, 1868, ER-A, National Archives; *Little Rock Evening Republican*, October 11, 1867; *Little Rock Daily Arkansas Gazette*, October 12, 1867; *Little Rock Weekly Arkansas State Gazette*, May 14, 1867.

67. *Little Rock Evening Republican*, October 11, 1868.

CHAPTER 6

1. Predmore to Mills, November 3, 1868, FOR-A, National Archives; George C. Rable, *But There Was No Peace: The Role of Violence in the Politics of Reconstruction* (Athens: University of Georgia Press, 1984), 3.

2. Predmore to Smith, January 31, 1868, FOR-A, National Archives; Reed to Sprague, January 10, 1866, AC-A, National Archives; Thibaut to Tyler, November 6, 1866, AC-A, National Archives.

3. Richard Slotkin, *Regeneration through Violence: The Mythology of the American Frontier, 1600–1860* (Middletown, Conn.: Wesleyan University Press, 1973); John Hope Franklin, *The Militant South* (Cambridge, Mass.: Belknap Press, 1956); Dickson D. Bruce Jr., *Violence and Culture in the Antebellum South* (Austin: University of Texas Press, 1979); Sheldon Hackney, "Southern Violence," in *Violence in America*, ed. Hugh D. Graham and Ted Robert Gurr (New York: Bantam Books, 1969), 505–27; Don Higginbotham, "The Martial Spirit in the Antebellum South: Some Further Speculations in a National Context," *Journal of Southern History* 58 (February 1992): 3–36.

4. Smith to Howard, August 21, 1867, AC-A, National Archives; Geisreiter to Mills, October 18, 1868, AC-A, National Archives; Stuart to Sargent, July 19, 1865, FOR-A, National Archives.

5. Charles Royster, *The Destructive War* (New York: Alfred A. Knopf, 1991), 144–92; Dan T. Carter, "The Anatomy of Fear: The Christmas Day Insurrection Scare of 1865," *Journal of Southern History* 42 (August 1976): 345–65; Geisreiter to Bennett, September 30, 1867, FOR-A, National Archives; Campbell to Bennett, December 31, 1867, FOR-A, National Archives; Martin to Smith, October 31, 1868, FOR-A, National Archives.

6. Thorp Report, February 2, 1867, FOR-A, National Archives; Morgan Report, January 8, 1867, FOR-A, National Archives; Inman to Bennett, March 31, 1868, AC-A, National Archives; Mason to Smith, January 31, 1868, AC-A, National Archives.

7. Register of Complaints, August 13, 1867, Entry 362, FOR-A, National Archives; Kenneth Stampp, *The Peculiar Institution: Slavery in the Antebellum South* (New York: Vintage Books, 1956), 173; *Little Rock Weekly Arkansas State Gazette,* June 24, 1865.

8. Thorp Report, November 21, 1867, Entry 297, FOR-A, National Archives; Barker Report, March 18, 1868, Entry 387, FOR-A, National Archives; Hale to Page, February 28, 1867, FOR-A, National Archives; Barnard to Mills, August 14, 1868, FOR-A, National Archives.

9. Watson Report, December 7, 1866, Entry 338, FOR-A, National Archives; Ballard to Thibaut, October 13, 1866, AC-A, National Archives; *Little Rock Weekly Arkansas State Gazette,* February 18, 1868.

10. Cain Report, September 29, 1865, Entry 296, FOR-A, National Archives; Geisreiter to Bennett, June 1, 1868, AC-A, National Archives; Abel Report, September 30, 1866, Entry 351, FOR-A, National Archives; Stuart to Sargent, October 31, 1865, AC-A, National Archives.

11. Stuart to Sargent, July 19, 1865, FOR-A, National Archives; Helena Report, August 8, 1866, AC-A, National Archives; Sprague to Howard, June 7, 1866, AC-A, National Archives.

12. Wiley Deposition, May 24, 1867, Entry 331, FOR-A, National Archives; McCullough Deposition, May 24, 1867, Entry 331, FOR-A, National Archives; Holanary Deposition, October 29, 1866, Entry 303, FOR-A, National Archives; Taylor Report, March 21, 1867, Entry 326, FOR-A, National Archives; Cobb Deposition, June 14, 1867, AC-A, National Archives; Watson to Williams, December 8, 1867, FOR-A, National Archives.

13. McCullough Report, January 4, 1867, Entry 315, FOR-A, National Archives; Carhart to Sargent, October 30, 1865, FOR-A, National Archives; Mott Deposition, April 9, 1868, FOR-A, National Archives; Sweeney to Tyler, March 12, 1867, AC-A, National Archives; Colby Reports, July 1, 1870, ER-A, National Archives.

14. Williams Report, December 31, 1866, FOR-A, National Archives; Habricht Report, March 21, 1868, FOR-A, National Archives; Cunningham to Mills, August 1868, AC-A, National Archives; Sprague to Reynolds, January 17, 1866, AC-A, National Archives; Barker Report, August 14, 1866, FOR-A, National Archives; Martin Report, November 11, 1868, AC-A, National Archives; William Richter, "'A Dear Little Job': Second Lieutenant Hiram Willis, Freedmen's Bureau Agent in Southwestern Arkansas, 1865–68," *Arkansas Historical Quarterly* 50 (summer 1990): 197–98,; Mason to Murphy, January 26, 1868, FOR-A, National Archives.

15. Willis to Tyler, December 31, 1868, FOR-A, National Archives; Willis to Bennett, September 30, 1867, FOR-A, National Archives; Willis to Tyler, March 18, 1867, FOR-A, National Archives; Willis to Tourtellotte, September 14, 1867, FOR-A, National Archives.

16. Willis to Tyler, December 31, 1866, FOR-A, National Archives; Richter, "A Dear Little Job," 190; Willis to Bennett, January 4, 1868, FOR-A, National Archives; Willis to Tyler, November 6, 1866, FOR-A, National Archives.

17. Boyd W. Johnson, "Cullen Montgomery Baker: The Arkansas-Texas Desperado," *Arkansas Historical Quarterly* 25 (autumn 1966): 229–30, 232–34, 236; Smith to Bennett, November 30, 1867, FOR-A, National Archives.

18. Martin to Smith, October 31, 1868, FOR-A, National Archives; Allen W. Trelease, *White Terror: The Ku Klux Klan Conspiracy and Southern Reconstruction* (New York: Harper & Row, 1971), 151–52.

19. Mason to Colby, May 31, 1868, FOR-A, National Archives; Ord to Howard, March 15, 1867, AC-A, National Archives; Watson to Tyler, November 30, 1866, AC-A, National Archives; Dyer to Lattimore, May 24, 1866, FOR-A, National Archives.

20. Banzhoff Report, March 7, 1867, AC-A, National Archives; Banzhoff to Ord, March 7, 1867, AC-A, National Archives.

21. Wallace Report, August 7, 1866, AC-A, National Archives.

22. Trelease, *White Terror*, 99; Stanley Horn, *Invisible Empire: The Story of the Ku Klux Klan, 1866–1871* (Montclair, N. J.: Patterson Smith, 1969), 4–73.

23. William Brian Report, November 30, 1868, AC-A, National Archives; *Little Rock Morning Republican*, May 2, 1868; Deposition of T. H. Peck, April 9, 1868, FOR-A, National Archives; Simpson to Smith, April 30, 1868, AC-A, National Archives.

24. Barker to Mills, October 31, 1868, AC-A, National Archives; Rawick, *Arkansas Narratives*, 1st ser., 11:30.

25. Trelease, *White Terror*, 55; *Little Rock Weekly Arkansas State Gazette*, June 30, 1868; Mott Deposition, April 9, 1868, FOR-A, National Archives; Carhart to Bennett, April 30, 1868, AC-A, National Archives; Thorp Report, April 30, 1868, AC-A, National Archives.

26. Rawick, *Arkansas Narratives*, 1st ser., 9:94, 41; Geisreiter to Mills, November 2, 1868, AC-A, National Archives; Trelease, *White Terror*, 56–57.

27. Trelease, *White Terror*, 170, 180; Predmore to Smith, November 3, 1868, AC-A, National Archives.

28. Main to Mills, October 31, 1868, AC-A, National Archives; Rawick, *Arkansas Narratives*, 1st ser., 9:191, 149.

29. Barnard to Mills, August 31, 1868, FOR-A, National Archives; Barnard to Mills, August 31, 1868, AC-A, National Archives; Miller to Mills, November 1, 1868, AC-A, National Archives.

30. *Little Rock Daily Arkansas Gazette*, November 26, 28, and June 10, 1868.

31. Hale to Tyler, January 28, 1867, AC-A, National Archives; Benson to Smith, September 12, 1867, FOR-A, National Archives; *Little Rock Daily Arkansas Gazette*, May 12, 1867.

32. Margaret Ross, "Retaliation against Arkansas Newspaper Editors during Reconstruction," *Arkansas Historical Quarterly* 31 (summer 1972): 151; *Little Rock Daily Arkansas Gazette*, October 23, 1867.

33. Gantt to Sprague, December 23, 1865, FOR-A, National Archives.

34. Ord to Taylor, January 24 and 27, 1867, FOR-A, National Archives; Willis Report, October 22, 1866, AC-A, National Archives.

35. Gantt to Sprague, January 13, 1866, FOR-A, National Archives; Stuart Report, *Young v. Hunt* Deposition, November 30, 1865, AC-A, National Archives; Barker to Moss, December 13, 1867, FOR-A, National Archives; Montgomery to Sargent, July 23, 1865, FOR-A, National Archives.

36. Coats to Bennett, November 7, 1867, FOR-A, National Archives; Gantt to Britton, December 23, 1865, FOR-A, National Archives; Circular #5, February 18, 1867, AC-A, National Archives.

37. Stuart Docket, August 22, 1865, FOR-A, National Archives; Depositions of Cole & Smith, 1867, Entry 362, FOR-A, National Archives.

38. Kirby to Smith, July 17, 1867, FOR-A, National Archives; Willis to Bennett, June 30, 1867, FOR-A, National Archives; *Little Rock Daily Arkansas Gazette*, April 24, 1866.

39. Ord to Howard, February 22, 1867, AC-A, National Archives; Barker to Sprague, May 8, 1866, AC-A, National Archives; Reed to Sprague, January 10, 1866, AC-A, National Archives; Geisreiter to Mills, September 30, 1868, AC-A, National Archives.

40. Thorp to Watson, November 2, 1866, FOR-A, National Archives; Barker to Elliott, January 12, 1868, FOR-A, National Archives; Main to Mills, November 30, 1868, FOR-A, National Archives; Thibaut to Sprague, October 14, 1866, AC-A, National Archives; Predmore to Mills, November 3, 1868, FOR-A, National Archives; Willis to Tyler, December 31, 1866, FOR-A, National Archives; Cole to Tyler, January 6, 1867, FOR-A, National Archives; Watson to Smith, December 8, 1867, FOR-A, National Archives; Winters to Smith, October 25, 1867, AC-A, National Archives.

41. Thibaut Report, November 12, 1867, AC-A, National Archives; Morgan to Bennett, November 27, 1867, AC-A, National Archives; Barker to Sprague, October 12, 1866, FOR-A, National Archives; McCullough to Mills, August 31, 1868, AC-A, National Archives.

42. Smith to Bennett, July 31, 1867, AC-A, National Archives; Smith Report, June 3, 1868, AC-A, National Archives.

43. Sweeney to Tyler, March 12, 1867, AC-A, National Archives; *Little Rock Daily Arkansas Gazette*, November 17, 1867; Gross to Bennett, May 2, 1867, FOR-A, National Archives.

44. Willis to Tyler, December 31, 1866, AC-A, National Archives; Smith to Bennett, July 17, 1867, AC-A, National Archives.

45. Geisreiter to Watson, February 4, 1867, FOR-A, National Archives; Geisreiter Report, June 30, 1866, FOR-A, National Archives; Hersey to Bennett, June 25, 1867, FOR-A, National Archives; Bennett from Morgan, November 27, 1867, AC-A, National Archives.

46. Main to Mills, October 31, 1868, FOR-A, National Archives; Cole to Tyler, January 6, 1867, FOR-A, National Archives.

47. Morgan Report, November 29, 1867, FOR-A, National Archives.

48. Paige E. Mulhollan, "The Arkansas General Assembly and Its Effect on Reconstruction," *Arkansas Historical Quarterly* 20 (winter 1961): 334–40.

49. Arkansas Constitution, 1868; Ledbetter, "The Constitutional Convention of 1868," 39; *Acts of Arkansas,* 1868, 345, 39–40, 166–97, 224–27, 63–69.

50. Scroggins Report, February 4, 1867, AC-A, National Archives; Stuart to Sargent, July 19, 1865, FOR-A, National Archives; Habricht Report, November 24, 1866, FOR-A, National Archives; McCullough to Tyler, January 7, 1866, AC-A, National Archives; Morgan Report, January 29, 1867, FOR-A, National Archives; Sweeney to Bennett, September 10, 1867, AC-A, National Archives; Cunningham Report, August 25, 1868, AC-A, National Archives; Ord to Taylor, January 24, 1867, FOR-A, National Archives; Ord to Walker, January 24, 1867, FOR-A, National Archives.

51. Thorp Report, April 1, 1867, FOR-A, National Archives; Barker Report, March 20, 1866, AC-A, National Archives; Predmore to Dawes, October 14, 1866, FOR-A, National Archives; Ballard Report, February 28, 1866, AC-A, National Archives; Foner, *Reconstruction,* 276–77, 308.

52. Abel Report, May 31, 1866, FOR-A, National Archives; Bowler to Skilman, October 16, 1865, FOR-A, National Archives.

53. Ross, "Retaliation against Arkansas Newspaper Editors," 152–53.

54. Fort Smith Reports, May 4, 1866, Entry 318, FOR-A, National Archives; Mix to Smith, September 12, 1868, AC-A, National Archives.

55. William H. Burnside, "Powell Clayton," in *The Governors of Arkansas: Essays in Political Biography,* ed. Timothy Donovan and Willard Gatewood Jr. (Fayetteville: University of Arkansas Press, 1981), 46; William H. Burnside, *The Honorable Powell Clayton* (Conway: University of Central Arkansas Press, 1991); Powell Clayton, *The Aftermath of Civil War in Arkansas* (New York: Neale Pub. Co., 1915), 71; Trelease, *White Terror,* 154, 157; Otis A. Singletary, "Militia Disturbances in Arkansas during Reconstruction," *Arkansas Historical Quarterly* 15 (summer 1956): 142–43.

56. Trelease, *White Terror,* 159, 162–70; Clayton, *Aftermath of Civil War,* 66–67; Richard N. Current, *Those Terrible Carpetbaggers* (New York: Oxford University Press, 1988), 141; *Little Rock Daily Arkansas Gazette,* November 22, 24, and December 1, 1868; *Little Rock Evening Republican,* September 2 and November 19, 1868.

57. Dyer to Bennett, September 21, 1867, FOR-A, National Archives; Singletary, "Militia Disturbances," 140; Otis A. Singletary, *Negro Militia and Reconstruction* (Austin: University of Texas Press, 1957), 50–65.

58. *Little Rock Daily Arkansas Gazette,* August 8, 1868; Dyer to Bennett, September 21, 1867, FOR-A, National Archives; E. M. Main Report, August 31, 1868, Entry 387, FOR-A, National Archives; Willis to Mills, August 31, 1868, FOR-A, National Archives; Brusard to Mills, August 31, 1868, AC-A, National Archives; *Little Rock Daily Arkansas Gazette,* December 1, 1868, and January 14, 1869; Richter, "A Dear Little Job," 158–200; Brusard to Mills, August 31, 1868, AC-A, National Archives.

59. E. M. Main Report, August 31, 1868, Entry 387, FOR-A, National Archives; Willis to Mills, August 31, 1868, AC-A, National Archives; *Little Rock Daily Arkansas Gazette,* October 15, 1867, and January 16, 1869; Main to Mills, August 31, 1868, AC-A, National Archives.

60. Stuart to Gantt, December 18, 1865, FOR-A, National Archives; Barnard

to Mills, August 31, 1868, FOR-A, National Archives; Mix to Sprague, April 30, 1866, AC-A, National Archives; Sprague to Wallace, May 4, 1866, AC-A, National Archives; Predmore to Smith, January 31, 1868, AC-A, National Archives; Geisreiter to Cabel, August 2, 1866, FOR-A, National Archives; Sumners Report, November 14, 1867, AC-A, National Archives; *Little Rock Weekly Arkansas State Gazette,* December 17, 1867; *Little Rock Daily Arkansas Gazette,* December 13, 1867; Gross Report, June 3, 1867, AC-A, National Archives.

61. Staples, *Reconstruction in Arkansas,* 366–68; *Little Rock Daily Arkansas Gazette,* December 12, 16, and 23, 1871; *Pine Bluff Daily Dispatch,* February 8, 1872; Current, *Those Terrible Carpetbaggers,* 299–305.

CHAPTER 7

1. Peirce, *The Freedmen's Bureau,* 69–74.

2. Williams Report, December 31, 1866, FOR-A, National Archives; Habricht Report, March 21, 1868, FOR-A, National Archives; Cunningham to Mills, August 1868, AC-A, National Archives; Sprague to Reynolds, January 17, 1866, AC-A, National Archives; Barker Report, August 14, 1866, FOR-A, National Archives; Martin Report, October 11, 1868, AC-A, National Archives; Richter, "A Dear Little Job," 197–98.

3. Willis to Bennett, January 31 and July 13, 1868, FOR-A, National Archives.

4. *State of Arkansas v. Robert Hunt,* November 14, 1867, Entry 429, FOR-A, National Archives; *Little Rock Weekly Arkansas State Gazette,* February 11, 1868.

5. Thibaut to Sprague, August 22, 1866, FOR-A, National Archives; Laura Scott Butler, "History of Clark County," in *Publication of Arkansas History Association,* ed. John Hugh Reynolds (Little Rock, Ark.: Democratic Printing & Lithography, 1906), 1:391; Hamburg Citizens to Ord, February 13, 1867, AC-A, National Archives; Predmore to Dawes, October 14, 1866, AC-A, National Archives.

6. *Little Rock Weekly Arkansas State Gazette,* October 23, 1866; *Little Rock Daily Arkansas Gazette,* February 27 and August 21, 1866.

7. Williams to Ord, September 27, 1866, AC-A, National Archives; *Little Rock Daily Arkansas Gazette,* September 27, 1868.

8. *Arkansas Constitutional Convention: Debates and Proceedings, 1868* (Little Rock, Ark.: J. G. Price, 1868), 428, 437, 431, 429, 438–43, 433, 469.

9. Foner, *Reconstruction,* 170; Eric McKitrick, "Reconstruction: Ultraconservative Revolution" in *The Comparative Approach to American History,* ed. C. Vann Woodward (New York: Basic Books, 1968), 152; McFeely, *Yankee Stepfather,* 328.

10. William McFeely, *Sapelo's People: A Long Walk into Freedom* (New York: W. W. Norton & Co., 1994), 125–26.

11. *Little Rock Daily Pantograph,* May 23, 1865.

BIBLIOGRAPHY

GOVERNMENT DOCUMENTS

Acts of Congress Relative to Refugees, Freedmen, and Confiscated and Abandoned Lands. Washington, D.C.: Government Printing Office, 1865.

Army Adjutant General Reports. Personnel Branch Document File. Washington, D.C. National Archives.

Eighth Census of the United States. Washington, D.C.: Government Printing Office, 1866.

Fourth Military District: General Orders and Circulars. Washington, D.C.: Government Printing Office, 1867.

Journal of the Senate of Arkansas. Little Rock: Price and Barton, 1870.

Ninth Census of the United States. Washington, D.C.: Government Printing Office, 1872.

Report of the Commissioner of the United States Bureau of Refugees, Freedmen, and Abandoned Lands. Washington, D.C.: Government Printing Office, 1865.

United States Congress. Report of the Joint Committee on Reconstruction. 39th Cong., 1st sess., 1865. Reprint, Westport, Conn.: Negro Universities Press, 1989.

MANUSCRIPT COLLECTIONS

Alwood, Evan. Diary. Mary Lee Chapter, No. 87. Arkansas History Commission, Little Rock.

American Missionary Association Manuscripts. Mullins Library. Fayetteville: University of Arkansas, 1864–1873. Microfilm #894.

Hobbs, Fredericks. Papers. SMC, Box 9, No. 2. Arkansas History Commission, Little Rock.

Little Rock Republican Club. Minutes, 1867–1868. SMC, Box 65, No. 4. Arkansas History Commission, Little Rock.

Miller, Enoch K. Papers. Arkansas History Commission, Little Rock.

Ratcliff, W. E. Clipping Book. SMC, Box 14, No. 8. Arkansas History Commission, Little Rock.

Records of the Bureau of Refugees, Freedmen, and Abandoned Lands, District of Arkansas. Record Group 105, Reports of Field Offices, Reports and Files of Assistant Commissioners, and Records of Education Division. Washington, D.C. National Archives.

Union League of Arkansas. SMC, Box 21, No. 6. Arkansas History Commission, Little Rock.

Vance Family Papers. Arkansas History Commission, Little Rock.

Wyeth, John Allen. Reconstruction Days in Arkansas. SMC, Box 72, No. 1. Arkansas History Commission, Little Rock.

NEWSPAPERS

Batesville North Arkansas Times, 1866–1868.

Fort Smith New Era, 1863–1865.

Fort Smith Weekly Herald, 1867–1869.

The Freedman's Journal, 1865–1866.

Little Rock Daily Arkansas Gazette, 1865–1869.

Little Rock Daily National Democrat, 1864–1865.

Little Rock Daily Pantograph, 1865–1866.

Little Rock Evening Republican, 1867–1868.

Little Rock Morning Republican, 1868.

Little Rock Weekly Arkansas State Gazette, 1865–1868.

New York Times, 1865–1869.

Pine Bluff Daily Dispatch, 1866–1872.

BOOKS

Appleby, Joyce. *Capitalism and a New Social Order.* New York: New York University Press, 1984.

Bennett, Lerone, Jr. *Black Power USA: The Human Side of Reconstruction, 1867–77.* Cambridge: Cambridge University Press, 1967.

Bensel, Richard F. *Yankee Leviathan: The Origins of Central State Authority in America, 1858–77.* Cambridge: Cambridge University Press, 1990.

Bentley, George R. *A History of the Freedmen's Bureau.* New York: Octagon Books, 1970.

Berlin, Ira, ed. *Freedom: A Documentary History of Emancipation, 1865–67.* The Black Military Experience, 2nd ser. Cambridge: Cambridge University Press, 1971.

Billings, Dwight B., Jr. *Planters and the Making of a "New South": Class, Politics, and Development in North Carolina, 1865–1900.* Chapel Hill: University of North Carolina Press, 1979.

Blassingame, John. *The Slave Community: Plantation Life in the Antebellum South.* New York: Oxford University Press, 1973.

Blight, David W. *Frederick Douglass' Civil War: Keeping Faith in Jubilee.* Baton Rouge: Louisiana State University Press, 1989.

Boles, John. *Black Southerners, 1618–1869.* Lexington: University of Kentucky Press, 1983.

Bowers, Claude G. *The Tragic Era: The Revolution after Lincoln.* Cambridge: Riverside Press, 1929.

Bremner, Robert H. *The Public Good: Philanthropy and Welfare in the Civil War Era.* New York: Alfred A. Knopf, 1980.

Bruce, Dickson B., Jr. *Violence and Culture in the Antebellum South.* Austin: University of Texas Press, 1979.

Burns, Alan. *History of the British West Indies.* London: George Allen & Unwid, 1954.

Burnside, William H. "Powell Clayton." In *The Governors of Arkansas: Essays in Political Biography,* edited by Timothy Donovan and Willard B. Gatewood Jr. Fayetteville: University of Arkansas Press, 1981.

Butchart, Ronald E. *Northern Schools, Southern Blacks, and Reconstruction: Freedmen's Education, 1862–75.* Westport, Conn.: Greenwood Press, 1980.

Butler, Laura Scott. "History of Clark County." In *Publication of Arkansas Historical Association,* Vol. 1, edited by John H. Reynolds. Little Rock: Democratic Printing and Lithographing Co., 1906.

Carpenter, John. *Sword and Olive Branch: Oliver Otis Howard.* Pittsburgh, Pa.: University of Pittsburgh Press, 1964.

Cash, Wilbur J. *The Mind of the South.* New York: Alfred A. Knopf, 1941.

Clark, Thomas D. *Pills, Petticoats, and Plows: The Southern Country Store.* New York: Bobbs-Merrill Co., 1944.

Clayton, Powell. *The Aftermath of Civil War in Arkansas.* New York: Neale Publishing Co., 1915.

Coffman, Edward M. *The Old Army: A Portrait of the American Army in Peacetime, 1784–1898.* New York: Oxford University Press, 1986.

Cohen, William. *At Freedom's Edge: Black Mobility and the Southern White Quest for Racial Control, 1861–1915.* Baton Rouge: Louisiana State University Press, 1991.

Cornish, Dudley. *The Sable Arm: Black Troops in the Union Army, 1861–65.* Lawrence, Kans.: University Press, 1987.

Cox, LaWanda, and John H. Cox. *Politics, Principle, and Prejudice, 1865–66.* New York: Free Press of Glencoe, 1963.

Cresap, Bernarr. *Appomattox Commander: The Story of General E. O. C. Ord.* San Diego, Calif.: A. S. Barnes & Co., 1981.

Current, Richard N. *Old Thad Stevens: A Story of Ambition.* Madison: University of Wisconsin Press, 1942.

————. *Those Terrible Carpetbaggers*. New York: Oxford University Press, 1988.

Cypert, Eugene. "Constitutional Convention of 1868." In *Publications of the Arkansas Historical Association*, Vol. 4, edited by Eugene Cypert. Little Rock: Democrat Printing & Lithographing Co., 1917.

Daniel, Harriett Bailey Bullock. *A Remembrance of Eden: Harriett Bailey Bullock Daniel's Memories of a Frontier Plantation in Arkansas, 1849–72*. Edited by Margaret Jones Bolsterli. Fayetteville: University of Arkansas Press, 1993.

Davis, Ronald L. F. *Good and Faithful Labor: From Slavery to Sharecropping in the Natchez District, 1860–1890*. Westport, Conn.: Greenwood Press, 1982.

Donald, David. *Charles Sumner and the Coming of the Civil War*. New York: Alfred A. Knopf, 1960.

————. *Charles Sumner and the Rights of Man*. New York: Alfred A. Knopf, 1970.

Donald, Henderson H. *The Negro Freedman: Life Conditions of the American Negro in the Early Years after Emancipation*. New York: Henry Schuman, 1952.

Dougan, Michael B. *Confederate Arkansas: The People and Policies of a Frontier State in Wartime*. Tuscaloosa: University of Alabama Press, 1976.

DuBois, W. E. B. *Black Reconstruction in America: An Essay toward a History of the Past in Which Black Folk Played in the Attempt to Reconstruct Democracy in America, 1860–1880*. New York: Russell & Russell, 1935.

Dunning, William. *Reconstruction: Political and Economic, 1865–1877*. New York: Harper & Row, 1907.

Eaton, Clement. *A History of the Old South*. New York: Macmillan Co., 1966.

Eaton, John. *Grant, Lincoln, and the Freedmen*. New York: Negro Universities Press, 1969.

————. *Report of the General Superintendent of Freedmen, Department of the Tennessee and the State of Arkansas*. Memphis, Tenn.: n.p., 1865.

Ferguson, John L. *Arkansas and the Civil War*. Little Rock: Pioneer Press, 1961.

Fields, Barbara J. "Ideology and Race in American History." In *Region, Race, and Reconstruction: Essays in Honor of C. Vann Woodward*, edited by J. Morgan Kousser and James M. McPherson, 143–77. New York: Oxford University Press, 1982.

Fitzgerald, Michael W. *The Union League Movement in the Deep South: Politics and Agricultural Change during Reconstruction*. Baton Rouge: Louisiana State University Press, 1983.

Foner, Eric. *Nothing but Freedom: Emancipation and Its Legacy*. Baton Rouge: Louisiana State University Press, 1983.

————. *Politics and Ideology in the Age of the Civil War*. New York: Oxford University Press, 1980.

————. *Reconstruction: America's Unfinished Revolution, 1863–77*. New York: Harper & Row, 1988.

————. "Reconstruction and the Black Political Tradition." In *Political Parties and the Modern State*, edited by Richard L. McCormick. New Brunswick, N.J.: Rutgers University Press, 1984.

Fox-Genovese, Elizabeth. *Within the Plantation Household: Black and White Women of the Old South*. Chapel Hill: University of North Carolina Press, 1988.

Franklin, John Hope. *The Militant South*. Cambridge: Belknap Press, 1956.

Fredrickson, George M. *The Arrogance of Race: Historical Perspectives on Slavery, Racism, and Social Inequality*. Middletown, Conn.: Wesleyan University Press, 1988.

Genovese, Eugene. *Roll, Jordan, Roll: The World the Slaves Made*. New York: Random House, 1972.

Gerteis, Louis S. *From Contraband to Freedmen: Federal Policy toward Southern Blacks, 1861–65*. Westport, Conn.: Greenwood Press, 1973.

Glatthar, Joseph T. *The Civil War Alliance of Black Soldiers and White Officers*. New York: Free Press, 1990.

Grant, Ulysses. *Personal Memoirs of U. S. Grant*. Edited by E. B. Long. New York: World Publishing Co., 1952.

Gutman, Herbert G. *The Black Family in Slavery and Freedom, 1750–1925*. New York: Pantheon Books, 1976.

Hackney, Sheldon. "Southern Violence." In *Violence in America*, edited by Hugh D. Graham and Ted Robert Gurr. New York: Bantam Books, 1969.

Hahn, Steven. *The Roots of Southern Populism: Yeomen Farmers and the Transformation of the Georgia Upcountry, 1850–1890*. New York: Oxford University Press, 1983.

Harding, Vincent. *There is a River: The Black Struggle for Freedom in America*. New York: Random House, 1983.

Hempstead, Fay. *Centennial History of Arkansas*. Chicago: S. J. Clarke Publishing Co., 1922.

———. *Historical Review of Arkansas*. Chicago: S. J. Clarke Publishing Co., 1924.

———. *Historical Review of Arkansas*. Chicago: Lewis Publishing Co., 1924.

Herndon, Dallas Tabor. *Centennial History of Arkansas*. Chicago: S. J. Clarke Publishing Co., 1922.

Higgs, Robert. *Competition and Coercion: Blacks in the American Economy, 1865–1914*. Chicago: University of Chicago Press, 1980.

Holmes, Torlief S. *Horse Soldiers in Blue*. Gaithersburg, Md.: Butternut Press, 1985.

Horn, Stanley. *Invisible Empire: The Story of the Ku Klux Klan, 1866–1871*. Montclair, N.J.: Patterson Smith, 1969.

Howard, Oliver Otis. *Autobiography of Oliver Otis Howard*. New York: Baker & Taylor Co., 1907.

Hyman, Harold. *Lincoln's Reconstruction: Neither Failure of Vision nor Vision of Failure*. Fort Wayne, Ind.: Lincoln Library and Museum, 1980.

Johnson, Andrew. *Papers of Andrew Johnson*. Edited by Paul Bergeron. Knoxville: University of Tennessee Press, 1989.

Jones, Jacqueline. *Labor of Love, Labor of Sorrow: Black Women, Work, and the Family from Slavery to the Present*. New York: Vintage Books, 1985.

Jordan, Winthrop. *White over Black: Attitudes toward the Negro, 1550–1812*. Chapel Hill: University of North Carolina Press, 1968.

Joyner, Charles. *Down by the Riverside: A South Carolina Slave Community*. Urbana: University of Illinois Press, 1984.

Kolchin, Peter. *American Slavery, 1619–1877*. New York: Hill & Wang, 1993.

Lanza, Michael. *Agrarianism and Reconstruction: The Southern Homestead Act*. Baton Rouge: Louisiana State University Press, 1990.

Levine, Lawrence W. *Black Culture and Black Consciousness: African-American Folk Thought from Slavery to Freedom*. New York: Oxford University Press, 1977.

Litwack, Leon F. *Been in the Storm So Long: The Aftermath of Slavery*. New York: Alfred A. Knopf, 1979.

———. "The Ordeal of Black Freedom." In *The Southern Enigma: Essays on Race, Class, and Folk Culture*, edited by Walter J. Fraser Jr. and Winfred B. Moore Jr. Westport, Conn.: Greenwood Press, 1983.

Magdol, Edward. *A Right to the Land: Essays on the Freedmen's Community*. Westport, Conn.: Greenwood Press, 1977.

Mandle, Jay R. *Not Slave, Not Free: The African-American Experience since Emancipation*. Durham, N.C.: Duke University Press, 1992.

Mays, Joe H. *Black Americans and Their Contributions toward Union Victory in the American Civil War*. New York: University Press of America, 1984.

McFeely, William S. *Frederick Douglass*. New York: W. W. Norton & Co., 1991.

———. *Sapelo's People: A Long Walk into Freedom*. New York: W. W. Norton & Co., 1994.

———. *Yankee Stepfather: General O. O. Howard and the Freedmen*. New Haven, Conn.: Yale University Press, 1968.

McKitrick, Eric. *Andrew Johnson and Reconstruction*. New York: Oxford University Press, 1960.

McPherson, James. *The Civil War and Reconstruction*. New York: Alfred A. Knopf, 1982.

———. *The Negro's Civil War: How American Negroes Felt and Acted during the War for the Union*. New York: Random House, 1965.

———. "The New Puritanism: Values and Goals of the Freedmen's Education in America." In *The University in Society: Europe, Scotland, and the United States from the Sixteenth Century to the Twentieth Century*, Vol. 2, edited by Lawrence Stone. Princeton, N.J.: Princeton University Press, 1964.

———. *The Struggle for Equality, Abolitionism, and the Negro in the Civil War and Reconstruction*. Princeton, N.J.: Princeton University Press, 1964.

McWhiney, Grady. *Cracker Culture*. Tuscaloosa: University of Alabama Press, 1968.

Mintz, Steven. *A Prison of Expectations: The Family in Victorian Culture*. New York: New York University Press, 1983.

Moneyhon, Carl. *The Impact of the Civil War and Reconstruction on Arkansas: Persistence in the Midst of Ruin*. Baton Rouge: Louisiana State University Press, 1994.

Morris, Robert C. *Reading, 'Riting, and Reconstruction: The Education of Freedmen in the South, 1861–70*. Chicago: University of Chicago Press, 1976.

National Cyclopedia of American Biography, Vols. 3, 5, 8, and 9. New York: James T. White & Co., 1924

Nieman, Donald. *To Set the Law in Motion: The Freedmen's Bureau and the Legal Rights of Blacks, 1865–68*. Millwood, N.Y.: KTO Press, 1979.

Novak, Daniel. *The Wheel of Servitude: Black Forced Labor after Slavery*. Lexington: University Press of Kentucky, 1978.

Oubre, Claude F. *Forty Acres and a Mule: The Freedmen's Bureau and Black Land Ownership*. Baton Rouge: Louisiana State University Press, 1978.

Peirce, Paul Skeels. *The Freedmen's Bureau: A Chapter in the History of Reconstruction*. Iowa City, Iowa: University Press, 1904.

Powell, Lawrence N. *New Masters: Northern Planters during the Civil War and Reconstruction*. New Haven: Yale University Press, 1980.

Quarles, Benjamin. *Frederick Douglass*. Englewood Cliffs, N.J.: Prentice-Hall, 1968.

———. *The Negro in the Civil War*. New York: Russell & Russell, 1953.

Rabinowitz, Howard N., ed. *Southern Black Leaders of the Reconstruction Era*. Chicago: University of Illinois Press, 1982.

Rable, George C. *But There Was No Peace: The Role of Violence in the Politics of Reconstruction*. Athens: University of Georgia Press, 1984.

Ransom, Roger L., and Richard Sutch. *One Kind of Freedom: The Economic Consequences of Emancipation*. Cambridge: Cambridge University Press, 1977.

Rawick, George P., ed. *Arkansas Narratives*. The American Slave, 1st ser., vols. 8–11, 2nd ser., vols. 1–2. 1941. Reprint, Westport, Conn.: Greenwood Pub. Co., 1972.

———. *From Sundown to Sunup: The Making of the Black Community*. Westport, Conn.: Greenwood Pub. Co., 1972.

Richardson, Joe M. *Christian Reconstruction: The American Missionary Association and Southern Blacks, 1861–90*. Athens: University of Georgia Press, 1986.

Rose, Willie Lee. "Jubilee and Beyond: What Was Freedom?" In *What Was Freedom's Price?* edited by David G. Sansing. Jackson: University of Mississippi Press, 1978.

———. *Rehearsal for Reconstruction: The Port Royal Experiment*. Indianapolis: Bobbs-Merrill, 1964.

Royster, Charles. *The Destructive War*. New York: Alfred A. Knopf, 1991.

Schlozman, Kay Lehman, ed. *Elections in America*. Boston: Allen & Urwin, 1987.

Schwartz, Harold. *Samuel Gridley Howe: Social Reformer, 1801–1876*. Cambridge: Harvard University Press, 1956.

Scott, James C. *Weapons of the Weak: Everyday Forms of Peasant Resistance*. New Haven: Yale University Press, 1985.

Seagrave, Charles E. *The Southern Negro Agricultural Worker, 1850–1870*. New York: Arno Press, 1975.

Sefton, James E. *The United States Army and Reconstruction, 1865–1877*. Baton Rouge: Louisiana State University Press, 1967.

Shlomowitz, Ralph. "The Squad System on Postbellum Cotton Plantations." In *Toward a New South? Studies in Post–Civil War Southern Communities*, edited by Orville V. Burton and Robert C. McMath Jr., 265–80. Westport, Conn.: Greenwood Press, 1982.

Simon, John Y. *Papers of U. S. Grant*. Carbondale: Southern Illinois University Press, 1979.

Singletary, Otis A. *Negro Militia and Reconstruction*. Austin: University of Texas Press, 1957.

Slotkin, Richard. *Regeneration through Violence: The Mythology of the American Frontier, 1600–1860*. Middletown, Conn.: Wesleyan University Press, 1973.

Smith, H. Shelton. *In His Image, But . . . : Racism in Southern Religion, 1780–1910.* Durham, N.C.: Duke University Press, 1972.

Stampp, Kenneth. *Andrew Johnson and the Failure of the Agrarian Dream.* Oxford: Clarendon Press, 1962.

———. *The Era of Reconstruction, 1865–77.* New York: Alfred A. Knopf, 1965.

———. *The Peculiar Institution: Slavery in the Antebellum South.* New York: Vintage Books, 1956.

Staples, Thomas. *Reconstruction in Arkansas, 1862–74.* Gloucester, Mass.: Peter Smith, 1923.

Strickland, John Scott. "Traditional Culture and Moral Economy: Social and Economic Change in the South Carolina Low Country, 1865–1910." In *The Countryside in the Age of Capitalist Transformation: Essays in the Social History of Rural America*, edited by Steven Hahn and Jonathan Pride, 141–78. Chapel Hill: University of North Carolina, 1985.

Stuckey, Sterling. *Slave Culture: Nationalist Theory and the Foundations of Black America.* New York: Oxford University Press, 1987.

Summers, Mark W. *Railroads, Reconstruction, and the Gospel of Prosperity: Aid under the Radical Republicans, 1865–1877.* Princeton, N.J.: Princeton University Press, 1984.

Sumner, Charles. *The Works of Charles Sumner.* Boston: Lee & Shepard, 1874.

Swint, Henry Lee. *The Northern Teacher in the South, 1862–70.* Nashville, Tenn.: Vanderbilt University Press, 1941.

Taylor, Arnold H. *Travail and Triumph: Black Life and Culture in the South since the Civil War.* Westport, Conn.: Greenwood Press, 1976.

Thomas, Benjamin P., and Harold M. Hyman. *The Life and Times of Lincoln's Secretary of War.* New York: Alfred A. Knopf, 1962.

Thomas, David Y. *Arkansas in War and Reconstruction, 1861–74.* Little Rock: Arkansas Division, United Daughters of the Confederacy, 1926.

Thomas, Dean S. *Civil War Commanders.* Arendtsville, Pa.: Thomas Publications, 1986.

Thomas, Emory. *The Confederate Nation, 1861–1865.* New York: Harper and Row, 1979.

Thompson, George H. *Arkansas and Reconstruction: The Influence of Geography, Economics, and Personality.* Port Washington, N.Y.: National University Publications, 1976.

Trefousse, Hans L. *Andrew Johnson: A Biography.* New York: W. W. Norton & Co., 1989.

———. *The Radical Republicans: Lincoln's Vanguard for Racial Justice.* New York: Alfred A. Knopf, 1969.

Trelease, Allen W. *White Terror: The Ku Klux Klan Conspiracy and Southern Reconstruction.* New York: Harper and Row, 1971.

Trowbridge, John Townsend. *A Picture of the Desolated States; and the Work of Restoration, 1865–68.* Hartford, Conn.: L. Stebbins, 1868.

Vaughn, William Preston. *Schools for All: The Blacks and Public Education in the South, 1865–77.* Lexington: University of Kentucky Press, 1974.

Walker, Clarence W. *A Rock in a Weary Land: The African Methodist Episcopal Church during the Civil War and Reconstruction.* Baton Rouge: Louisiana State University Press, 1982.

Walter, John F. *Capsule History of Arkansas: Military Units in the Civil War.* Middle Village, N.Y.: privately printed, 1971.

Wayne, Michael. *The Reshaping of Plantation Society: The Natchez District, 1860–1880.* Chicago: University of Illinois Press, 1990.

Whayne, Jeannie, ed. *Shadows over Sunnyside: An Arkansas Plantation in Transition, 1830–1945.* Fayetteville: University of Arkansas Press, 1993.

Williamson, Joel. *The Crucible of Race: Black-White Relations in the American South since Emancipation.* New York: Oxford University Press, 1984.

———. *New People: Miscegenation and Mulattoes in the United States.* New York: Free Press, 1980.

Woodman, Harold. *King Cotton and His Retainers: Financing and Marketing the Cotton Crop of the South, 1800–1925.* Lexington: University of Kentucky Press, 1968.

———. *New South–New Law: The Legal Foundations of Credit and Labor Relations in the Postbellum Agricultural South.* Baton Rouge: Louisiana State University Press, 1995.

Woodson, Carter G. *The History of the Negro Church.* Washington, D.C.: The Associated Publishers, 1921.

Woodward, C. Vann. *The Burden of Southern History.* Baton Rouge: Louisiana State University Press, 1968.

Wright, Gavin. *Old South, New South: Revolutions in the Southern Economy since the Civil War.* New York: Basic Books, 1986.

———. *The Political Economy of the Cotton South: Households, Markets, and Wealth in the Nineteenth Century.* New York: W. W. Norton & Co., 1978.

JOURNAL ARTICLES

Abbott, Martin. "Free Land, Free Labor, and the Freedmen's Bureau." *Agricultural History* 30 (October 1956): 150–56.

Bigelow, Martha Mitchell. "Freedmen of the Mississippi Valley, 1862–65." *Civil War History* 8 (March 1962): 38–47.

Blassingame, John. "The Union Army as an Educational Institution for Negroes." *Journal of Negro History* 34 (spring 1965): 152–59.

Carter, Dan T. "The Anatomy of Fear: The Christmas Day Insurrection Scare of 1865." *Journal of Southern History* 42 (August 1976): 345–65.

Cohen, William. "Black Immobility and Free Labor: The Freedmen's Bureau and the Relocation of Black Labor, 1865–1868." *Civil War History* 30 (September 1984): 221–34.

Coulter, Nate. "The Impact of the Civil War upon Pulaski County, Arkansas." *Arkansas Historical Quarterly* 41 (spring 1982): 67–82.

Cox, LaWanda. "The Promise of Land for the Freedmen." *Mississippi Valley Historical Review* 45 (December 1958): 413–40.

Cox, LaWanda, and John Cox. "General O. O. Howard and the 'Misrepresented Bureau.'" *Journal of Southern History* 29 (November 1953): 427–56.

Daniel, Pete. "The Metamorphosis of Slavery, 1865–1900." *Journal of American History* 66 (June 1979): 89–99.

Dillard, Tom. "To the Back of the Elephant: Racial Conflict in the Arkansas Republican Party." *Arkansas Historical Quarterly* 33 (spring 1974): 3–15.

Eggleston, G. K. "The Work of Relief Societies during the Civil War." *Journal of Negro History* 14 (July 1929): 251–99.

Foster, Gaines M. "The Limitations of Federal Health Care for Freedmen, 1862–68." *Journal of Southern History* 48 (August 1982): 349–72.

Gates, Paul W. "Federal Land Policy in the South, 1866–68." *Journal of Southern History* 6 (August 1940): 303–30.

Higginbotham, R. Don. "The Martial Spirit in the Antebellum South: Some Further Speculations in a National Context." *Journal of Southern History* 58 (February 1992): 3–36.

Johnson, Boyd W. "Cullen Montgomery Baker: The Arkansas-Texas Desperado." *Arkansas Historical Quarterly* 25 (autumn 1966): 229–39.

Kennan, Clara B. "Dr. Thomas Smith, Forgotten Man of Arkansas Education." *Arkansas Historical Quarterly* 20 (winter 1964): 303–17.

———. "The First Negro Teacher in Little Rock." *Arkansas Historical Quarterly* 9 (autumn 1950): 194–204.

Kennedy, Thomas. "Southland College: The Society of Friends and Black Education in Arkansas." *Arkansas Historical Quarterly* 42 (autumn 1983): 207–38.

Ledbetter, Cal, Jr. "The Constitution of 1868: Conqueror's Constitution or Constitutional Continuity?" *Arkansas Historical Quarterly* 44 (spring 1985): 16–41.

Lovett, Bobby L. "African Americans, Civil War, and Aftermath in Arkansas." *Arkansas Historical Quarterly* 54 (autumn 1995): 304–58.

May, J. Thomas. "Continuity and Change in the Labor Program of the Union Army and the Freedmen's Bureau." *Civil War History* 17 (September 1971): 245–54.

McPherson, James. "Who Freed the Slaves?" *Reconstruction* 2 (1994): 35–44.

Meier, August. "Negroes in the First and Second Reconstructions of the South." *Civil War History* 12 (June 1967): 114–30.

Moneyhon, Carl H. "From Slave to Free Labor: The Federal Plantation Experiment in Arkansas." *Arkansas Historical Quarterly* 53 (summer 1994): 137–60.

Mulhollan, Paige E. "The Arkansas General Assembly and Its Effect on Reconstruction." *Arkansas Historical Quarterly* 20 (winter 1961): 331–43.

Nash, Horace D. "Blacks in Arkansas during Reconstruction: The Ex-Slave Narratives." *Arkansas Historical Quarterly* 48 (autumn 1989): 243–59.

Neal, Diane. "Seduction, Accommodation, or Realism? Tabbs Gross and the *Arkansas Freeman*." *Arkansas Historical Quarterly* 48 (spring 1989): 57–64.

Nieman, Donald G. "Andrew Johnson, the Freedmen's Bureau, and the Problem of Equal Rights, 1865–66." *Journal of Southern History* 44 (August 1978): 399–420.

Palmer, Paul C. "Miscegenation as an Issue in the Arkansas Constitutional Convention of 1868." *Arkansas Historical Quarterly* 24 (summer 1965): 99–119.

Pearce, Larry W. "The AMA and the Freedmen in Arkansas, 1863–78." *Arkansas Historical Quarterly* 30 (summer 1971): 123–44.

———. "The AMA and the Freedmen's Bureau in Arkansas, 1863–78." *Arkansas Historical Quarterly* 31 (autumn 1972): 246–61.

———. "The American Missionary Association and the Freedmen's Bureau in Arkansas, 1866–68." *Arkansas Historical Quarterly* 30 (autumn 1971): 242–59.

———. "Enoch K. Miller and the Freedmen's Schools." *Arkansas Historical Quarterly* 31 (winter 1972): 305–27.

Reid, Joseph D. "Antebellum Southern Rental Contracts." *Explorations in Economic History* 13 (January 1976): 69–84.

———. "Sharecropping as an Understandable Market Response—The Postbellum South." *Journal of Economic History* 33 (March 1973): 106–30.

Richards, Ira Don. "The Battle of Poison Springs." *Arkansas Historical Quarterly* 18 (winter 1959): 312–35.

Richter, William F. "'A Dear Little Job': Second Lieutenant Hiram F. Willis, Freedmen's Bureau Agent in Southwestern Arkansas, 1866–68." *Arkansas Historical Quarterly* 50 (summer 1991): 158–200.

Ross, Margaret. "Retaliation against Arkansas Newspaper Editors during Reconstruction." *Arkansas Historical Quarterly* 31 (summer 1972): 150–65.

St. Hilaire, Joseph M. "The Negro Delegates in the Arkansas Constitutional Convention of 1868: A Group Profile." *Arkansas Historical Quarterly* 33 (spring 1974): 38–69.

Sellers, James. "The Economic Incidence of the Civil War in the South." *Mississippi Valley Historical Review* 14 (September 1927): 179–91.

Simmons, Hugh. "Black History of Okolona." *Clark County Historical Journal* 2 (spring 1978): 24.

Singletary, Otis A. "Militia Disturbances in Arkansas during Reconstruction." *Arkansas Historical Quarterly* 15 (summer 1956): 140–50.

Small, Sandra E. "The Yankee Schoolmarm in Freedmen's Schools: An Analysis of Attitudes." *Journal of Southern History* 45 (August 1979): 381–402.

Sproat, John G. "Blueprint for Reconstruction." *Journal of Southern History* 23 (February 1957): 25–44.

Swint, Henry L. "Northern Interest in the Shoeless Southerner." *Journal of Southern History* 16 (November 1950): 457–71.

Woodman, Harold. "Post–Civil War Agriculture and the Law." *Agricultural History* 53 (January 1979): 319–37.

———. "Sequel to Slavery: The New History Views the Postbellum South." *Journal of Southern History* 43 (November 1977): 523–54.

DISSERTATIONS AND THESES

Huff, Leo E. "Confederate Arkansas: A History of Arkansas during the Civil War." M.A. thesis, University of Arkansas, 1964.

Hunt, George Murrell. "A History of the Prohibition Movement in Arkansas." M.A. thesis, University of Arkansas, 1933.

Pfanz, Harry Wilcox. "Soldiers in the South during the Reconstruction Period, 1865–77." Ph.D. diss., Ohio State University, 1958.

INDEX

abandoned land, 2, 29, 74, 77, 78

Abel, Thomas: adjudicates, 35, 80, 101; health care, 114; violence, 144, 158

Abramson, Laura, 1, 45

abuse: physical, 43–44; sexual, 43–44

Adair, Isaac, 29, 50

Adkins, Green, 126

African American: African heritage, 31; children, 34–35, 83–85, 99, 117–18; community formation, 24, 26, 40, 47–48, 49–67, 168–69; demographics, 24; diets, 96–97; disease, 4, 111–13, 114–19; economics, 69–110, 167–68; education, 5, 61, 66, 103, 122–40, 157; elites, 22, 63–64, 76, 134, 168–69; emancipation, 1–2; family, xiv, 26, 33–36, 75, 84; folk cures, 122; group empowerment, xv; health care, xv, 3–5, 96–97, 100–101; 111–22; housing, 95–96, 103; identity, 23, 31–67; leaders, 22, 63–64; leisure, 66; marriages, 19, 40–42, 45; men, 43–44, 73, 83–86, 99, 104; mobility, 24, 71–72, 75, 98–101; mortality rates, 4, 114–19; names, 32–33, 44; paramilitary organizations, 64; politics, 23, 53–64, 105, 108, 148–51; poverty, xv; preachers, 50–51, 131, 132, 143, 151; racial beliefs, xiv, 134–35, 168–69; religion, 49–53; residency, 23–24; schools, xv, 122–40; self-defense, xv, 65, 160–61, 166; self-reliance, 121, 128–30, 134, 143, 166, 168; sexuality, xiv, 20, 36–41, 137, 143–44; soldiers, 2, 22; teachers, 134–36; theology, 51–52; time, xiv; urban life, 24; voting, 61–63; wages during Civil War, 3; weddings, 40; women, 41–44, 73, 75, 82, 83–86, 99; work ethic, 26–27, 75, 81, 82, 97–101, 108, 137–38

African Methodist Episcopal Church: congregations, 50; politics, 52, 57; race, 47; supports schools, 139; work ethic, 26; youth rallies, 51

African Methodist Episcopal Zion Church, 50

Aiken, Liddie, 24
Alabama: family, 35; health care, 115; labor, 99
Alexander, Amsy O., 99
Alexander, David, 117
Alexander, J. M., 134
Alexandria, Virginia, 100
Allen and Beson, 87
Alvord, John, 137
American Freedmen's Inquiry Commission, 6
American Missionary Association: education, 127, 128, 136; health care, 3–4; help for destitute, 24, 111; labor, 5
amnesty, 78
Anderson, America, 143
Anderson, Charles, 1, 62
Anderson, W. H., 21
Anderson, W. R., 117
Andrews, M. L., 4
Andrews, P. J., 126
arbitration, 74, 80–81
Arkadelphia: adjudication, 74, 153, 154; attitude toward bureau, 28; bureau agents, 21; bureau office, 13; economics, 74, 92; labor, 27, 72, 73; marriages, 41; schools, 123, 126, 128, 130; violence, 144, 146, 152, 157, 163
Arkadelphia Standard, 46, 151–52
Arkansas: black militias, 160; health care, 115; land, 99–101; literacy, 122; wages, 99
Arkansas County: bureau agent, 40; bureau office, 12; destitution, 103; elections, 54; labor, 74, 84, 104; violence, 103, 117, 118, 144
Arkansas Freeman, 54
Arkansas Gazette, 51, 56, 57, 58, 62, 102, 125, 151, 154, 164
Arkansas River Valley, 87, 97, 123, 148

Arkansas State Gazette, 112
arson, 130
Ashley County: anti-bureau sentiment, 165; black soldiers, 22; bureau offices, 12; deaths, 118; labor, 83, 84, 87; violence, 27, 142, 146, 150, 154
Atlanta, Georgia, 100
Auburn, 12
Augusta: agent adjudicates, 155, 156; bureau offices, 17; elections, 62; health care, 121; labor, 70, 71
Ayers, A., 104
Ayers, Willard, 117

Backwell, Isaac, 148
bail, 155
Baker, Cullen, 146, 147, 160
Bale, J. H., 87
Ballard, A. W., 71, 72, 158
Ballard, H. W., 29
Banzhoff, Charles, 81
Baptist, 47, 49–50, 52, 53
Barker, E. G.: adjudicates, 38, 43, 74, 81, 101, 105; aid requested, 52; attitude toward black preachers, 52; community assessment, 103; education, 131, 136, 137; labor, 22, 105, 131; land policy, 29; racial attitudes, 21, 38; violence, 146, 149, 153, 154, 158
barley, 106
Barnard, R. W., 144
Barnes and Burr, 138
Barnett, J. R., 137
Barnett, Lizzie, 96
Batesville: bureau office, 14; Caribbean ties, 47; education, 128, 129, 134; health care, 113; mobility, 101; politics, 56, 59
Batesville North Arkansas Times, 96
Batteman, Andrew, 38

Bayner Plantation, 27, 86–91. *See also* Pine Bluff
Bean, Brown, 34
Bell, J. H., 85
Bell, Martha, 36
Bell, Moses, 58
Bell, S. S., 85
Bennett, Lt. John, 80
Bennett, Lizzie, 116
Bennett's Bayou, 143
Benson, George, 22, 151
Bethlehem Baptist Church, 47
Big Rock, 83, 85
Black, Amanda, 115
Black River, 79
Blair, Henderson, 115
Blair, Louisa, 115
Blassingame, John, 31
Board of Health, 121
Boles, John, 31
Bowler, J. M., 158
Bradley, John, 46, 165
Bradley County: anti-bureau sentiment, 165; bureau location, 12; racial attitudes, 46; violence, 48, 104
Brady, Hugh, 5, 136
Branch, Ann, 40
Branch, Col. Joseph, 117
Branch's Plantation, 123
Brasfield, 24
Bremen, 115
Brian, William: adjudicates, 43; labor, 94, 105; politics, 42, 59; violence, 148.
Bridges, Newton, 73
Bright Star, 61, 146
Brinkley: deaths, 116; families, 26, 36; Ku Klux Klan, 149–50; slaves freed, 75
Brisbin, Gen. James S., 77
Britton, N. A., 125

Brooks, W. P., 117
Brown, Diana, 35
Brown, F. H., 62
Brown, John, 10
Brownsville, Texas, 2
burial societies, 65
Burt and Cox, 87
Burton, J. B., 126
Butler, M. L., 85
Byers, W., 164

Cabell, W. L., 87
Cain, Capt. J. M., 79, 144
Caledonia Iron Works, 77
Calhoun, John C., 99
Calhoun County: bureau offices, 12; death, 118; labor, 84, 87
Callaway, William, 164
Camden: adjudicates, 34, 154; anti-bureau sentiment, 164; black community, 24; bureau offices, 15; churches, 53; debt, 92, 98; education, 5, 124, 128, 131, 132, 134, 138; health care, 114, 118; labor, 70, 71; literary league, 66; marriages, 29; politics, 56, 59; poverty, 111; prostitution, 38; temperance rallies, 65; violence, 2, 29, 48, 53, 79, 143, 144, 145, 149, 158
Camden Constitutional Eagle, 151, 158–59
Campbell, Bishop Jabez P., 57
Campbell, John, 104
Carhart, Lewis: adjudicates, 34, 154; education, 124; labor, 70, 71, 111; requests troops, 29
Caribbean, 47
Carlton, R. C., 156
carpetbaggers, 24, 58, 141, 146, 166
Carrigan, H. H., 87
Carroll, John, 26
Carter, T., 85

Case, Charles, 134
cattle, 107
Center Point, 160
Chambers, Liney, 116
Chandler, Edward R., 123
Chapman, Eli, 81
Cheatham, M. V., 87
Cherokee County, Texas, 100
Cherokee Nation, 115
Chicago, Illinois, 127, 138
Chicot County: black elite, 63, 64;
    bureau agents, 12; education, 22,
    124, 125, 126, 128, 136; labor, 80,
    83, 84; mobility, 99; mortality, 114,
    118; planters, 21; pro-bureau senti-
    ment, 165; transportation, 29; vio-
    lence, 79, 103, 144, 146
Chicot Press, 56, 151
children, 34–35, 83–85
Childs, Thomas, 144
cholera, 112, 114, 116, 121
Christmas, 66–67, 74, 142
churches: education support, 125–26,
    132; origins, 49–53; politics, 51–52
Churchill, T. J., 80
Civil Rights Act of 1866, 153, 154, 156
Civil War, 27
Clarendon, 34, 36, 149
Clark, Adam, 151
Clark, Thomas, 92
Clark County: anti-bureau sentiment,
    164; bureau offices, 13; deaths, 118;
    education, 125, 133; labor, 84; vio-
    lence, 103
Clarksville: bureau offices, 15; land,
    101; violence, 149
Clarksville Standard, 149
class conflict, 28, 168–69
Clay, Robert, 21
Clayton, Powell, 151, 159–60, 161
Coats, Albert: concerned over African-
    American debt, 93, 103; requests

Civil Rights Act, 153; sexual
    behavior, 20, 40; worries over land
    for blacks, 102
Cobb, James, 145
Cockrell Plantation, 126
Cohen, William, 72
Colby, Abraham, 103
Colby, William: political factions, 58;
    religion, 49–51; schools, 122, 123,
    124, 130, 131, 132, 135, 136, 138;
    temperance, 64
Cole, F. M., 81
Cole, Nathan, 21, 28
Colfax, Schuyler, 54
Colored Missionary Baptist Church,
    52
Columbia County: bureau offices, 13;
    politics, 55, 61; violence, 79, 155
Columbus, 157
Commack, N. T., 85
congestive fever, 116
Congregational Baptist, 49
constitutional convention (1868): dele-
    gates, 63; education, 133; elections,
    42, 58, 62, 155; equal protection,
    157; miscegenation, 46; supporting
    bureau, 164–65
consumption, 116
contraband, 3–4
contracts, 70, 73–75, 80, 81, 82, 83
Conway, 96
Conway County: bureau offices, 13;
    labor, 83; miscegenation, 38;
    violence, 151, 160
cooking utensils, 96
Coons, Albert, 143
Cooper, Lewis, 21
corn, 88, 97, 105, 106
Cotley, W. C., 82
Cotley, W. D., 82
cotton: interferes with schools, 131,

132; production, 75, 77, 87, 88, 92, 99, 105; sale, 70, 82, 98
Coulter, D. E., 126
Coulter, J. M., 130
coupons, 82
courts, 155, 156
Cox, Samuel, 7
Cragin, Ellen, 41
Craig, J. M., 126
Craighead County: bureau offices, 13; schools, 51, 131; violence, 151, 160
Crane, Sallie, 32
Crittenden County: conflict adjudication, 104, 105; bureau offices 13; poor whites, 28; work ethic, 22
Crocker, E. L., 85
Cunningham, A. G., 146
currency, 71, 73
curriculum, 136–38
cut worm, 97

Daily Arkansas Gazette, 122, 164
Daily Pantograph, 138
Dale, Hammett, 24
Dallas County: bureau offices, 13; deaths, 118; labor, 83, 84, 86, 88–89; racial attitudes 48
Dangerfield, Texas, 35
Daniel, Harriet, 48
Daniel, Pete, 70
Dardanelle: aid to destitute, 51; bureau offices, 17; conflict adjudicated, 155; economics, 98; education, 124; politics, 58; requests army, 157
Davis, Jefferson, 77
Davis, Joseph, 77
Davis Bend Plantation, 77
Davis Lake, 136
Dawes, William: attitudes on black preachers, 52; attitudes on black

sexuality, 36; health care, 112, 114, 117; labor, 98; politics, 56; violence, 66–67
Deal, Wade, 75
debating clubs, 65
debt, 74, 91–93, 108
Delaney, Samuel, 145, 155
Democratic clubs, 58
Democratic party: opposed by blacks, 23, 78; supported by blacks, 58–59
Des Arc, 24, 101
Desha County: bureau offices, 14; deaths, 118; sexual behavior, 39–40; work, 84
Detroit, Michigan, 159
De Valls Bluff: bureau offices, 16; education, 5, 128, 129, 134; health care, 120; Ku Klux Klan, 60; labor, 73; religion, 53; requests army, 157; trials, 155; violence, 53, 145
De Witt, 150
DeWolf, H. C., 30
diarrhea, 116, 122
Dibrell, Dr. J. A., 121
diet, 96–97
diphtheria, 113
disease, 114–19
doctors, 80, 113–14, 121
Doharty, William, 115
Donaldson and Bell, 85
Douglass, Frederick, 26
drama societies, 65
Draper, W. C., 72
Drennan Plantation, 93
Dressim Plantation, 21
Drew County: bureau offices, 14; politics, 60; violence, 146, 151
Du Bois, W. E. B., 107
Dumas, 82
Dunn, G. S., 83
Duvell, Dr. E. V., 121

Dyer, A. S., 79, 81
dysentery, 114, 116

Easter, 67
Eaton, James D., 136
Eaton, Col. John, 2–4
economics, 69–110, 166–67
Edington, A. A., 117
Edmondson, 113
Education: curriculum, 61, 66;
    funding, 5, 103; bureau work,
    122–40
Edwards, John, 2
Edwards, L. A., 113
El Dorado: bureau office, 17; housing,
    96; politics, 55; violence, 145, 150
elections, 61–63, 159
Eliot, Thomas D., 6
emancipation, 1–2, 46, 75
England, 98, 133
English Birmingham Association, 127
epidemics, 112, 114
Episcopalians, 126
Equal Rights League, 65
Evans, Charity, 115
Evans, W. J., 130, 145
Evening Shade, 16

factions, political, 57–58
Fair Dale Plantation, 117
family, xiv, 26, 33–36
farm animals, 80, 107
farm implements, 71
farming, 97–101
Farrar, Maggie, 134
Fawnwood Plantation, 21
Fayetteville: bureau office, 17; schools,
    132
Fifteenth Amendment, 54, 153, 156
fire companies, 65
Fisher, N. P. and Jill, 85

Fisk Place, 126
floods, 97
· Florida, 99, 160
folk cures, 122
Foner, Eric, 166
Fort Smith: aid to freedmen, 52;
    barbers, 44; bureau agents, 18, 29;
    bureau office, 16; education, 126,
    128, 132, 137; family reunions, 35;
    health care, 4, 114, 116, 117, 118,
    121; judiciary, 156; land, 76, 101,
    103; mobility, 75, 101; politics, 56,
    59; violence, 148, 158
"Forty acres and a mule," 76, 77, 78
Fountain Hill, 22, 54
Fourteenth Amendment, 114, 145, 153,
    154, 156, 157
Fourth Military District, 158
Fourth of July, 67
Fowler, C. H., 130
Fox-Genovese, 31
franchise, 157
Franklin, Lulaman, 126
Franklin, Saul, 94
Franklin County, 87, 103
Freedmen's Bureau: closing of,
    164–65; creation, 6; goals, 7; histo-
    rian's assessment of, 107, 165–70;
    location (map), 11; opposition to, 7,
    27; personnel, 11, 12–17, 114; prob-
    lems faced, 28–30, 103
Freedmen's Bureau agents: adjudicate
    conflict, 37–40, 74, 81–84, 105,
    108, 153–54; attitude toward
    planters, 22, 152–54; hierarchy, 22,
    108; ideologies, 19–23;
    independence, 28; health care, 120;
    labor arrangements, 73, 74, 81–84,
    101–3, 105, 108; political beliefs,
    59, 61–62; racial attitudes, 19–22,
    36–40; religious beliefs, 52;
    violence, 146; work ethic 23, 71–72
Free Will Baptist, 49

French Revolution, 166
Fulton, 126
Fulton County: bureau office, 14; death, 118; education, 123; labor, 79, 84; violence, 143, 146, 147, 163

gangs, 146–48
Gantt, E. W.: courts, 153; labor, 22, 98; politics, 55; violence, 152
Garland, A. H., 164
Garrett, Curtis, 21
Gatewood, Philip, 151
Gattling, Jesse, 34
Gualding, Col. J. W., 151
Geisreiter, Sebastian: attitude toward planters, 21; biography, 19; class consciousness, 22; education, 130; health care, 113; labor, 92–93, 101; law, 142, 156; politics, 55, 61; racial attitudes, 20, 52; violence, 43, 144
gender: role in school curriculum, 137–38; self-concepts, 41–44; teachers, 135
General Assembly, Arkansas, 157
General Order Number 7, 61
General Order Number 8, 120
General Order Number 11, 120
General Order Number 68, 71
General Order Number 138, 71
Genovese, Eugene, 31
Georgia, 99, 100, 102, 115, 160
Gettysburg, 133
Gibbs' Store, 138
Gibson, Thomas, 104
Gibson, William, 148
Gilbert, Charles C., 158–59
Gill, James, 24
Gillam, Cora, 73, 75, 106
Goodrum, John, 24, 101
Goodwin, 122
graduation ceremonies, 138
Granger, W. W., 102

Grant, Joel, 122
Grant, Ulysses, 18, 54
Grave, Wesley, 130
Great Society, 167
Green, Henry, 99
Green County, Georgia, 102
Greene, Gen. O. D., 120
Greene, O. O., 61
Greene County, 51, 131, 160
Grey, William, 46, 64, 165
Grinds, Dr. E. S., 126
Griswold, Ruby, 115
Gross, Frank: appointment, 18; racial attitudes, 22, 156
Grundy, Henry, 134
guns, 154, 161
Gwin, A. B., 148

Habricht, A. E.: attitude about planters, 21; violence, 146, 163
Hagg, Beulah, 48, 62
Hale, Plymouth, 45
Hamburg: attitudes toward bureau, 164; bureau office, 12; labor, 83, 84, 93; politics, 54, 58; racial attitudes, 36, 47; violence, 145
Hamlin, Nancy, 43
Hampton: bureau office, 12; education, 124, 126, 137; racial attitudes, 36
Haney, Julia, 96
Hanna, Carolina, 115
Hanna, Catherine, 20
Hanover, James, 144
Harbison, I. P., 87
Harlan, A. N., 3
Harlanson, J. P., 85
Harper, Ida, 1
Harris, John, 58
Harris, Rachel, 150
Harris, Richard, 38, 67
Harrisburgh, 146

Jacksonport: adjudication, 35; bureau office, 14; economics, 81, 92, 93, 104, 105; marriages, 41; mobility, 75; politics, 42, 59; racial attitudes, 112; rape, 43; schools, 126, 129, 130, 131; slavery, 70, 79; violence, 144, 158
Jacksonville, 15
James, John, 83
James, Peter, 104
Jefferson, Thomas, 76, 169
Jefferson County: black elite, 64; bureau office, 15; Christmas, 67; economics, 86–91, 87; politics, 55, 56; violence, 67, 163
Jeffries, Moses, 149
Jim Crow laws, 47
Johnson, Andrew, 8, 77, 133, 163, 167
Johnson, Betsy, 43
Johnson, Elda, 48
Johnson, George, 100
Johnson, Henry, 43
Johnson, John, 62, 104, 149
Johnson, Lucinda, 35
Johnson, Lyndon, 167
Johnson, Marion, 96
Johnson, Thomas, 64
Johnson County, 15
Johnston, Amy Ann, 38, 80–81
Johnston, Mamala, 19
Joint Committee on Reconstruction, 77
Jones, Ann, 72
Jones, Maj. Henry, 94, 126
Jones, John, 150
Jones, Orlando, 45
Jones, Thomas, 115
Jones, Vergil, 149
Jones, Willie, 72
Jonesboro: bureau office, 13; planters opposition, 60; politics, 54, 58, 59; religion, 51

Jordan, Margaret, 38
Jordan, Winthrop, 37
Joyner, Charles, 31
Julian, George Washington, 77, 78
juries, 153, 156
Justice, A. S., 34
justices of the peace, 63

Kettrell, W. E., 85
kidnapping, 154
King, G. R., 85
King, Mary, 115
Kinman, Riley, 149
Knowlton, Dr. Knox, 35, 117
Krull, Christian, 115
Ku Klux Klan: acquitted in Marion, 156; anti-miscegenation, 38; anti-bureau, 146; anti-education, 130; anti-religion, 51; beat doctor, 114; disrupts dance, 67; political violence, 60, 62, 64, 148–51, 159–61

labor agent, 72, 74, 99–101
labor systems: during Civil War, 2–3; ideologies, 22–26; varieties, 70–92, 97–101, 104
Laconia Landing, 100
Lafayette County: black elite, 64; bureau agent, 29; bureau office, 15; economics, 48, 82, 83; juries, 156; violence, 28, 143
Lake Village: bureau agent, 20; bureau office, 12; economics, 93; judiciary, 156; schools, 22, 123, 125
land, 76–79, 101–3, 108
Landers, Mandy, 155
Lanza, Michael, 103
Latter, Russell, 80
laudanum, 112
law, 74, 80, 142
Lawrence, Dr. George, 112

Lawrence County, 79
Lee, A. N., 80
Lee, Nancy, 115
Leek's Plantation, 122
leg ulcer, 116
Levine, Lawrence, 31
Lewis, Alvin, 38
Lewis, John, 115
Lewis, Col. M. W., 126
Lewis, Washington, 38
Lewis, William, 115
Lewisburg: army requested, 157; bureau office, 13; judiciary, 156; labor, 82, 83, 98, 104, 130; miscegenation, 38; politics, 23, 54, 57, 61; violence, 143, 145
lien, 80, 104, 157
Lilly, Henry, 119
Lincoln, Abraham, 8, 18, 46, 57, 77
Linscott, Rufus Lycurgus, 151
literary society, 66, 131
Little River County: planters, 59; schools, 128, 133; violence, 62, 146, 150, 163
Little Rock: black militias, 64; black networks, 64, 161; bureau agents, 20, 153; bureau office, 16; Caribbean celebrations, 47; diet, 97; health care, 4, 112, 113, 114, 116, 118, 119, 120, 121; home farm, 4; housing, 96; judiciary, 156; labor, 71, 73, 74, 75, 80, 99; land desire, 77, 101; marriages, 41; mortality, 4; mulatto, 45; politics, 52, 55, 56, 57, 58, 59, 60, 61, 62; population, 24; prostitution, 38; religion, 102; schools, 5, 122, 123, 124, 127, 128, 132, 134, 136, 138, 139; slavery, 23, 106; temperance, 65, 66; violence, 149
Little Rock Board of Health, 121
Little Rock Daily Arkansas Gazette, 27
Little Rock Daily Pantograph, 169

Little Rock Evening Republican, 55
Little Rock Morning Republican, 136
Litwack, Leon, 107
livestock, 71, 107
London, Sam, 115
Lonoke County, 15
Louisiana, 99, 122, 160
Lugenbeel, Pinkeny, 29, 126
Luna Landing, 12
Lyman, James G., 126

McClelland, B. T., 136
McClemm, J., 21
McCoy, Smart, 145
McCullough, W. S., 120, 134
McFeely, William, 166–67
McGarock, Dr., 100
McGee, Milly, 113
McGuffey's Reader, 136, 137
McKaye, Col. James, 6
McKaye, Samuel, 82, 83
McKinney, Warren, 97, 116
McKitrick, Eric, 166
McMillen, Granville, 143
McMurty, James, 43
McPherson, James, 137
Madison: blacks' despondency, 103, 163; bureau office, 17; economics, 80, 82; emancipation, 1; health care, 116, 122; judiciary, 155; marriages, 41; politics, 54, 59, 61, 105; violence, 143, 144
Magnolia: bureau office, 13; politics, 54, 55, 62; religion, 47, 48
Main, E. M., 105, 160
Malcom, Israel, 73
Malcom, Julia, 73
Mann, Maria, 3
Marianna, 75
Marion: blacks' despondency, 103; blacks' self-defense, 160; bureau agents, 21; bureau office, 13;

economics, 98, 104, 105; education, 126, 131, 136; planters, 81, 105, 153; politics, 58, 60, 61, 64; trials, 43, 156; violence, 60, 61, 64, 81, 105, 143, 149, 150

Marion County, 28, 80

Markham Street, Little Rock, 52, 57

Mark's Mill, 2

marriages, 19, 40–42, 45

Marroll, Sally, 115

Martin, Joni, 106, 122

Marvel, 24

Mason, James, 63, 64, 165

Mason, Simpson, 79, 129, 146, 147, 163

Masonic lodges, 65

Matthews, Caroline, 54

Maxwell Plantation, 26

Meal, J. W., 117

measles, 116

medical personnel, 113–15

medicine, 86, 88, 93, 100–101, 111–22

Memphis, Tennessee, 2, 39, 71, 90, 94, 95, 96, 116, 159

men, 73, 83–86, 104, 135

merchants, 80, 91–96

Merriman, Easter, 81

Merriman, W. B., 81

Methodist, 49, 50

Methodist Episcopal North, 50

Methodist Episcopal South, 49, 51

Meyer, L., 55

Military Reconstruction Act (1867), 54

Millard, Rev. William, 50

millenialism, 51

Miller, Enoch K., 126, 128, 129, 133, 135

Miller County, 147

Millerd, Coryden, 50

Millikens Bend, Louisiana, 2

Millios, Joel, 85

Mills, Lt. S. M., 61

miscegenation, 46–47

Mississippi, 77, 99, 100, 122, 151, 158

Mississippi County: bureau office, 15; deaths, 118; economics, 84, 100; politics, 62; violence, 143, 149, 160

Mississippi River, 97, 99, 100, 159

Missouri, 78, 115, 147

Mitchell, C., 104

Mix, Eli, 43

Monks, William, 147

Monroe County, 150, 156

Montgomery, Alabama, 99

Montgomery, Charles, 105

Montgomery, John R., 27, 72, 74, 165

Monticello: agent adjudicates, 82; bureau office, 14, 29; Civil Rights Act agitation, 154; education, 123, 130, 137; trials, 38, 155; violence, 158, 160

Monticello Guardian, 125

Moody, David, 94

Moore, C. E., 87

Moore, Col. D. H. C., 117

Moore, Patsy, 1

Moore, W. D., 165

Mooreman, Mattie, 97

Morgan, William: economics, 98; politics, 54, 61; schools, 124; violence, 143

Morrison, James, 115

Morton, Oliver, 57

mulattoes, 45

mules, 107

murders, 48, 105, 150–51, 154, 155

Murphy, Gov. Isaac, 35, 146

Murphy, William, 64, 87

Napoleon: anti-bureau sentiment, 27, 164; black self-defense, 65, 161; black sexual behavior, 36; bureau

Walker, Thomas, 124, 125
Walker, William, 18
Wallace, Bob, 144
Wallace, Edward T., 18, 20, 148, 160
Warren, 12
Warren, E. A., 60
Warren, Tobey, 153
Warren Place, 126
Washington: bureau office, 14;
    children, 34; education, 123, 129,
    132, 133, 135, 138; emancipation,
    27; health care, 114, 118; labor, 72,
    74, 93, 98, 99, 100, 101; mobility,
    75, 103; politics, 55, 58, 60; temper-
    ance, 65; trials, 155; violence, 142,
    152, 157, 160
Washington, George, 115
Washington, Lucinda, 113
Washington County, 17
Watson, J. T., 92, 101
Watts, Phillips, 34
Weatherford, W. G., 117
Webb, Dr. A. W., 121
Webb, Ishe, 100
Weekly Arkansas Gazette, 24, 46, 122,
    126, 164
Weekly Republican, 54, 61
Wells, John, 113
Western Freedmen's Aid Commission,
    127
Western Sanitary Commission, 5
wheat, 97, 106
Wheatley, 24
whippings, 114–45, 152–53, 154
White, Deborah, 31
White, James T., 64
White County, 17
White River, 3
whites: attitudes toward blacks, 2,
    52–53, 56–57, 60; attitudes toward
    bureau, 27, 164; attitudes toward
    schools, 5, 130–31; class conflict,

28; jurors, 156; violence, 60–62,
    143, 146–48
Wiggins and McCurdy, 85
Wilburn, John, 149
Wiley, Nancy, 81, 145
Wilkinson, Robert, 81
Williams, A. B., 164
Williams, D. H., 71, 119
Williams, Green, 151
Williams, Capt. John, 126, 146, 163
Williams, Dr. L. G., 43
Williams, R. N., 81
Williams, Reuben, 94
Williams, Thomas, 54, 61, 103, 105,
    163
Willis, Hiram: government, 155; guns,
    153; judiciary, 156; labor, 82, 92,
    101; militia, 160; schools, 134, 137;
    violence, 146, 152, 163
Womack, T. P., 85
women: black gender constructs, 42;
    labor, 73, 75, 82, 83–86; schools
    135, 137–38
Wood County, 87
Woodruff County, 17, 147, 160
Woods, Ellen, 115
Woods, Gen. Thomas J., 120
Woodson, Carter G., 50
worms, 113
Worthington, Elisha, 63
WPA slave narratives, 33, 48, 137
Wright, A. A., 20, 40

Yambert, N. B. D., 85
Yampert, J. L. D., 85
Yazoo Valley, 99
Yell County, 17, 156
yellow fever, 113, 116
Young, E. A., 5
youth organizations, 66